Reconciliation in the Asia-Pacific

Reconciliation in the Asia-Pacific

edited by Yoichi Funabashi

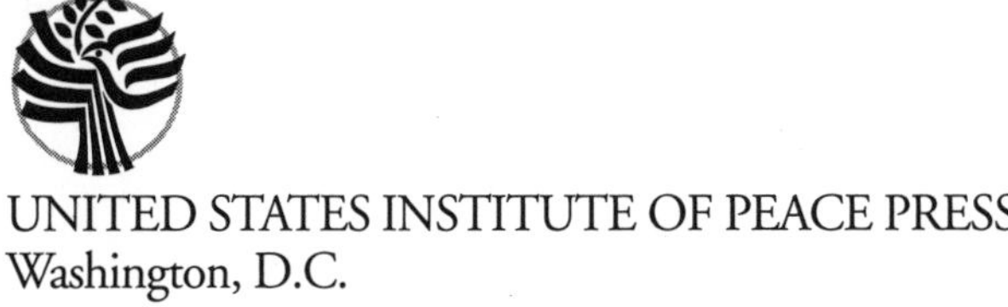

UNITED STATES INSTITUTE OF PEACE PRESS
Washington, D.C.

The views expressed in this book are those of the authors alone. They do not necessarily reflect views of the United States Institute of Peace.

UNITED STATES INSTITUTE OF PEACE
1200 17th Street NW, Suite 200
Washington, DC 20036-3011

First published 2003

Printed in the United States of America

The paper used in this publication meets the minimum requirements of American National Standards for Information Science—Permanence of Paper for Printed Library Materials, ANSI Z39.48-1984.

Library of Congress Cataloging-in-Publication Data
Reconciliation in the Asia-Pacific / edited by Yoichi Funabashi.
p. cm.
Includes bibliographical references and index.
ISBN 1-929223-47-1 (alk. paper)
1. Conflict management—Case studies. 2. Ethnic conflict—Case studies. 3. Pacific settlement of international disputes—Case studies. 4. Reconciliation —Case studies. 5. Asia—Politics and government. 6. Pacific Area—Politics and government. I. Funabashi, Yoichi, 1944–

HM1126.R413 2003
303.6'9—dc21 2003044988

Contents

Foreword

Ezra Vogel

IT IS NOW ALL TOO CLEAR that globalization does not mean homogenization. As the forces of globalization bring peoples of the world into closer contact, is it inevitable that different ethnic groups, different religions, different civilizations will clash? Are nations and peoples that have fought in the past destined to repeat their conflicts?

In 1945, looking back at the history of wars between Germany and Poland, one might have said that the bitter hatreds from past conflicts would condemn them to fight again. Yet today, future fighting between them is almost unthinkable. How did Germany and Poland achieve such reconciliation?

Those of us who work in the Asia-Pacific region know that no issue is more important for the future of the region than overcoming the hatreds that history has spawned. Yet very little has been done to understand why some peoples have achieved reconciliation and others have not. One can only admire the pioneering efforts of Richard Solomon and his colleagues at the United States Institute of Peace, and of Yoichi Funabashi and other Japanese, who have worked together to assemble a talented and thoughtful group of scholars, journalists, and government officials to find ways to advance reconciliation in the Asia-Pacific region.

The authors in this volume address a broad range of cases of interethnic and international animosity fueled by histories and memories of injustices and human rights abuses. Masahiro Wakabayashi, for instance, examines the infamous 2-28 Incident that occurred in Taiwan in February 1947, when the KMT military forces that took over Taiwan slaughtered thousands of local leaders who might have led resistance to the KMT. For the next forty years—as the percentage of "Mainlanders" among Taiwan's population rose from 1 percent in 1947 to 8 percent in 1952 to 14 percent in 1990—the KMT leadership maintained a tight crackdown on dissent. But beneath the surface hostility simmered. In the 1980s the two sides finally began to face their history. The issue has not died down and may flare up again as Taiwan debates how to respond to mainland pressure for reunification. But historical grievances have been faced squarely and tensions have been greatly reduced. Wakabayashi explains how this progress was achieved.

Other authors in the volume address such problems as hatred between North and South Korea that lingers from the Korean War, the animosities between different groups within Cambodia and between Cambodia and Vietnam, and the strained relations between Indonesia and East Timor and among the East Timorese themselves. Another problem examined in this volume—a problem that in sheer scale dominates East Asia—is relations between Japan and its two large neighbors in East Asia, China and Korea. Here national differences reinforce cultural differences and historical memories have become powerful symbols for a host of problems that stymie efforts at reconciliation. The animosity has a powerful internal aspect, too, for within China and Korea enmity continues to smolder between those who worked with the Japanese during World War II and those who hated such "collaborators."

■ ■ ■

Bold leaders who seek reconciliation can accomplish a great deal. When Deng Xiaoping came to power in China in 1978 he had to contend with deep divisions between, on the one side, victims of the Cultural Revolution who wanted to settle accounts and, on the other side, those who wanted to forget the entire episode or who refused to acknowledge that its victims deserved any form of restitution or rehabilitation. He worked hard to create a climate in which history could be reexamined and realities faced, but rather than allow retribution to be vented, he moved on to deal pragmatically with the problems ahead.

In the same way, when Deng was about to launch his policy of reform and opening, he realized that China's growth required peaceful relations with other major countries. Relations with Japan were particularly strained. In the fall of 1978, just before he launched his new policies, Deng visited Japan. He stressed that the two countries should concentrate on the future rather than on the past. At the time, with Japan and China (along with the United States) cooperating against the Soviet Union, the geostrategic climate was very favorable. The historical issue did not go away, but for fifteen years it remained relatively quiet. In the early 1990s, however, the issue again broke out and has hobbled Sino-Japanese relations ever since.

In 1965, President Park Chung Hee, knowing that South Korean economic growth required cooperation with Japan, boldly concluded a peace treaty with Japan. The treaty brought economic assistance from Japan for South Korea's economic takeoff, but Park's policy was forced on the South Korean people and protests were suppressed. The process of reconciliation was superficial; public attitudes were not changed.

In 1998 President Kim Dae Jong made a dramatic visit to Japan in which he advocated thinking about the future, not the past. His speech took on added meaning because he had been kidnapped in Japan by the Korean Central Intelligence Agency, which then prepared to kill him. In a heartfelt speech in Japan, Kim thanked his Japanese friends who had helped save his life. A few weeks later President Jiang Zemin of China also visited Japan, but his repeated attacks on Japan for inadequately dealing with its history led Prime Minister Obuchi to refuse to issue an apology. In contrast, during Kim Dae Jong's visit, Obuchi was deeply moved by Kim's efforts to put the past behind. He happily signed an apology and Korean-Japanese relations took a dramatic turn for the better.

In the wake of Kim Dae Jong's 1998 visit to Japan, individual Koreans and Japanese—in business, in government, in universities, in the press, and in casual tourist encounters—reported a dramatic improvement in their mutual relations. Public opinion polls in Japan reflected a marked increase in positive attitudes toward Japan. But in 2001, when a new textbook in Japan sought to minimize the suffering that Japan had caused to the Korean people, the progress threatened to unravel. Many

Koreans who had begun to feel more positively toward Japan became enraged again.

Leadership alone clearly is not enough. In an era when much of the public follows national news through the media, reconciliation cannot work unless it enjoys broad support among the people.

■ ■ ■

Many Japanese in the 1970s and 1980s hoped that, with the passage of time, painful memories of World War II and the powerful emotions of the families of those who suffered during the war would gradually fade. Within Japan, when Japanese quarrel, they do often deal with the problem by remaining silent and going about their business, and with the passage of time, enmities do often begin to fade away. But between nations this approach evidently has not been working. Other nations will not forget Japan's past conduct, whether because they cannot suppress spontaneous public expressions of outrage and injustice, or because they want to promote national unity against outsiders, or because they want to contain Japanese power and guard against a rebirth of Japanese militarism, or because they hope to secure further compensation from Japan.

Within China and Korea, the stories of those who bravely fought the Japanese have never been entirely forgotten. In China, the songs, stories, novels, and movies from the 1930s and 1940s of heroic Chinese fighting against the cruel invaders are periodically revived, refreshing the public's sense of Japanese iniquity. In Korea, painful memories can still be stirred by the essays written before 1945 by Koreans living outside the reach of imperial Japan, essays intended to appeal to global public opinion. It is through such material, and through the reminiscences of those who suffered at the hands of the Japanese, that Koreans and Japanese pass on the pain of injustice to later generations. Today young Chinese boys, in tune with the world by mastering electronic games, play games in which they are Chinese guerrillas fighting Japanese invaders.

Furthermore, Chinese and Korean spokesmen now criticize not only those Japanese who participated in wartime atrocities but also present-day Japanese who refuse to acknowledge the full extent of such atrocities and who fail to display public sorrow and make further compensation.

Time alone will not heal the wounds.

■ ■ ■

Chinese and Koreans ask why the Japanese cannot apologize more thoroughly, show real remorse, make a clean breast of all the atrocities they caused, and offer more generous compensation. "Why," they ask, "do not the Japanese condemn their history as roundly as the Germans do?" In fact, most Japanese, as shown in polls, do acknowledge that Japan committed atrocities in Asia, do believe that Japan should have apologized, and do want to achieve reconciliation. Nonetheless, clearly they have not been sufficiently forthcoming to satisfy their Asian neighbors. Why?

In Europe after World War II, Germany, bordered by France and Poland, was an integral part of the economic reconstruction of Europe. The building of NATO and of the European Economic Community—and later of the European Union—forced Germany to address the issues that divided it from its neighbors. By contrast, Japan after 1949 had almost no contact with communist China or North Korea, and even relations with South Korea, separated from Japan by an ocean, were never as close as the relations between Germany and its neighbors.

One atrocity perpetrated by the Germans—the attempt to exterminate an entire people—was never attempted by the Japanese. The horrors of the Holocaust created demands for expiation not only among Germany's neighbors but among Germans as well. Japanese could more easily persuade themselves that their atrocities were inseparable from war and that Japan's behavior was not qualitatively worse than that of other colonial and warlike powers.

Many Japanese people who lived under the military in the 1930s and early 1940s have long argued that they, the ordinary people, were not responsible for the decisions of their government. After all, they contend, they had been subjects of the Japanese military in World War II and, like the Koreans, had suffered at the hands of that military. Those Japanese who were born after 1945 feel even less responsible for the actions of Japan's military government.

The issue of war apology and atonement became a political issue in Japan soon after World War II. Japanese socialists and communists attacked mainstream politicians for not doing more to make amends for the country's atrocities, and quickly passed on to Korea and China news of incidents and of efforts to whitewash atrocities. In response, Liberal Democratic

Party officials often tended to play down the atrocities and to dismiss their domestic opponents as tools of foreign interests.

China and Korea have sometimes given extraordinary publicity to certain Japanese textbooks that try to explain away the horrors that Japan perpetrated in the war and to certain politicians who outrageously understate the scope of human rights abuses committed by Japanese forces. These textbooks and politicians do not necessarily reflect broad segments of Japanese public opinion but, when widely publicized, they can have an enormous impact on opinion in China and Korea.

The effects can be felt in Japan, too, especially when it appears that the Chinese and Korean media have reminded their audiences of Japanese atrocities in order to stir up anti-Japanese sentiments in other parts of Asia and to elicit more economic aid or more compensation from Japanese. Even Japanese who are prepared to apologize for their country's past behavior become annoyed when they feel they are being manipulated.

Japanese point out that Japan agreed in 1965 to give large sums to South Korea, either directly or indirectly through industrial assistance. Japanese are also well aware that they will have to give comparable amounts to North Korea as and when relations between Tokyo and Pyongyang are normalized. China's leaders agreed not to ask for reparation, so Japan has given far more economic aid to China than to other countries. In the view of the Japanese, these aid programs are at least psychologically an effort to offer some compensation for the horrors of World War II. In Japanese eyes, the Chinese media has shown almost no recognition of Japanese generosity.

Many Japanese feel that Japan has apologized enough. The emperor apologized in China in 1992, and prime ministers who have visited China have repeatedly offered apologies. They have come to believe that they can never satisfy Chinese and Korean requests for apology. Enough is enough, they conclude. Other colonialists have done horrible things: the British in India, the Dutch in Indonesia, the French in Indochina, the Americans in the Philippines. No one any longer asks these nations to apologize. Why should only Japan be asked to apologize?

By the 1990s, as the Chinese economy was taking off and Chinese military expenses were growing rapidly, many Japanese came to suspect that China might be taking advantage of Japan's contrition. At the same time, many Japanese who used to feel somewhat condescending toward Chinese achievements began to fear what might happen as China grows stronger. Such sentiments help explain why Chinese demands for apologies—like that made by President Jiang in 1998—may make the Japanese less willing, not more willing, to apologize.

This explanation of Japanese attitudes is not intended to justify those attitudes. But it is necessary to understand the complex emotional and psychological dynamics of the situation if full reconciliation is to be achieved. And full reconciliation must also deal with the fact that some people in China and Korea use historical issues for their own ends.

■ ■ ■

What, then, is to be done? It is clear that reconciliation is a many-sided process that requires a variety of ingredients and action at many levels. Among other things, it requires the following:

- Political leadership that can provide a vision for the future and can pilot a steady course toward that future.
- More objective textbooks and media in all the affected countries. Japanese textbooks sometimes understate the horrors, but textbooks in China and Korea often overstate the horrors and understate the peaceful efforts of the Japanese since 1945. Commissions made up of widely respected and relatively objective scholars from various countries could help to pinpoint and correct errors and exaggerations in textbooks and media.
- Objective research to create the basis for a more accurate understanding of disputed historical events. Working together, scholars from various countries—including countries directly affected by a particular historical dispute as well as countries not involved in that dispute—can help create a relatively objective picture of what is known and, no less important, what cannot be known and thus cannot be fully resolved on the basis of historical understanding.
- Opportunities for former belligerents to work together in common projects of mutual benefit.

Some potentially valuable elements of a reconciliation process can also be provided by outsiders. For instance, outsiders such as Americans can convene meetings and facilitate discussions that enable the parties to a dispute to adopt a more objective tone than they employ in purely bilateral encounters.

Clearly, all of us who believe in the importance of reconciliation have ample opportunity to contribute to the process of restoring relationships poisoned by historical animosities. The chapters in this volume provide an excellent basis for us to move forward in our search for reconciliation in the Asia-Pacific.

Preface

IT MUST HAVE BEEN AROUND 1996 when Dr. Richard Solomon, president of the United States Institute of Peace, asked me whether I would be interested in conducting a research project on Japan's historical issues.

Dr. Solomon and I had known each other for some time, dating back to his days as assistant secretary of state for East Asian and Pacific affairs in the Reagan administration. We had often met and exchanged views on a range of issues, particularly issues on the relations of the United States, Japan, and China. On such occasions, our conversation would inevitably gravitate to the persistent historical issues. Despite the fact that World War II ended over fifty years ago, Japan's historical past refuses to fade away quietly. On the contrary, it is becoming an increasingly entangled Gordian knot of emotion and ideology, complicating Japan's diplomatic relationships with its neighbors.

Dr. Solomon once asked me how exactly Japan is attempting to resolve this persistent problem, and whether, if the problem is left unresolved, there is not a danger of Japan being saddled with this heavy burden indefinitely. He suggested that I conduct a research project on the subject, which he thought would offer an excellent opportunity for intellectual cross-stimulation.

At the time, I had little choice but to decline his kind invitation as I was busy with my duties as *Asahi*'s bureau chief in America. Nonetheless, it was indeed a compelling proposition, particularly given my long interest in the issue. Later, my interest in historical reconciliation grew even keener, especially after the 1990s, when it had become all too apparent that Japan's unresolved historical problems were posing a roadblock to the success of new diplomatic initiatives in Asia, such as the Asia-Pacific Economic Cooperation Conference, the ASEAN Regional Forum, and ASEAN+3 summit meeting.

Upon returning to Japan from Washington, I had the good fortune to meet and make friends with the German ambassador, Frank Elbe. A lawyer-turned-diplomat, Ambassador Elbe was first posted to Poland; ever since, he has been working on the issue of reconciliation between West Germany and Poland. Through my extensive discussions with him, I learned two salient points about how issues of historical reconciliation should be addressed: first, the problem must be tackled not only in moral terms of what should be done but also in pragmatic terms of what can be done; and second, that whoever addresses the problem should have a policy-oriented perspective, that is, a clear and feasible policy on how to pursue reconciliation.

Reminded of Dr. Solomon's invitation, I met with him in Washington. I noted that it would still be difficult for me personally to conduct a research project at the United States Institute of Peace, but that I would be interested in organizing an international workshop in order to address the issue in a more broadly defined global context. Dr. Solomon readily acceded to my request for the support of the Institute in this endeavor.

It was through this chain of events that the International Workshop on Reconciliation in the Asia-Pacific came to be organized and held on February 16–17, 2001, at the International House of Japan in Tokyo, cosponsored by the United States Institute of Peace and the Tokyo Foundation. Dr. Solomon and I served as cochairs of the workshop. We were joined by seven scholars who presented papers and five commentators, each of whom I had had the opportunity to meet previously and who offered rich insights on historical reconciliation. We were also favored with keynote speeches by Gareth Evans, the former Australian foreign minister, and Yasuhiro Nakasone, the former Japanese prime minister.

All of these individuals participated in the workshop of their own volition. The discussions among them were lively, with much give-and-take.

Scholars presented papers and practitioners offered commentaries, stimulating further discussion and honing sharper insights on the topics addressed.

In the twenty-four months following the workshop, the authors of the papers revised their contributions to incorporate new insights, refine analyses, and reflect recent developments. Those developments, it should be noted, have been significant. In several of the cases discussed in this volume, the first years of the twenty-first century have seen bold and surprising steps being taken toward reconciliation. For instance, governments in North Korea and Japan have candidly acknowledged and apologized for past wrongs, although normalization talks have subsequently appeared to stall over the abduction cases and the nuclear issue. In other cases, recent developments have been less positive. For example, many in the international community have been disappointed by the outcomes of trials of Indonesian military officers charged with human rights abuses in East Timor.

Whether recent events are seen as encouraging or discouraging overall, there is no doubt that reconciliation is high on the agenda of many people in the Asia-Pacific region. This book reflects and, we trust, enhances that interest. It offers seven case studies spanning a considerable geographical area and a remarkably wide range of issues. It also includes as an appendix comments made at the workshop by Ambassador Elbe, Ambassador Yukio Sato, and Dr. Marianne Heiberg. Regretfully, because of limitations of space, the comments of other speakers and participants at the workshop had to be omitted. However, I have done my best to capture the essence of their observations in the concluding chapter, which tries to identify many of the keys that can unlock the paths to reconciliation.

Acknowledgments

THIS PROJECT ON RECONCILIATION IN THE ASIA-PACIFIC began as a workshop in February 2001 and has since evolved into the present volume. Throughout the course of the project, I have been blessed with both the moral and the material support of many individuals and institutions. First and foremost, I wish to thank the workshop participants for their active and insightful contributions. I am also most grateful to Gareth Evans and Yasuhiro Nakasone for having kindly agreed to serve as our keynote speakers. Furthermore, I am deeply indebted to Richard Solomon and the United States Institute of Peace, whose generous and kind support has been vital to achieving this project's success.

I am honored that Ezra Vogel of Harvard University has written the foreword to this volume. As an understanding friend of not only Japan but also China and South Korea, he has over a long span of years organized a wide range of projects on war and history at Harvard and elsewhere. There is simply no other Asia expert in the world who is as well versed in the languages, histories, and societies of all three of these countries. Nor is anyone better respected in both the scholarly and the policymaking communities. I am, therefore, delighted to express our deepest gratitude to him for the distinguished contribution he has made to this publication.

Numerous other colleagues and associates have supported these efforts in a variety of ways. Among them, I would like to thank the staff of the

United States Institute of Peace, particularly Patrick M. Cronin (former director of the Research and Studies Program), Neil J. Kritz (director of the Rule of Law Program), William M. Drennan (deputy director of the Research and Studies Program), Judy Barsalou (director of the Grant Program), Deepa M. Ollapally (a program officer in the Grant Program), and April R. Hall (grant administrator in the Grant Program), for so kindly extending to this endeavor their intellectual, logistical, and financial support. I also wish to express my appreciation to the affiliated members of the Tokyo Foundation, which cosponsored and co-organized the workshop, for providing their strong support in implementing the project. My thanks go to Kimindo Kusaka (chairman), Heizo Takenaka (president), and Takahiro Suzuki (director of the Research Division), as well as to the staff: Nami Uesugi, Takeshi Tamamura, and Kori Urayama.

Finally, I am grateful to Nigel Quinney, the editor of this publication, for his deep interest in the topic, strong encouragement, and unrelenting moral support. This volume could not have been realized without his editorial expertise and support.

Contributors

Yoichi Funabashi is a columnist and the chief diplomatic correspondent for the *Asahi Shimbun.* A leading journalist in the field of Japanese foreign policy, he has served as correspondent for the *Asahi Shimbun* in Beijing (1980–81) and Washington, D.C. (1984–87), and as American general bureau chief (1993–97). He won the Japan Press Award, known as Japan's "Pulitzer Prize," in 1994 for his columns on foreign policy, and his articles in *Foreign Policy* (of which he is a contributing editor) and *Foreign Affairs* won the Ishibashi Tanzan Prize in 1992.

His books in English include *Alliance Tomorrow,* ed. Tokyo Foundation (2001); *Alliance Adrift* (1998), winner of the Shincho Arts and Sciences Award; *Asia-Pacific Fusion: Japan's Role in APEC* (1995), winner of the Mainichi Shimbun Asia Pacific Grand Prix Award; and *Managing the Dollar: From the Plaza to the Louvre* (1988), winner of the Yoshino Sakuzo Prize. His books in Japanese include *Globalization Trick* (2002) and *How to Come to Terms with Japan's War Responsibility* (2002).

He received his B.A. from the University of Tokyo in 1968 and his Ph.D. from Keio University in 1992. He was a Nieman Fellow at Harvard University in 1975–76 and a visiting fellow at the Institute for International Economics in 1987 and at Columbia University's Donald Keene Center of Japanese Culture in the spring of 2003.

Among his current responsibilities, he is a visiting professor at the University of Tokyo, an executive board member of the International Crisis Group, and a board member of the Brooking Institution's Center for Northeast Asian Policy Studies.

■ ■ ■

Victor D. Cha holds the D. S. Song Chair in Asian Studies and Government in the Edmund Walsh School of Foreign Service, Georgetown University. He is the author of *Alignment despite Antagonism: The United States–Korea-Japan Security Triangle,* which won the 2000 Ohira Book Prize, and coauthor of *Nuclear North Korea? A Debate on Strategies of Engagement* (forthcoming in 2003). He has written articles on international relations and East Asia that have appeared in numerous journals, including *Foreign Affairs, International Security, Political Science Quarterly, Survival, International Studies Quarterly, Journal of Strategic Studies, Washington Quarterly,* and *Orbis.*

Cha, who has a B.A. and an M.A. from Oxford University and a Ph.D. from Columbia University, is the director of the American Alliances in Asia Project at Georgetown. He is a consultant to various branches of the U.S. government and has testified before Congress.

Nayan Chanda is the director of publications at the Yale Center for the Study of Globalization and editor of YaleGlobal Online. He is a fellow of the Pierson College, Yale University, and a nonresident fellow of the Brookings Institution, Washington, D.C. For nearly thirty years before he joined Yale University, Chanda served as editor, editor-at-large, and correspondent for the Hong Kong–based *Far Eastern Economic Review.* In 1989–90 Chanda was a senior fellow at the Carnegie Endowment for International Peace in Washington. From 1990 through 1992 he was editor of the *Asian Wall Street Journal Weekly,* published from New York.

Chanda is the author of *Brother Enemy: The War after the War* and coauthor of over a dozen books on Asian politics, security, and foreign policy, including *Soldiers and Stability in Southeast Asia* and *The Political Economy of Foreign Policy in Southeast Asia.* His most recent book is the *Age of Terror: America and the World after September 11,* which he coedited with

Strobe Talbott. He is a frequent contributor to the opinion page of the *International Herald Tribune.*

Todung Mulya Lubis is a senior partner of Lubis, Santosa & Maulana Law Offices in Jakarta and a lecturer on human rights in the Faculty of Law, University of Indonesia. He has defended a number of important and widely publicized cases, among them HR. Dharsono (1985), Prioritas (judicial review, 1992), Tempo (1995), Jakarta Post (1997), Time Magazine (1999), and Washington Post (2002). Between 1971 and 1986 he worked as a legal aid lawyer and chaired the Indonesian Institute of Legal Aid (1983–86) and its Jakarta chapter (1979–85). Currently, he is the chairman of the Board of Ethics at Indonesian Corruption Watch and vice president of the Indonesian Bar Association.

He has written and edited numerous articles, papers, and books on legal aid, human rights, and economic laws, and has been a regular columnist for various newspapers and magazines in Indonesia, among them *Kompas,* the *Jakarta Post,* and *Tempo.*

A graduate of the University of Indonesia, he also studied at the Institute of American and International Law in Dallas, the Boalt Law School of the University of California at Berkeley, and Harvard Law School. He is a member of various international and national organizations, including the International Bar Association, the Regional Council for Human Rights in Asia, Human Rights Internet, Human Rights Advocate, and the International Crisis Group.

Greg Sheridan is foreign editor of the *Australian.* He has also been its diplomatic correspondent in Canberra, chief editorial writer, and correspondent in Washington, D.C., and Beijing. His work has appeared in the *Sunday Times* (London), *Asian Wall Street Journal, Quadrant, South China Morning Post,* and numerous anthologies. He is the author of *Tigers: Leaders of the New Asia Pacific* (1997).

Scott Snyder is the Asia Foundation's representative in Korea. Previously, he was an Asia specialist in the Research and Studies Program of the United States Institute of Peace, where he wrote *Negotiating on the Edge: North Korean Negotiating Behavior* (1999). A former Abe Fellow of the Social

Sciences Research Council, Snyder has written extensively on Korean affairs and has also conducted research on the political and security implications of the Asian financial crisis and on the conflicting maritime claims in the South China Sea.

Snyder received his B.A. from Rice University and an M.A. from the Regional Studies East Asia Program at Harvard University. He was the recipient of a Thomas G. Watson Fellowship in 1987–88 and attended Yonsei University in South Korea.

Masahiro Wakabayashi is professor at and director of the Department of Area Studies, Graduate School of Arts and Sciences, University of Tokyo. He earned his Ph.D. in sociology from the University of Tokyo in 1985. His academic interests focus on the role of Taiwanese intellectuals in anti-Japanese movements, Taiwan's democratic transition, and identity politics in Taiwan. Wakabayashi's publications include *Taiwan: Democratization in a Divided Country* (in Japanese, 1992; in Chinese, 1994) and *Chiang Ching-kuo and Lee Teng-hui* (in Japanese, 1996; in Chinese, 1998). He was a visiting research fellow at the Institute of Ethnology, Academia Sinica, Taiwan, in 1995 and 1996. He served as president of the Japan Association for Taiwan Studies in 1998–2002.

Daqing Yang teaches modern Japanese history at the George Washington University in Washington, D.C., where he is an associate professor of history and international affairs. He also regularly lectures on modern Japan at the U.S. Foreign Service Institute.

A native of Nanjing, Yang received his Ph.D. from Harvard University. He has twice studied at Keio University in Tokyo and is a recipient of the Japan Foundation Research Fellowship, the ACLS/SSRC/NEH International and Area Studies Fellowship, and the Abe Fellowship sponsored by the Center for Global Partnership and the Social Sciences Research Council. He is author of *Technology of Empire* (forthcoming), which deals with telecommunications networks and Japanese expansion before 1945. His articles have appeared in the *American Historical Review, Journal of Asian Studies, Monumenta Nipponica, Gunji Shigaku, Shiso,* and *Ronza.*

Reconciliation in the Asia-Pacific

Introduction
Why Reconciliation?

Yoichi Funabashi

I must confess that I feel a certain hesitation in using the term *reconciliation* in the title of this volume. After all, how likely is it that the victims and the victimizers in such incidences of gross injustice as mass slaughter can achieve reconciliation when even coexistence between them is fraught with difficulties? However, I am one of many Japanese who, while not having been directly involved in Japan's military aggression and colonial behavior before and during World War II, nonetheless feel a sense of responsibility for those actions. Furthermore, I believe that Japan's inability to deal adequately with its historical legacy has prevented it from developing constructive security relations with its neighbors, which in turn has impeded the emergence of a multilateral security framework in the region. Japan can become a "normal country" only if it addresses this legacy more earnestly and pursues a path toward historical reconciliation with its neighbors.

Japan's record is not unique, but rather one example of an experience common within human society, and I believe that by reexamining Japan's past from various perspectives, we can enhance our knowledge and understanding of painful historical issues in a way that will better enable us to resolve them. Similarly, we can learn from the wisdom of those elsewhere in the world who have already accomplished some level of reconciliation. In that spirit, this volume addresses not only Japan's past but also the histories of several relationships in the Asia-Pacific region between countries and peoples who harbor a profound sense of injustice.

Relationships between Japan and China, North and South Korea, Japan and South Korea, Taiwan and China, Indonesia and East Timor, Cambodia and Vietnam all still resonate with traditional geopolitical conflicts. The historical issues unresolved between these and other countries have become key factors contributing to tensions between them. Since the end of the Cold War, Asia has not experienced the kind of mass genocide seen in Europe and Africa, but we cannot afford to relax even for a moment our vigilance against such a possibility, as was seen in East Timor. We must maintain a constant effort to lighten the burden of history. In Japan's case, pressure from various groups that have suffered from Japan's aggression and oppressive rule—among them, prisoners of war, "comfort women," and conscript laborers—has added a new dimension to this already complicated issue.

The seven case studies presented in this book cover diverse forms of conflict and reconciliation, including those between different nation-states, nation-states of the same ethnic group, groups within the same nation, and different ethnic groups. There are, however, many other instances of ethnic strife and unresolved historical issues within the Asia-Pacific region that this volume does not address—notably, the conflicts between India and Pakistan, China and Tibet, the Tamil and Sinhalese communities in Sri Lanka, and ethnic groups in Afghanistan. Such limitations in the scope of our coverage must be acknowledged and should be borne in mind by our readers.

A Global Trend toward Apology

More or less in step with the advent of the post–Cold War era, there has emerged a global trend toward offering apologies for past wrongs. One after another, nations and organizations in various parts of the world are voicing apologies for past actions that caused suffering for many people.

One of the earliest manifestations of this trend came in 1990, when the administration of President George Bush provided compensation to Japanese-Americans who had been interned in the United States during the war in the Pacific. Of the approximately 120,000 internees, some

65,000 survivors received, along with their compensation checks, a presidential letter that read: "A monetary sum and words alone cannot restore lost years or erase painful memories; neither can they fully convey our nation's resolve to rectify injustice and to uphold the right of individuals. But we can take a clear stand for justice and recognize that serious injustices were done to Japanese-Americans during World War II."

Similar efforts have been made in a variety of contexts. Mikhail Gorbachev admitted in 1990 with "profound regret" that Joseph Stalin's secret police had murdered fifteen thousand Polish officers in Katyn Forest in 1940. Pope John Paul II apologized for the Catholic Church's failure to help save the Jews from the Holocaust. Britain's Queen Elizabeth II apologized for her country's persecution of the Maori people of New Zealand, and laid a wreath and offered a silent prayer at the site of the British army's massacre of Sikhs at Amritsar. The British prime minister Tony Blair expressed deep regret for Britain's actions during the potato famine in Ireland in the nineteenth century. President Bill Clinton expressed regret during his African tour of 1998 for the role of the United States in African slavery. The government of Germany established the special Remembrance, Responsibility and Future Fund to provide individual compensation to Jews and other Eastern European and Soviet citizens conscripted for forced labor by German enterprises prior to and during World War II. The thrust of these gestures is essentially one of symbolic recompense for debts of a moral nature.

Japan, too, has grown apologetic. In his 1993 general-policy address to the Diet, Prime Minister Morihiro Hosokawa expressed "profound remorse and apologies for the fact that Japan's actions, including acts of aggression and colonial rule, caused unbearable suffering and sorrow for so many people." In 1995, in a statement on the occasion of the fiftieth anniversary of the end of World War II, Prime Minister Tomiichi Murayama also expressed "feelings of deep remorse and . . . heartfelt apology" for Japan's "colonial rule and aggression." In the joint statement issued by President Kim Dae Jung of South Korea and Prime Minister Keizo Obuchi of Japan in 1998, the two countries took a significant step toward reconciliation, with Japan expressing "deep remorse and heartfelt apology" for its wartime colonial rule, and South Korea voicing appreciation for "the role that Japan has played in promoting peace and prosperity within the international community through its security policies—foremost its exclusively defense-oriented policy and three nonnuclear principles under the postwar Japanese Peace Constitution—its contributions to the global economy, and its economic assistance to developing countries."

This global trend of expressing sorrow has been driven by the emergence on a worldwide scale of victims of past human rights violations who, feeling they have yet to receive due redress, are raising their voices in protest and in demands that lost rights be restored. This phenomenon may be regarded as the flip side to the globalization of issues arising from past injustices, or "historical issues."

This global interest in revisiting painful historical issues has been spurred by several factors, among them democratization in various parts of the world throughout the 1980s and into the 1990s, and the consequent prominence of so-called transitional justice as an issue demanding immediate attention. In their respective transitions from military to democratic rule, countries such as South Africa, Guatemala, South Korea, the Philippines, Argentina, Chile, and El Salvador have faced a common problem of how to redress the serious injustices perpetrated by earlier regimes so as to achieve transitional justice without destroying either the fledgling process of democratization or people's rising hopes of building a better society. This became an even more pressing issue during the 1990s as former Soviet and Eastern European communist-bloc countries began their own processes of democratization.

However, historical issues are far from limited to questions of transitional justice in newly democratizing countries. Even in mature democracies such as the United States, Japan, Germany, Switzerland, and France, questions are being raised about how to deal with lingering issues of a troubled past, including slavery, treatment of aboriginal peoples, colonialism and colonial wars of independence, war crimes, and collaboration with Nazi authorities. The "ethnic cleansing" that flared up on the Balkan peninsula with the end of the Cold War stands as grim testimony to the fact that even Europe is far from being completely free of "revenge cycles" over historical issues. Nonetheless, European countries have achieved considerable progress in reconciliation. In 1999, for example, the French parliament unanimously passed a bill formally recognizing the 1954–69 conflict that led to Algeria's independence as being a "war," and not simply an operation to "maintain law and order," as the French government had formerly claimed. Furthermore, during the visit of President Abdelaziz Bouteflika of Algeria to France in 2000, President Jacques Chirac heralded a new era in the relationship between France and Algeria by calling for the two countries to face the future "side by side."

In a very twisted way, the terrorist attacks on the World Trade Center and the Pentagon highlighted the dangers of leaving historical scars to fester. The roots of terrorism can usually be found in the (mis)teaching of history, and certainly the perpetrators of the September 11 attacks were schooled to believe that most of the problems facing the Muslim world were the result of a long history of malign Western—and especially American—influence and interference.

Worryingly, as outlined in the report issued in July 2002 by the Council on Foreign Relations (CFR), it is not only al Qaeda terrorists and radical Islamists who view the United States in such a poor light. "America does indeed have a serious image problem," remark the authors of *Public Diplomacy: A Strategy for Reform.* "Gallup's poll of nearly ten thousand people in nine Muslim countries—including Indonesia, Iran, Jordan, Kuwait, Lebanon, Morocco, Pakistan, Saudi Arabia, and Turkey—found that 53 percent of respondents viewed the United States unfavorably."[1] This disquieting discovery was further confirmed by the results, released in December 2002, of a survey by the Pew Research Center for the People and the Press. According to the survey, the percentage of people regarding the United States favorably fell significantly compared with that in 1999/2000: in Turkey, for example, the percentage fell from 52 to 30 percent; in Pakistan, from 23 to 10 percent; and in Indonesia, from 75 to 61 percent.[2] The CFR report urged that the U.S. government launch a public diplomacy campaign aimed at countering one-sided depictions of the United States. In August 2002 the Bush administration did just that, deciding to establish the Office of Global Communications to promote and explain U.S. policies and actions to the rest of the world.

The importance of countering historical misrepresentations is not limited to the relationship of the United States with Muslim societies. In respect to China, for instance, President Bush has drawn attention to the biased view of the United States presented in Chinese classrooms:

> As America learns more about China, I am concerned that the Chinese people do not always see a clear picture of my country. . . . My friend, the Ambassador to China, tells me some Chinese textbooks talk of Americans as "bullying the

weak and repressing the poor." Another Chinese textbook, published just last year, teaches that special agents of the FBI are used to "repress the working people." Now, neither of these is true—and while the words may be leftovers from a previous era, they are misleading and they're harmful.[3]

The End of the Cold War and the "Beginning of History"

The end of the Cold War has brought not, as some commentators famously expected, an "end to history" but rather a new beginning, albeit a beginning shaken by eruptions over issues concerning historical injustices and grievances. Several factors can be identified that have contributed to this unsettling but potentially positive development.

- With the lifting of ideological and political constraints on efforts to expose and renew demands for the redress of past injustices long suppressed under Cold War regimes, the victims have begun to make their voices heard both in their own countries and abroad.
- As democratization movements get under way throughout the world, legal structures enabling more active assertion of individual human rights have become more widespread, both in the developed world and in developing countries. These conditions have enabled the victims of past injustices to stage protests and press claims that could not be advanced before.
- The democratization process is in some respects conducive to the fostering of ethnic-nationalistic sentiment, which in turn can easily lead to oppressive rule by the majority ethnic group and to human rights violations against minorities. The heightening of ethnic-nationalistic sentiment also increases the likelihood of strained relations with neighboring countries.
- As prevailing ideologies and ruling regimes have collapsed, ethnic groups have sought to reestablish their identities. In many cases, this has resulted in a redefining of collective identity in narrower and more exclusive terms. Furthermore, there is a growing tendency to invoke history in an effort to cement such redefinition. This kind of identity politics is apt to foster a sense of victimization and aggressive exclusionism. Such a process is typified by the "ethnic cleansing" that took place in Bosnia, Kosovo, and the Caucasus.

- With heightened awareness of ethnic identity as one aspect of human rights, more and more of the victimized are taking the view that any violation of their identity as a member of a distinct group prevents them from enjoying a full complement of human rights. Among the victimizers as well, there is a growing sense that ignominious aspects of their past and the manner in which they are addressed significantly affect a nation's image and identity.[4]
- Rather than seeking to cultivate a broad perspective on issues of historical interest, the mass media is increasingly focusing on the oral recollections of particular individuals and groups; in many cases, these recollections are becoming the prevailing mode of historical description in a visually oriented popular culture. This process is giving rise to a phenomenon whereby, according to Professor Carol Gluck of Columbia University, history loses out to memory.[5] The trend of multiculturalism in which various groups contend with one another to assert their respective identities is apt to engender a "culture of revering victims" and a mass media that typically pays most attention to those who can be portrayed as wronged and victimized.
- Among groups who feel that their identity is being threatened by advancing globalization, there is a growing trend to reorganize and reunify under the catchwords of *history* and *culture*. This process is susceptible to efforts to revise the group's history in ethnic-nationalistic terms.
- Technological advances in the Internet and other global media at the command of individuals have vastly increased the potential for individual empowerment and enabled victims' claims to reach a global audience. As a corollary, individual and collective feelings and protests have come to enjoy a more direct influence not only within the country in question but also throughout the international community.

A case in point concerns a public lecture that was held at the Osaka government's International Peace Center in January 2000 under the title "The Verification of the Rape of Nanjing: The Biggest Lie of the Twentieth Century." In response to the lecture, Chinese computer hackers attacked Japanese government websites, besmearing them with anti-Japanese text. The incident marked the opening of a new phase in the problem of lingering historical issues between Japan and China.

Recollections of the experiences of individual Chinese (and their claims for compensation) had been largely ignored in the earlier process of historical reconciliation, which proceeded from the normalization of relations between Japan and China in the 1970s to a treaty on peace and friendly relations between the two countries. Now, however, such personal memories have the potential to strain the bilateral relationship. If China should embrace full-fledged democracy, such memories could burst to the fore in more striking ways.

A Regionwide Phenomenon

How each country addresses its historical issues—that is, how it manages the remembering and the forgetting of the past—will influence the future direction of strategic realignment among countries in Asia, not least among them Japan, China, and North and South Korea. Relations between Japan and China are particularly susceptible to being swept up in a revenge cycle. However, the reemergence of historical issues in the post–Cold War era is not a phenomenon that is limited to one country or one bilateral relationship. Rather, the trend has become highly visible in the Asia-Pacific region as a whole. For example:

- The post–Cold War democratization process that took place in South Korea and Taiwan has made it possible for South Korean and Taiwanese civilians to bring lawsuits for individual compensation for Japanese war crimes. To a large extent, tensions between South Korea and Japan in the 1990s over such issues as the sex slave legacy and history textbooks have been a side effect of this process.
- Australian aborigines have addressed historical issues as part of efforts to rediscover and reinstate their identity. Such a search for identity by minorities must inevitably occur within a complex dynamic of reaction and counteraction as the majority attempts to reestablish its own identity.
- South Africa's Truth and Reconciliation Commission and the UN-led war crime tribunals for Bosnia and Rwanda have prompted strong interest in such measures within the Asia-Pacific, most particularly in Cambodia.

All of these examples attest to the fact that interest in historical issues has been stimulated not only by regional factors but also by global (and globalizing) forces, not the least of which are the global media.

Nevertheless, historical issues have been defined in the historical, strategic, and social contexts unique to each case. Each case is peculiar in its own way, and as an aggregate, they defy universal definition. Various factors complicate the situation even further: Is a given issue interstate or intrastate in nature? Is it ethnic or religious? Does it fall within an international political or geopolitical environment? Given such variables, it is critical to analyze such issues on a case-by-case basis, paying special attention to the inherent dynamics of each.

The Case Studies

In this volume, we present seven such case studies. They feature both interethnic and international antagonisms and cover a broad geographic area that includes Korea, Japan, China, Taiwan, Cambodia, East Timor, and Australia.

In the first case study, "Evaluating the Inter-Korean Peace Process," Scott Snyder argues that the recent attempt at reconciliation between North and South Korea differs from all previous attempts because, this time, the two countries are the primary players. As a result, he views the prospects for reconciliation as positive but warns that real reconciliation on the Korean peninsula may take several decades to achieve. Snyder notes that while unique, the recent manner of attempting reconciliation is still inherently fragile. There is pressure to deal too quickly with "hard" issues that could cause negotiations to break down, while a decline in domestic political support within South Korea could easily undermine the process. Another major obstacle to the process is the long period of time required for the institutions and societies of both countries to adapt to the prospect of reunification. The recent slowdown in the South Korean economy is yet another problem.

Snyder concludes with four points: South Korea's willingness to provide the North with economic assistance makes this process unique; since South Korean aid is dependent on public opinion, North Korea will have to make concessions or risk losing the assistance; since North and South

Korea are the primary actors in this drama, it will take considerable time for the two sides to truly reconcile; and reconciliation on the peninsula will affect other reconciliation efforts in Asia either by providing an example for joint cooperation or by spurring renewed confrontation.

The second case study also features Korea but in this instance focuses on South Korea and its historically sensitive relationship with Japan. Victor Cha, the author of "Hypotheses on History and Hate in Asia: Japan and the Korean Peninsula," asserts that since the end of the Cold War Japan and the Republic of Korea (ROK) have reconciled themselves to a point that a fundamental "identity change" has occurred in their relationship. He argues that material (as distinguished from emotional) imperatives such as security, democratization (especially on the Korean side), and economic development have forced Japan and the ROK to engage in episodic cooperation. Cha finds evidence of the fundamental change in the relationship between Japan and the ROK in statements made by Kim Dae Jung and Keizo Obuchi during their summit meeting in 1998—statements that emphasized the positive aspects of the two countries' relations while expressing admiration for each other's accomplishments.

The case of Japan and the ROK may help to inspire a new way of thinking about historical enmity in international relations. Cha outlines the following seven lessons drawn from his hypothesis on reconciliation: reconciliation is driven by material imperatives; an apology is necessary, but not sufficient, for reconciliation to begin; reconciliation is a two-way street; no formula for reconciliation will succeed—the process is a natural one; institutional linkages between the reconciling countries are essential; domestic legitimacy is key; and regional precedent is useful.

Whereas Japan's relations with the ROK have improved since the end of the Cold War, its relationship with China has actually worsened in recent years. In "Reconciliation between Japan and China: Problems and Prospects," Daqing Yang notes that Japan's and China's perceptions of each other's attitudes toward historical issues have seriously deteriorated, creating a problem that has significant implications for the foreign policy of both countries.

While many analysts agree that the 1982 textbook controversy brought the problem of historical perception into the open, there is no general agreement about its underlying cause. Instead, there are three theories.

The first places blame on contemporary Chinese tactics of realpolitik, that is, the tendency of China to play the "history card" to leverage Japanese concessions. The second argues that Japanese right-wing revisionism and collective amnesia are at the root of the problem. The third avoids a purely domestic analysis by looking at the relationship's bilateral dynamics along with broader international trends such as generational changes in Japan and China, a global rise in nationalism, and the phenomenon of redressing historical injustices.

Yang notes that, when discussing the prospects for solving historical issues between Japan and China, one must take into account the fact that the relationship between the two countries is now entering a phase of "competition and coexistence." It is in the national interest of both countries to prevent the relationship from becoming a rivalry and to work toward creating a political environment conducive to solving history issues. Both short- and long-term solutions—ranging from official to track-two and track-three exchanges in historical research and educational programs—must be implemented to effect changes in the social and political systems of the two countries. Equally, for reconciliation to be lasting, the process must be carried out not only between governments but also between individuals and between and within civil societies.

Masahiro Wakabayashi turns the spotlight on interethnic reconciliation in his case study, "Overcoming the Difficult Past: Rectification of the 2-28 Incident and the Politics of Reconciliation in Taiwan." Wakabayashi argues that, as the process of democratization has advanced, the Taiwanese people have shown a growing desire to settle past accounts, particularly with regard to past acts of oppression such as the "2-28 Incident." This bloody episode began on February 27–28, 1947, when Nationalist (Mainlander) troops cracked down on native Taiwanese protesters; between eighteen and twenty-eight thousand people are estimated to have been killed. The incident had two important ramifications for Taiwanese society: first, it deprived native Taiwanese of the ability to protest persecution at the hands of the Mainlanders; second, it marked the start of ethnic conflict in Taiwan.

The process of settling past accounts began in 1987 with a small movement, which expanded incrementally to involve larger numbers of legislators. The process culminated in the enactment of an ordinance in 1995 to compensate the victims and establish a memorial foundation.

Wakabayashi notes that these attempts at settling the 2-28 Incident have inspired discussions on other sensitive historical issues such as the White Terror campaign. He warns, however, that while the process of settling past accounts has allowed more open discussion, the issue of whether this process has led to real ethnic reconciliation remains unclear as the Mainland minority continues to retain great influence in various spheres of Taiwan's society. Wakabayashi concludes that ethnic reconciliation in contemporary Taiwan is still unstable.

The situation in Cambodia is perhaps less encouraging than that in Taiwan. As Nayan Chanda points out in "Cambodia: Unable to Confront the Past," at first glance Cambodia appears to have achieved a remarkable degree of reconciliation, but a closer look reveals that the country needs a three-way reconciliation process to heal the wounds caused by three decades of war and genocide. The first axis of reconciliation must be between the victims and their oppressors; the second, between the minority Vietnamese living in Cambodia and the Khmers; and the third, between Cambodia and Vietnam.

The possibility of a mixed international court trying the Khmer Rouge is stronger today than in the past due to a combination of external pressures and growing internal demands, but the outcome, Chanda contends, may still fall short of a fair trial of all the responsible leaders. There is certainly a need for a special tribunal both to ascertain the facts about what the Khmer Rouge did and to facilitate national soul searching so as to prevent a recurrence of similar atrocities in the future. Chanda suspects, however, that even if a tribunal were to be held, it would not, owing to the corrupt nature of Cambodia's judiciary system, go beyond establishing a few facts related to the killing. The fundamental difference between what the Cambodia government wants (i.e., social stability) and what the nongovernmental and international communities desire (i.e., a public trial and convictions) adds to Chanda's rather pessimistic outlook.

Such pessimism may apply equally to the case of East Timor. In "East Timor: A Nation Divided," Todung Mulya Lubis examines the impact of the substantial human rights abuses that occurred in East Timor under Indonesian administration, even after the referendum on independence was passed in September 1999. The legal process for prosecuting the perpetrators of these violations and crimes remains unclearly defined to this day. Lubis asserts that this will undoubtedly delay the settlement of the East Timor issue.

He argues that reconciliation is the key to resolving the East Timor problem and to avoiding disintegration or separatism. The reconciliation process is beginning to take place, with the creation of the Commission for Reception, Truth, and Reconciliation in East Timor, which will deal with relatively minor offenses committed between 1974 and 1999. For the process to be sustainable, however, historical truths must be revealed and incorporated into the country's future teaching of its history. In addition, legal prosecution of the parties directly involved in crimes against humanity during the pre- and post-referendum periods must continue.

Unfortunately, the trials being held in Jakarta have at times appeared farcical. As Lubis explains, in the current geopolitical climate, the international will to bring the members of the Indonesian military and police elites to justice has waned significantly. By allowing misconceptions regarding the role of the military and the United Nations in the East Timor massacres to go unchecked, the trials threaten to have widespread negative implications for reconciliation in other parts of the Indonesian archipelago. Lubis asserts that the solution of the East Timor problem does not rest with the East Timorese alone and should be a critical concern for the entire international community.

In the final case study, "Aboriginal Reconciliation, Asian Australians, and Some Heretical Thoughts," Greg Sheridan argues that for reconciliation to take place between aboriginal Australians and the Australian nation as a whole, less emphasis should be placed on symbols of reconciliation and more time should be devoted to substantive rectification of the way in which aborigines are treated in Australian society today. Sheridan outlines the historical and contemporary contexts in which Australia's native population has sought redress for injustices committed against them. But, while admitting that aborigines have suffered grave human rights abuses in the past and continue to be disadvantaged in terms of health, education, life expectancy, and other factors, Sheridan asserts that some of the aborigines' demands are counterproductive. He argues that little progress has been made on symbolic issues precisely because aboriginal demands in this category conflict with the deep-seated Australian belief in the universality of citizenship.

Sheridan concludes by admonishing the aborigines to follow the example of Asian Australians. Although he admits that the circumstances and history of discrimination against the aborigines and Asians are quite different, he points out that Asians have worked within the Australian system to improve their situation. And while their participation in society is far from complete, Asian Australians' willingness to focus on issues of substance, rather than on symbolic ones, has won them considerable success and the acceptance of their fellow citizens. He conjectures that aboriginal Australians would, therefore, do well to accept mainstream, modern Australian society and to de-emphasize symbols that undermine national principles. Insistence on a stance that runs counter to the beliefs of most Australians increases the threat of a majority backlash and risks civic exhaustion and a general lapse into disregard for aboriginal issues.

Drawing Lessons

As noted at the outset, the purpose of the essays in this volume is not only to improve our understanding of the impact of painful historical issues on international and interethnic relations but also to learn from the experiences of others how we might best come to terms with the past and transform conflict into cooperation. Fortunately, the case studies offer many lessons for the future, revealing a variety of common patterns, themes, and key elements in efforts to promote reconciliation in very different circumstances. These lessons, which are discussed in detail in the concluding chapter, include the following.

1. *Human rights violations are a universal human experience.* Large-scale, serious human rights violations of the kind that inspire and sustain long-standing grievances occur in all societies. We should not seek the causes of our historical problems in supposed ethnic "traits"; no ethnic group or nation has a monopoly on cruelty or on suffering.
2. *"Our" history is everyone's history.* While each community's or ethnic group's history is in an obvious sense its own, it is also part of the history of all ethnic and national groups and of the world as a whole. It is dangerous to try to describe one's own country's history as if it were completely self-contained and entirely detached from world history.

3. *Reconciliation over the past is a process.* Reconciliation is necessarily a long-term process. Unless the process is begun, however, no visions of peace or coexistence will be able to endure and no links between civil societies will be able to develop.
4. *There is no universal formula.* We must analyze and take into account the specific circumstances under which each violation of human rights took place. There is no universal formula for reconciliation.
5. *Reconciliation must be a joint effort by victimizers and victimized.* Efforts toward reconciliation will not take root unless they are made by both the victimizers and the victimized, working in collaboration.
6. *Use a forward-looking, realistic approach.* Moralistic arguments are not an effective way to transcend the problems of the past. Instead, we need more discussion on how to resolve these problems realistically with a common vision.
7. *Cultivate democracy.* In order for reconciliation to take firm root, it is important for all the societies involved to expand and strengthen their democratic institutions.
8. *The approach should be based on multilateralism and regionalism.* Efforts to promote bilateral reconciliation should reinforce multilateral and regional cooperation to nurture a "culture of dialogue" and a "custom of dialogue."
9. *Political leadership is key.* Whatever vision is pursued, the process of reconciliation over the past will not move forward without appropriate political leadership.
10. *Individual initiative is essential.* Ultimately, however, the key to success in the reconciliation process lies in the commitment of people at the individual level.
11. *Our behavior should reflect the kind of nation we hope to build.* Facing up to history and transcending the lingering troubles of the past are not tasks to be approached passively. The way in which we tackle these issues will itself make up part of our country's national identity. Loving one's country or ethnic group should not mean idealizing it and its past. Ultimately, the task of reconciliation requires the kind of grace that arises in individuals at the intersection of heartfelt remorse and heartfelt forgiveness.

1

Evaluating the Inter-Korean Peace Process

Scott Snyder

As one examines the legacy of unresolved conflicts in the Asia-Pacific region, the situation on the Korean peninsula stands out as a pivotal case. The conflict and its origins are long-standing, but active efforts that might finally un-make the conflict and establish a lasting inter-Korean reconciliation are still relatively recent. The contribution of such efforts to the consolidation of a true rapprochement remains uncertain, although the long-term trend on the peninsula itself suggests positive movement, despite occasional setbacks and periods of inertia—even the nuclear crisis that began in late 2002, unlike the crisis of 1993–94, has been played down by some players, who have expressed determination not to let the situation devolve into a military conflict. The drama of the first-ever summit meeting between the two Korean leaders held in June 2000 underscored the promise accompanying hopes for reconciliation on the Korean peninsula, but it also marked only the beginning of what may be a decades-long process of accommodation between the two very different systems, cultures, and societies, which have been almost completely isolated from each other for over half a century. Such accommodation is bound to be the most difficult aspect of reconciliation on the Korean peninsula and will have profound implications not only for the domestic politics of the two Koreas but also for other legacies of unresolved confrontation in the region that may shape the future of relations within Northeast Asia.

When compared with other Asian conflicts, the Korean conflict is distinctive in two important respects. First, it had no interethnic component; it was a war among an ethnically homogeneous people divided by ideology and system and led by powerfully stubborn personalities on both sides. Second, it was to a greater extent than any other conflict in Asia directly influenced by the emergence of the global confrontation of the United States and the Soviet Union that marked the Cold War. There is no need to delve too deeply into the arguments among historians over which factors were predominant, but it is important to recognize that the conflict itself was fueled by a coincidence of both domestic and international factors; therefore, the inter-Korean reconciliation process is likely to have both domestic and international implications.[1] In this chapter I will briefly review failed attempts to initiate inter-Korean dialogue as a vehicle for resolving the conflict, analyze the prospects and potential weaknesses of the nascent inter-Korean peace process that has grown out of the inter-Korean summit, and explore the domestic (i.e., within South and North Korea) and international implications of reconciliation on the Korean peninsula.

Historical Overview of Inter-Korean Dialogue

The first attempts at inter-Korean dialogue stemmed directly from the need to end the military conflict on the Korean peninsula. Armistice negotiations were aimed not at resolving the conflict but at trying to stop the "hot" war by establishing the parameters for the end of confrontation and the management of the resulting stalemate. The Korean armistice in 1953 ended the military confrontation, but negotiations through the resulting Military Armistice Commission quickly became a primary vehicle for scoring propaganda points over the other side, i.e., for representatives from both sides, the negotiations became a war by other means.[2] Thus, the earliest steps away from conflict and toward reconciliation through negotiation on the Korean peninsula have their origins in interaction that effectively substituted for military conflict while perpetuating so-called peaceful competition for legitimacy, accompanied by occasional small-scale skirmishes between the two sides.

It was not until almost two decades after the end of the armed conflict that the two Koreas themselves engaged in direct dialogue, because the management of the Military Armistice Commission remained under the control of the Democratic People's Republic of Korea (DPRK) and the UN Command at Panmunjom. A review of relations between North and South during the course of more than a quarter century since the opening of inter-Korean dialogue in 1972 shows that initial dialogues seeking reconciliation were really an extension of inter-Korean competition for legitimacy, but in a new venue. Political talks through the Red Cross were initiated in 1972 under the leadership of President Park Chung Hee of South Korea and the North Korean leader, Kim Il Sung, and resulted in the North-South Joint Communiqué of July 4, 1972, which laid out the three principles for national unification, namely that reunification should be achieved through "independent Korean efforts without being subject to external imposition or interference; through peaceful means, not through the use of force against each other; and through the pursuit of national unity, transcending differences in ideas, ideologies, and systems."[3] In the wake of the shock that accompanied Nixon's historic visit to Beijing, both Kim Il Sung and Park Chung Hee were sufficiently unsettled to be willing to take a chance on talks.[4]

The most significant agreements between North and South Korea during the Cold War period came as a result of changes elsewhere. The 1972 Red Cross talks were authorized by the two leaders as a direct result of the opening of U.S. diplomacy with China, a development that must have been as shocking to Pyongyang as it was to Seoul. However, the Red Cross talks broke down once both sides had been sufficiently reassured through their dialogue and their observations of the international environment that they would be able to adapt to the new environment created by the rapprochement between the United States and the People's Republic of China (the PRC). Likewise, the Agreement on Reconciliation, Nonaggression, Exchanges, and Cooperation (known as the Basic Agreement) of December 1991 occurred following the collapse of the Soviet Union, another shock to North Korea. On other occasions—when, for example, North Korea proposed a dialogue during a period of political instability in South Korea in 1980, or in the context of international outrage following the bombing in Rangoon in 1983, when seventeen South Korean officials were killed—North Korea has taken the initiative to propose dialogue to press a perceived advantage or to counter international criticism.

After a period of assessment in each case, it appears, however, that North Korea backed away from implementation as old patterns settled in and the country adapted to new structural circumstances. Only in the context of a perceived immediate external threat to North Korea's system have radical changes been contemplated. The passage of time and renewed confidence in the ability to cope with perceived external threats, or false threats, have resulted in a return to the core processes and traditional modes of behavior that marked inter-Korean interactions during the Cold War, namely, one-upmanship and a zero-sum attitude toward the prospect of any compromise or concession that might benefit the opposing side, regardless of whether benefits might also accrue to one's own side.

The Inter-Korean Summit and Post–Cold War Reconciliation

The June 2000 inter-Korean summit began the first truly post–Cold War series of high-level inter-Korean dialogues. The atmosphere of competition and occasional conflict between the West and the Communist world had been replaced by the mid-1990s with an essential convergence of the objectives of all the major-power neighbors of the two Koreas. The three essential objectives were the prevention of war, the prevention of instability that might result from the collapse of North Korea, and the prevention of nuclear proliferation on the Korean peninsula. Thus, the external factors that had previously limited progress in inter-Korean dialogue and that had provided the two Koreas with the luxury of gamesmanship and competition for legitimacy during the Cold War had been replaced by a very different situation, one in which North Korea desperately needed external inputs from its neighbors, including South Korea, to ensure the survival of the regime.

Both the South Korean president, Kim Dae Jung, and the North Korean leader, Kim Jong Il, clearly had a large stake in pushing forward the reconciliation process they have led. Most remarkable is that the Kims have become politically dependent on each other for cooperation in order to convince critics at home that the process is real. By the same token, many of the measures used in the initial stages of the process have appealed to symbolism and emotion and have occurred in fits and starts (manipulated by the North Korean side as a vehicle for turning the flow of humanitarian aid back on and for breaking periodic stalemates); the core issues of confrontation have not yet been dealt with in concrete terms—neither can they be easily or quickly resolved. North Korea's own recognition of the severity of its economic needs, the political consolidation of Kim Jong Il, and Kim Dae Jung's consistent and principled pursuit of engagement on terms that would provide North Korea with tangible economic benefits were all necessary conditions for a breakthrough in the dialogue. The process of moving toward reconciliation will, however, involve considerable institutional adaptation and social accommodation on both sides, a process that, if Germany is any example, is likely to take decades.

In fact, the relative stagnation in inter-Korean relations that had set in within six months of the historic summit provides evidence of just how formidable are the institutional and structural barriers to reconciliation, bringing the process to a halt despite the dramatic political risks and commitment shown by both leaders. The deepening of internal political divisions and debates in South Korea over the nature and process of reconciliation in the aftermath of the summit illustrates the stakes involved and the institutional and political resistance to and hesitancy about structural accommodations that may accompany reconciliation.[5] Likewise, Kim Jong Il's mysterious inability to make good on his promises to Kim Dae Jung suggests the possibility of a similar internal struggle on the North Korean side, in which vested interests must be overcome to forge the institutional adaptations necessary to support a reconciliation process. However, its economic dependency is the overarching factor that continues periodically to drive North Korea to reopen negotiations with the South, despite evident institutional and internal hesitancy and even resistance.

In its first few months the inter-Korean peace process took on a number of characteristics that have made it quite distinct from other peace processes. First, the historic meeting between Korean leaders took place without the mediation of a third party, unlike with the processes in Ireland and the Middle East during the late 1990s, in which American and Norwegian brokers invested considerable effort to bring former warring parties together. The fact that it was possible to set aside differences and directly arrange an inter-Korean summit through purely Korean efforts is a tribute to both sides, and it underscores the character of inter-Korean reconciliation as an *autonomous* process. The principle of autonomy is enshrined in the 1972 North-South Joint Communiqué and reaffirmed in the June Declaration.[6] It is clearly an important starting point and reflects a context and history that is unique to Korea.

Two potential drawbacks of an unmediated peace process are the difficulty of overcoming temporary setbacks or apparently intractable differences and that of incorporating verification measures as part of the implementation. Indeed, just those difficulties—managing setbacks and ensuring verification—have become issues as the dialogue has lost its momentum, and the lowering of public expectations has created new challenges for the respective leaderships. If the two sides find that they do need the assistance of a mediator, it is useful to recognize that the third parties that may usefully be incorporated into such a process may not necessarily be nation-states or even foreigners, but they do have to be trusted by both sides as fair and impartial intermediaries, even if not necessarily neutral.

A second distinctive characteristic of the inter-Korean peace process is that, unlike with the Irish and Middle East peace processes, in which the symbolic handshake between leaders of opposing sides represented a consolidation and institutionalization of the first phase of an already existing process, the handshake between Kim Dae Jung and Kim Jong Il came before the formal institutionalization of the process, as a symbol of the hope of future reconciliation rather than as the consolidation of work already accomplished. This fact underscores the fragility of the process, but it also suggests the positive role that political leadership on both sides of a dispute may play in the attempt to create a new reality or context for interaction and negotiation. The role of leadership is certainly relevant to the North Korean case, where all decision-making power still flows to the top and where Kim Jong Il's public emergence on the international stage has been an essential prerequisite for substantive progress in the inter-Korean relationship. Likewise, leadership remains a key factor in South Korea's democratic society, where the legacy of state-led development cedes a significant role for the South Korean president in setting the direction of government policy.

The symbolism of reconciliation has provided a powerful emotional and psychological boost for efforts by both sides to live up to the promise embodied in the June summit. Kim Jong Il himself acknowledged in his initial meeting with Kim Dae Jung that "the world is watching," and both sides have made extraordinary efforts to overcome vast system differences in the initial stages of the process. Many of those efforts have, however, been designed primarily to win psychological validation of the process. The second stage, in which practical cooperation at the working level might be institutionalized, has been a critical test for the process and, quite frankly, remains the major stumbling block to progress. The North-South meeting of defense ministers held on Cheju Island in late September 2000 envisaged the establishment of working-level cooperation between the two military establishments to provide the necessary security support to reconnect rail and highway links across the demilitarized zone (DMZ).[7] The agreements reached at the working-level inter-Korean talks in November 2000 about building the infrastructure for economic cooperation, including investment guarantees and taxation, will need to be implemented if trade and investment between North and South Korea are to be sustained in the future. However, through the summer of 2002, North Korea had not yet formally ratified or implemented those agreements. North Korean demands for the supply of energy from South Korea constitute yet another field in which further institutionalization of cooperation between the two sides will be required—in this case, technical cooperation will be needed to survey North Korea's energy sector and to determine how to supply North Korea's energy needs. If the Korean peace process is to move into a second stage of institutionalization and consolidation, these working-level meetings must be held regularly as envisaged in the 1991–92 Basic Agreement.

The experience of other peace and reconciliation processes also provides two cautionary lessons. First, the principle of starting with easier issues and moving on to harder issues is the right way to build momentum, but it is also important that the negotiators not feel compelled to address the hard issues prematurely. The principle appears to be flouted by the tendency, in the inter-Korean context, of the top political leadership to seek a whole host of visionary objectives in order to achieve a symbolic political "breakthrough" or "package deal." Thus, there is a real risk that a breakdown and an accompanying cycle of recrimination may occur unless there is a clear determination of firm and concrete standards for measuring performance in implementing the agreements made.

Second, domestic political support is essential in sustaining momentum for a peace process. In South Korea, it will not be enough to ride the wave of international support for inter-Korean reconciliation if domestic support for such a process cannot be secured. South Korean public opinion is a central factor in determining the pace and substance of the process and neither Kim Dae Jung nor Kim Jong Il can afford to ignore it without forfeiting the gains that have been realized thus far.

Domestic Implications in South Korea

Another major obstacle to furthering the inter-Korean reconciliation process has emerged in South Korea in the wake of the inter-Korean summit, and that is the recognition that any reconciliation or accommodation with the North that might eventually lead to Korean reunification will require extensive institutional and social adaptation within South Korea. This possibility is extraordinarily contentious within South Korean society because it threatens long-standing vested interests on elite and institutional levels and because of the difficulties of calibrating necessary institutional change with the pace of rapprochement with the North. In fact, the prospect of rapprochement with North Korea under Kim Jong Il is truly revolutionary if one considers that the raison d'être of the government of the Republic of Korea (ROK), as embodied in the legal foundations of the state constitution, is anticommunism. For example, President Kim Dae Jung's visit to Pyongyang was, strictly speaking, a violation of the National Security Law. The primary South Korean interlocutor in preparations for the summit was the chief of the National Intelligence Service, Lim Dong-won, who appeared publicly with Kim Dae Jung and Kim Jong Il in Pyongyang, a fact that has stimulated a debate over the future direction of the National Intelligence Service's intelligence collection activities vis-à-vis North Korea.[8]

If, therefore, the process of reconciliation with North Korea represents the beginning of "the end of history," to borrow Francis Fukuyama's phrase describing the ideational and ideological impact of the end of the Cold War,[9] for Korean politics it also means the beginning of ideology as a factor in a national political debate heretofore constrained by anticommunism as an essential prerequisite for participation. Thus, a domestic political debate that has for decades been driven by personality and regionalism is now being infused with ideology when, in other parts of the world, ideology as a political force is declining. Ideological division has come to the surface most strongly in initial debates over whether the National Security Law should be revised and in comments made by an opposition party lawmaker characterizing the Kim Dae Jung government as a wing of the North Korean Workers' Party.[10] Immediately after the summit in South Korea, there was a torrent of debate over its implications for South Korean politics, the educational system, the social adaptations that would be required as part of reconciliation with the North, and expectations of what North Korea should do in response. This debate has continued, in the context of any future visit of Kim Jong Il to Seoul, by way of a campaign to require Kim Jong Il to apologize for North Korea's invasion of the South and for such terrorist acts attributed to the North as the bombing deaths of over half of the South Korean cabinet in Rangoon in the mid-1980s and the downing of a Korean Airlines flight shortly before the Seoul Olympics in 1987.[11]

The ideological division over the intent of engagement is also clearly revealed in rationales that have been put forward for pursuing Kim Dae Jung's Sunshine Policy. As president, Kim Dae Jung almost always gave a liberal rationale for pursuing engagement with North Korea, arguing that the leadership in Pyongyang has finally recognized the "true intentions" of the Sunshine Policy and has decided that it is possible to trust South Korea.[12] According to this rationale, unconditional giving to North Korea is an essential vehicle for showing good faith, and eventually North Korea will respond in good faith as trust will have been built between the two sides. However, there is also a realist rationale for opening a political dialogue: It is a vehicle for inducing economic dependency and thereby defanging the North. This line of argument appeals to most South Korean conservatives but is almost never used by the ROK government, no doubt partly in recognition that such a construction would only intensify North Korea's mistrust of and hesitancy to engage with South Korea. Thus, it is important to recognize that, in many respects, the Sunshine Policy toward North Korea represents a continuation of past South Korean efforts to engage with North Korea, beginning when President Roh Tae Woo decided to pursue *nordpolitik* in 1988; however, the liberal justification for engagement is particularly provocative to South Korean conservatives who suspect that such arguments may represent the leading edge of a progressive ideological wave that could revolutionize South Korean politics.

As a result of the summit, many conservatives felt beleaguered and complained that a "new orthodoxy" of political correctness in favor of reconciliation with North Korea has detracted from the very real need for substantive change to occur in North Korea's military alignments and its targeting of Seoul before true reconciliation can be said to be at hand. Likewise, these conservatives continue to feel that the material price of reconciliation has thus far been too high or has consisted primarily of one-way economic support for North Korea with little in the way of reciprocity from the North. The Kim Dae Jung administration's handling of the return to North Korea of long-term unconverted prisoners (North Koreans who had refused to renounce their support for the North Korean regime despite being held in South Korea for decades) without pressing a reciprocal demand for the return of South Korean spies or prisoners of war still held by the North is perhaps the most politically salient example of such frustrations.[13] At the same time, some conservatives may feel that, because of the essentially anticommunist orientation of South Korea's institutional and social structure during the Cold War, they have much to lose in the process of institutional reform that is likely to accompany reconciliation. In addition, Kim Dae Jung's seeming inattention to serious domestic economic problems and the continuing domestic political deadlocks between the ruling and opposition parties serve to dramatize political divisions over the Sunshine Policy and weaken critical South Korean domestic political support for inter-Korean rapprochement. Although ruling party candidate Roh Moo-hyun's victory in the December 2002 presidential election has ensured that South Korea will continue to favor diplomatic and economic engagement with North Korea and appears to have revived South Korean public support for such policies, South Korean public opinion will remain deeply divided in the absence of North Korea's cooperation with the new government to continue dialogue and reconciliation.[14]

Public Opinion and Inter-Korean Reconciliation

Although President Kim Dae Jung's leadership in relentlessly pursuing engagement with North Korea has been critical in achieving an opening in high-level dialogue with the DPRK regime, South Korean public opinion remains the principal determinant of the pace, substance, and sustainability of the process. President Kim's power steadily waned as he entered the last stages of his presidency. Despite achievements beyond anything most Koreans would have imagined possible at the beginning of the year 2000, success has bred not political credit for Kim Dae Jung but rather higher expectations and the initiation of more substantive projects that will both induce real change in North Korea and show clearly that North Korea no longer need be considered an adversary. In fact, public disapproval of the Sunshine Policy was a factor in hastening the onset of President Kim's lame-duck status. It is clear that South Korea simply cannot afford the levels of generosity offered to the North in the initial stages. North Korea's insatiable demands for assistance are likely to reveal clearly the limits of South Korea's capacity to render humanitarian aid.

Another emerging factor that has had an influence on South Korean public opinion is the reservoir of public support for reaching out to brothers in the North through humanitarian assistance. Even at the post–Cold War low point of the official inter-Korean relationship following Kim Il Sung's death in 1994, South Korean religious organizations continued a campaign that had begun in the early 1990s to deliver "rice of love" to compatriots in the North. Despite governmental disapproval, a stream of assistance flowed from South Korea via Chinese border towns into North Korea. South Korean nongovernmental organizations (NGOs) with the mission of providing assistance to North Korea thus grew up under adverse circumstances, and they welcomed the change in policy and even financial support from the South Korean government that was initiated with the Kim Dae Jung administration. Between 1995 and 2000, South Korean NGOs contributed almost U.S. $100 million in assistance to North Korea, more than 25 percent of South Korea's overall assistance during that period. Ironically, the summit had a mixed effect on South Korean NGOs' efforts to work in North Korea: on the one hand, the summit opened the way for greater direct inter-Korean engagement, including South Korean NGO projects conducted through more active direct channels and exchanges of visits with North Korean counterparts; on the other hand, improvements in the inter-Korean official relationship actually marginalized some South Korean NGO work, making it harder for those NGOs to receive attention from North Korean counterparts.[15]

Economics and Inter-Korean Rapprochement

Despite mixed public opinion toward engagement, there is a growing recognition in South Korea of the opportunity for mutually beneficial long-term cooperation in the economic sphere, most notably through the provision to North Korea of "social overhead capital" through the rebuilding of North Korea's infrastructure, which may provide momentum for further progress in relaxing tensions between the two sides.[16] Hyundai's development of North Korea's Mount Kumgang as a tourist destination may be regarded as a demonstration project in the economic sphere, testing the possibilities for such cooperation; it remains to be seen, however, whether more realistic and profitable forms of economic cooperation will develop in the future. Both the negotiations by Hyundai to develop an industrial complex near the North Korean city of Kaesong and governmental discussions about the rebuilding of railroad and highway connections between the two Koreas will be litmus tests of the extent to which broadened economic cooperation is possible.

Domestic Implications in North Korea

Kim Jong Il's carefully choreographed entry onto the world stage through live satellite telecasts of his welcome to Kim Dae Jung in June 2000 underscored his primacy as the key decision maker. Even so, it will take time to prove that a process driven by top leaders can avoid the pitfalls of previous so-called breakthroughs in inter-Korean negotiations by establishing broad parameters for interaction and engagement. If politics is in command and the top political leader has not pre-authorized a specific position or response to agenda items raised in the course of even ministerial-level negotiations between the two Koreas, it is unlikely that there will be any progress on such items.

For instance, there were clear limitations on the ability of the North Korean negotiators to respond to South Korean proposals of concrete steps for economic cooperation or to initiate military confidence-building measures in the absence of explicit approval by Kim Jong Il. At the first round of inter-Korean ministerial talks less than two months after the summit in Pyongyang, it was difficult for the North Korean delegation to respond concretely to specific proposals on reestablishing rail connections, and the group flatly refused to consider dialogue on military confidence building, despite the fact that the South Korean government has been increasingly under pressure to show progress in that area if the South Korean public is to believe that the inter-Korean rapprochement is real. Only in direct dialogue with North Korea's top leader can substantive progress be made on key political issues; otherwise, the communication process remains indirect, embodied in the reports of the North Korean delegation.

Such cooperation also represents a potentially major challenge to North Korea's system, as it will be more and more difficult to build fences around South Korean economic investments and business practices or to isolate South Korean economic penetration of North Korea from the rest of the North Korean economy. Kim Jong Il must be acutely aware of the dilemmas accompanying economic dependency on South Korea, yet that is his country's only realistic option for economic rehabilitation. Depending on how it is implemented, increased economic integration between the two Koreas may have a major impact on the North Korean system. It is no wonder that North Korean officials have been so hesitant in working-level negotiations to go forward with substantive cooperation in the economic sphere absent explicit approval from Kim Jong Il.

The natural political strategy of the North is to keep politics in command and use political symbolism as a vehicle for drawing the economic resources necessary to keep the DPRK running. Available tools that the leadership may use to achieve these objectives include political sloganeering, propagandizing, and the strengthening of Kim Jong Il's political leadership by using increased economic benefits to consolidate and justify his rule despite the North's broken economic system. Giving Kim Jong Il political credit may also provide cover for substantive economic reforms that are necessary to rehabilitate North Korea's economy, but the costs of such a project are not yet clear; neither is it clear whether such a rehabilitation project can succeed. In fact, there is a risk that North Korea may gain just enough resources to get by without engaging in serious economic reforms—a risk underscored by the Mount Kumgang "demonstration project," in which the cash gained by North Korea might be used for expanded military exercises or other activities that heighten the risk of renewed confrontation.

Regional Implications

Because the Korean conflict has both inter-Korean and Cold War origins, the inter-Korean reconciliation process is likely to unravel the remnants of the Cold War confrontation in Northeast Asia. President Kim Dae Jung routinely referred to the major task of inter-Korean reconciliation as including "dismantling the Cold War structure."[17] The revamping of the conditions that have shaped international relations in Northeast Asia will clearly not be complete without inter-Korean rapprochement; neither has it been possible thus far for major powers surrounding the Korean peninsula to formulate a new structure for managing relations in the region absent the resolution of tensions there. In fact, it is increasingly clear that the inter-Korean reconciliation process itself is likely to be the major vehicle for reshaping the regional security environment. In particular, whether neighboring powers view the tasks of North Korea's rehabilitation cooperatively or competitively will determine the possibilities for cooperation, define new rivalries, or reawaken historical competition in Northeast Asia.

One significant structural factor that becomes apparent as one examines the influence of inter-Korean reconciliation on interstate relations in Northeast Asia is the emergence of Korean leaders as actors shaping regional events rather than simply as historic objects of major-power rivalry. From the late nineteenth century through the Cold War, the weakness of Korean national leadership made the peninsula a venue for major-power confrontation and the doormat for major-power conflict in the region. The Sino-Japanese Wars and Russo-Japanese Wars that occurred about a century ago were fought in Korea, and the beginning of the Cold War immediately following World War II left a newly liberated Korea divided, once again a victim of major-power intrigues. Kim Dae Jung's ability to improve South Korea's relations with all of its major-power neighbors simultaneously is a potentially important model for the future of Korean diplomacy as a bridge and constructive actor rather than as an object of major-power diplomacy. Likewise, Kim Jong Il's emergence has involved visits to China and Russia and constructive meetings with President Jiang Zemin of the PRC, President Vladimir Putin of Russia, and Goran Persson of Sweden, the chairman-in-office of the European Union. Despite certain peculiarities, Kim Jong Il's emergence as a diplomatic and political actor on the world stage reveals the nature and working of the North Korean leadership in ways that cannot easily be put back behind the screen.

One significant implication of the emergence of the two Koreas as actors shaping the environment for possible inter-Korean reconciliation is that all the major powers have reacted to events on the Korean peninsula rather than determined them. Whether they respond constructively or inter-Korean reconciliation engenders a renewed confrontation between major powers in Northeast Asia will influence the pace and progress of that reconciliation. For instance, it is widely assumed that a good relationship between the United States and the People's Republic of China is necessary for progress in inter-Korean relations. Likewise, China and Japan both see a favorable security environment in Korea as essential to their own security and will be watching the negotiations closely to determine whether new developments are favorable to their own respective interests.

The only possible exception to this pattern lies with the United States and the Bush administration's apparent revisionist impulses toward North Korea. Clearly, Washington can have a decisive impact on Korean peninsula affairs when its attention is directly focused on the issue. North Korea's inclusion in President Bush's "axis of evil" and the repercussions of that statement demonstrate the influence of U.S. policy and the need for cooperation from Washington if South Korea is to manage an effective policy toward North Korea. The Bush administration has in the past two years been able to stop Kim Dae Jung's Sunshine Policy in its tracks and has given North Korean leaders plenty of false excuses to hide behind as reasons for their lack of cooperation. Perhaps most damaging has been the negative effect of the Bush administration's rhetoric about North Korea on public opinion in South Korea. One result is that the younger generation of South Koreans have focused on President Bush as the primary cause of increased tensions involving North Korea rather than North Korea's own intransigence.

But the Sunshine Policy has arguably also moderated the policy of the Bush administration toward North Korea, and the South Korean government retains a veto power over the most dramatic policy options that the Bush administration might contemplate. The unilateral pursuit by the United States of any policy toward North Korea without acquiescence from Seoul would clearly signal the unraveling of the alliance between the United States and the Republic of Korea—ultimately at great cost to future U.S. influence on the Korean peninsula and in the region.

If indeed the inter-Korean reconciliation process can be kept on track, the danger of confrontation between the two Koreas would no longer be the most important issue in the security of the region. Other potential conflicts or long-buried historical rivalries would then dominate a new security environment in Northeast Asia. Most immediately, the focus would turn to the prospects for confrontation between Beijing and Taipei, a possibility that could also impair the relationship between the United States and the People's Republic of China. Another possibility is that competition between Tokyo and Beijing, each driven by security concerns, to gain influence over a unified Korean peninsula could catalyze the historical but long-buried Sino-Japanese rivalry.

These, however, are distant concerns compared with the immediate need to manage the dynamics of the inter-Korean reconciliation process, which will require international involvement and assistance if it is to be successful. The economic task of rehabilitating North Korea will require assistance from, among other sources, Japan, international financial institutions, and even China. The extent to which coordinated economic assistance to the North can be provided will help shape the choices, pace, and prospects for economic reform there and for the integration of the two Koreas. The transparency of South Korea's own economic system and the degree of economic and political stability in both South and North Korea will also determine the extent to which private versus public funding may be available to finance such a process. Such rehabilitation and integration will take decades, regardless of whether Korean unification occurs early or late in the process.

Conclusion

The inter-Korean peace and reconciliation process remains characterized by false starts and temporary setbacks—and the escalation in late 2002 of nuclear tensions between North Korea and the United States is but another reminder of the interrelationship between inter-Korean reconciliation and the relationships of major powers to the two Koreas—yet it is possible to draw a few conclusions about its future prospects. First, the willingness of the South Korean government to provide economic assistance to meet Pyongyang's increasingly desperate economic needs is the factor on which the success or failure of current efforts ultimately depends and is probably the underlying driver that makes the current rapprochement effort different from the numerous false starts of the past, which were characterized primarily by opportunism and propagandistic motives of bolstering competing claims of legitimacy.

Second, a shortcoming of the current process is that it continues to be perceived by many as a "one-sided love affair" in which only the South is giving, while reciprocal concessions from Pyongyang have not yet been forthcoming, a theme that received much attention in the South Korean presidential campaign of 2002. If Kim Jong Il is, indeed, increasingly motivated by the North's growing dependency on external humanitarian assistance and other economic aid, the pace and generosity of South Korean giving in the future is likely to be determined by local public opinion, a factor that may demand greater flexibility and reciprocity from North Korea. Likewise, it is inevitable that symbolism and emotion must give way to the difficult process of institutional adjustments designed to foster and in turn reflect reduced tensions on the Korean peninsula.

Third, the inter-Korean reconciliation process as it has developed thus far is a protracted negotiation process that is likely to be contested both between the two Koreas and internally in South and North Korea. It will take time to derive the consensus necessary to achieve reconciliation; the major outstanding question remains whether internal or international conditions will allow sufficient time for the process to develop fully.

Last, developments on the Korean peninsula may affect other reconciliation processes in the Northeast Asia region, either by providing a vehicle for joint cooperation to assure lasting stability on the Korean peninsula or by engendering confrontation among regional neighbors that have historically failed to achieve full reconciliation.

Hypotheses on History and Hate in Asia

Japan and the Korean Peninsula

Victor D. Cha

History, Passion, and International Relations

The causal significance of affect and emotion on state behavior is an understudied aspect of international relations.[1] In spite of this, such variables have been used frequently and in a self-evidently important and unproblematic fashion to explain or predict behavior between states.[2] Nowhere is this analytic practice more apparent than in Asia, where in post–Cold War assessments of the region's security and politics national "passions" deriving from unresolved histories are seen as a critical driver of relations.

For the realist school of thought in international relations, Asia's historical animosities are seen as reinforcing realism's already pessimistic outlook for regional peace, given the unstable multipolar distributions of power, the dangerous security vacuums emerging as a result of the United States' post–Cold War retrenchment, the emboldening effects of economic prosperity (manifested in Chinese ambitions and a regional arms race), and the lack of peace-building and transparency-enhancing institutions. Historical mistrust and hate only fuel scenarios of self-help and conflict deriving from these material factors.[3] Neoliberals, by contrast, hold out hope that Asia's nascent institutionalism and vibrant economies will create unbreakable ties and mutually beneficial relationships that might mute deep historical enmities.[4] Culturalists see history as an important and permanent factor in Asia, but their predictions are less determinate, more case specific, and often at odds with those of realists and neoliberals. Deeply ingrained enmity and history could explain, for example, why certain material incentives for economic cooperation and integration were not capitalized on. Historical factors could also explain why certain states (e.g., Japan) are unlikely to be aggressive despite realistic reasons for being so, or why the potential for regional cooperation is greater than the existing material institutions or levels of integration might suggest.[5]

The Problem with History

The basic problem with the way international relations treats history (particularly in the realist and neoliberal traditions) is one of underspecification and overemphasis. There are three dimensions to the problem. First, history is defined in a unidimensional manner—that is, as a source of animosity and enmity. Second, the literature on international relations does not specify rigorously how such enmity affects relations in Asia. The literature *asserts* that historical animosity is a genuine driver of conflict in the region but does not *explain* the requisite causal rationales and linkages for such an assertion. For example, does this subjective enmity affect the "rationality" of states? Does it cause states to forgo opportunities that are objectively in their interests or, conversely, to undertake actions that are clearly self-detrimental? Can states and national governments really hate one another? And third, with almost the same degree of certainty with which they unidimensionally define history as conflictual, scholars of international relations also define history in static terms—that is, historical animosity in Asia is deep seated and unchanging; moreover, it cannot be overcome to the betterment of regional politics and security.

The purpose of this chapter is to try to address these gaps in the scholarly treatment of historical enmity in Asia.[6] The method is inductive, using the case of relations between Japan and the Republic of Korea (ROK, or South Korea) to build an elementary model for understanding history's role. Japan and South Korea offer a good example because of the dramatic transformation of their relationship over the past decade. What was once an extremely acerbic relationship that has been persistently marred by historical animosity since 1945 has now been trumpeted in the post–Cold War era as one of Japan's successes in the slow, prodding task of reconciliation in Asia.

An understanding of the way in which this transformation took place provides the initial propositions of a more general model, which would then have to be tested against other cases. Essentially, I argue that historical animosity undoubtedly constitutes the initial negative template that informs behavior in Asia, but this is in no way all-determining and, under the right conditions, is subject to change. In particular, acute material factors can force cooperative behavior notwithstanding the template. Moreover, if these material forces for change are persistent and sustained over a long period of time, what was once episodic cooperation can become embedded in the existing negative historical template and eventually result in a transformation of this template. In this vein, the arguments made in this chapter are consonant with the lessons drawn in Yoichi Funabashi's introductory chapter of this volume on the process of reconciliation (point 3) and the "jointness" of this process (point 5). My argument and the situation involving Japan and Korea in particular highlight the importance that democracy plays in historical reconciliation (point 7) and the role of political leadership (point 9).

In this chapter I first describe the causal role of historical animosity in relations between Japan and South Korea, how it has affected the "rationality" of the relationship, and over what issues history rears its disruptive head. I then explain the sets of material factors that were responsible for causing first episodic, but then transformational, changes in favor of cooperative behavior in the relationship (i.e., security, democracy, and development). Then I deduce the policy implications of the argument for one of Japan's current and most vexing historical issues, namely, North Korea. I conclude with more general implications of the argument for future cases of historical reconciliation.

The Passions of History between Japan and Korea

The vexing question for Japan's relations with the ROK has always been why two countries with so much in common in terms of security, politics, economics, culture, and geography have had so much difficulty in their relationship.[7] For example, during the Korean War in 1950, ROK president Syngman Rhee warned the United States that he would rather surrender to the much-hated North Korean communists invading from the north than accept a Japanese role in the U.S.-led defense of the peninsula. Beginning in 1951, it took fourteen years of protracted and caustic negotiations before Seoul and Tokyo—despite common alliances with the United States—established formal ties, in June 1965. The resumption of diplomatic relations in 1965 was not celebrated with summit visits; indeed, there were no summit meetings until nearly two decades later. Moreover, the main channel of political dialogue, the annual joint ministerial conference, was suspended or postponed on countless occasions and diplomatic relations nearly ruptured on at least two separate occasions in the 1970s. Despite their shared Cold War environment (and their proximity), the two governments remained averse to a bilateral defense treaty.

The primary cause cited by students of this tortured relationship has been historical animosity. In essence, this view argues that deep-seated enmity and psychological barriers stemming from the turbulent histories shared by the two peoples are the primary causes of friction. Although disputes date back to Hideyoshi's invasions in the late sixteenth century, the defining event in a modern context was Korea's colonial subjugation to Japan from 1910 to 1945. Occupation policies sought to assimilate the Koreans by banning their language, mandating the adoption of Japanese surnames, and coercing worship in the Shinto state religion. The colonial police (many of whom were Korean) intruded extensively into every aspect of society and suppressed attempts at resistance, often brutally. Many colonial subjects were drafted into the military for the Japanese war effort. Even more were forced into labor conscription programs that abruptly moved nearly 20 percent of the rural population to unskilled mining and factory occupations in northern Korea, Manchuria, Sakhalin, and Japan under subhuman working conditions. All were the object of social discrimination and relegation to the lowest strata of society. In spite of these heavy-handed policies, the occupation period brought some benefits to Korea. Colonial policies aided the development of educational systems, provided an efficient government bureaucracy, and modernized agriculture and infrastructure.[8]

Admiration-Enmity Complex

Distilled from this history is a peculiar "admiration-enmity" complex. On the side of admiration is the view in Korea of Japanese organization, efficiency, and economic prowess as models to be emulated and aspired to. Similarly, Japanese liken Korea's modern development to that of a younger sibling—one to be nurtured and through which Japan vicariously relives its own earlier successes.

In spite of this mutual admiration, it is the enmity stemming from the colonial period that dominates. This historical memory has become deeply ingrained in the two peoples' mindsets through a variety of formal and informal institutions. Antagonistic images are passed down generationally through family folklore, chauvinist histories are taught in secondary schools (in both Korea and Japan), and popular stereotypes are perpetuated by the mass media such that the animosity becomes a part of one's identity. This is especially prevalent among Koreans for whom parts of the Korean self-identity have become constructed in linear opposition to Japan.[9] The two main national holidays in Korea, for example, March 1 (*samilchôl,* or Independence Day) and August 15 (*kwangbokchôl,* or Liberation Day), celebrate Korean patriotism through remembrance of the struggle for independence from Japanese colonial rule. At a deeper, psychological level, enmity is manifested in a victim's complex prevalent within the South Korean psyche known as *han,* or "unredeemed resentment for past injustices." In addition to the occupation, historical injustices recalled by Koreans include the aftermath of the Kanto earthquake in 1923, when thousands of Korean residents in Japan, condemned as scapegoats responsible for the natural disaster, were killed by angry citizens. Many also hold Japan partially liable for the postwar division of the peninsula and consider contemptible the economic benefits that accrued to the former colonizer as a result of the Korean War. *Han* often surfaces at elite and mass levels in the form of laborious lamentations about the historical victimization of Korea. Typical of this attitude was the opening statement by Korea at the first postwar meeting between the two sides in 1951:

> The years of Japanese occupation left us with problems which cannot be easily solved. . . . Our economic processes . . . were made to serve as subsidiaries

> to Japanese development. . . . Our own people were barred from technical and managerial training and experience. . . . We have never in our long history attacked you. We do not intend to do so. You have attacked against our will and engulfed us.[10]

For the Japanese, these negative attitudes surface in a general uneasiness about contending with their nation's past, and an annoyance at being eternally held responsible by the Koreans for their history. Some scholars have referred to this as Japan's "avoidance phenomenon" toward Korea.[11] Negative attitudes are also manifest in a superiority complex toward Koreans. Often described by Koreans and other Asians as "haughtiness," these attitudes are to some degree inherent in the collective mindset of Japan as a former colonizer of the region. And, while not openly stated, such views are occasionally expressed, as Richard Finn, a U.S. official, observed in 1949, in commenting on a statement made by Wajima Eiji (the director of the Control Bureau of the Foreign Ministry):

> The Japanese have always considered the Koreans to be an inferior race. [Wajima] said that a very elaborate study on the racial characteristics of Koreans had been prepared during the war and that it had concluded that the mental and social capacities of the Koreans were of a very primitive nature. He said that this feeling on the part of the Japanese that Koreans are inferior to a great extent motivates Japanese uncertainty and hostility in regard to the Koreans.[12]

Impressions of Koreans as "wild, savage, obstinate, and poor," and of Korea as a "country where there are many wars," were dominant among Japanese schoolchildren in 1956.[13] While a new level of respect for South Korean accomplishments is discernible today, the residue of these earlier impressions prevents the complete acceptance by the Japanese of Koreans as equals. In addition, the Japanese association with things Korean tends not to go beyond the novel: Korean cuisine, the Olympics, pop music. These "softer" images contrast with "harder" Korean images of Japan, which focus on negative issues such as the colonial period and economic dominance.[14]

Residual Historical Issues and Friction

This clash of negative attitudes gives rise to the *Han-Il ûng'ôri* (Korea-Japan tangle)—a fundamental lack of mutual understanding that plagues interaction between Japan and Korea at all levels.[15] The two countries consistently do not rank as highly liked in each other's public opinion polls. Koreans see the Japanese as untrustworthy and unrepentant. The Japanese see Koreans as overly emotional and blunt. These animosities peak whenever bilateral issues arise that invoke memories of the colonial past. For example, statements by Japanese leaders that hint even slightly at justification for the occupation period elicit strong protests from the Koreans. In 1953, when a senior Japanese official remarked that Japan's occupation policies provided many social and economic benefits to Korea, his statement precipitated a rupture in normalization talks lasting over four years.[16] Similar remarks by various Japanese cabinet officials in the 1970s and the 1980s elicited severe public reaction and government protest.

Another source of historical friction is the constant bickering over the sincerity of Japan's apology for past aggressions against Korea. South Koreans have been dissatisfied with the text of the 1965 normalization treaty as it omits any reference to Japanese contrition for the occupation period, and they were far from placated by the ambiguous wording of the apology proffered in 1984 by Emperor Hirohito.[17] Linked to this, the historical recollection of the occupation period leads to other persistent problems. The most prominent illustration of this was the revision, by the Monbusho (the education ministry), of Japanese history books to reflect a more conservative interpretation of past Japanese aggression in Asia. Public outrage over this issue in 1982 resulted in formal protests from the South Korean government, suspension of concurrent bilateral loan negotiations, and spontaneous acts of discrimination against Japanese nationals in Korea.[18]

Colonial legacies are inextricably intertwined with a number of other ongoing issues in the relationship. One of these concerns the *chaeil kyop'o* (overseas Koreans in Japan). Numbering around 650,000, they constitute the largest minority group in Japan. Many in this overseas community were victims of Japanese labor conscription policies during the occupation and have been subject to social and legal forms of discrimination. As a result, friction arises over Korean claims that Japan has a historical responsibility to redress the needs of this community. A related issue concerns Korean victims of the atomic bomb. As conscripted laborers who were innocent victims at Nagasaki and Hiroshima, these individuals (unofficially numbering between ten and twenty thousand) claim the historical right to seek reparations and medical treatment from the Japanese government. In addition, issues linked to the occupation period constantly arise. For example, in January 1992 the revelations confirming the Japanese government's involvement in the conscription of Korean "comfort women" *(chôngsintae)* during World War II resurrected dark colonial memories.

The Effects of Historical Enmity

In each of the disputes mentioned above, dialogue reverts to polemics and resolution becomes infinitely more difficult because of the historical-emotional baggage attached to the issues. Moreover, these negative attitudes filter down into all aspects of relations. For every failed diplomatic or trade negotiation, there arise Korean claims that Japanese intransigence reflects a lack of moral repentance for past aggressions and a desire to keep the Koreans in a subservient position. On the Japanese side, there is disdain for Korean attempts to use the colonial legacy to extort concessions, and a weariness at Korean emotional outbursts.

In sum, a systematic rendering of this psychohistorical explanation for friction could be expressed as follows: Historical animosity produces systematic biases of a "cold" cognitive or "hot" motivational nature among the government elite and the general public. These biases give rise to an atmosphere of distrust and contempt that makes compromise or concession in bilateral relations synonymous with treason, particularly for the Koreans. This, in turn, precludes the possibility of amiable or rationally based negotiations.

Today's Transformation of Relations

Many scholars agree that Japan's relations with South Korea have made significant strides in terms of overcoming the past. Bilateral discussions on security, which had been taboo given historical sensitivities, are now institutionalized from the working level to the ministry level and complemented by a growing set of military exchanges and combined exercises. Summit meetings (the first occurring as late as 1983) are now conducted on a regular and congenial basis. In 1998, the ROK abolished a long-standing ban on the import of Japanese popular culture, which had been instigated for fear of a second "cultural invasion." In October 1998, Japan, for the first time, included a statement of regret regarding the colonial past in a bilateral joint communiqué issued with the ROK. Seoul has extended an invitation to the Japanese emperor to visit Korea. Even the harshest critics of President Kim Dae Jung grudgingly admit that relations with Japan during his administration improved immensely.[19] Historical animosity certainly has not been eradicated, as was evident in the summer of 2001 when relations broke down over controversial Japanese history textbooks and Prime Minister Koizumi's visit to Yasakuni Shrine, but it has become muted. Gone are the days when a historically based dispute could lead to fundamental disruptions that spilled over into other aspects of relations (as occurred, for example, in the mid-1980s, when controversies over textbooks contributed to suspensions in bilateral loan negotiations). Even when the historical demons do impede relations, the two countries are much more capable of putting relations back on track than they have been in the past.[20] How does one explain this gradual transformation?

I believe that a confluence of several long-term material trends is responsible for the change. At first, these material imperatives led to episodic, pragmatic cooperation, but these sustained imperatives have eventually started a process of deeper change related not only to immediate interests but also to deeper attitudes and preferences that inform the two countries' views of each other.

Security Imperatives

The first of these trends relates to security. The Soviet collapse ended the Cold War bipolar conflict; however, quickly moving to the fore were two somewhat different security challenges for Tokyo and Seoul. The most obvious of these was the threat from the Democratic People's Republic of Korea (DPRK). Whether this took the form of provocation (by missile tests or naval incursions) or concern about imminent implosion (for which neither Japan nor the ROK was prepared), the DPRK threat was the proximate cause for the frenetic pace of security cooperation over the past few years.

Activities started in earnest in 1997 with the establishment of director-general-level security consultations (see table 1, p. 49). In May 1999, the two governments established communication hot lines between the Korean Ministry of National Defense and the Japanese Defense Agency as well as between air and naval components. The same month Korean and Japanese air force chiefs held successful meetings in Seoul, making commitments to increase bilateral exchanges and strengthen cooperation. In August 1999, the two navies held unprecedented joint naval exercises followed by goodwill port calls. In various diplomatic forums, Japanese officials consulted with Korean counterparts on the positive implications for Korean security of the new U.S.-Japan Defense Guidelines. And in April 1999, Washington, Seoul, and Tokyo created the Trilateral Coordination and Oversight Group (TCOG) to meet quarterly to coordinate policy on North Korea.

Clearly, the causes for much of this cooperation are jointly held and expedient concerns about the DPRK security threat.[21] From a broader perspective, however, what is distinct about these activities is that they represent the first step in the evolution from pragmatic and transitory cooperation to a more deeply rooted and preplanned security relationship. The naval exercise in August 1999, for example, while only a small-scale search-and-rescue exercise, was unprecedented in the history of modern relations between Japan and the Republic of Korea.[22] Combined exercises and exchange visits of military officers appear to be minor accomplishments, but taken as a whole they represent a vast improvement in substantive interaction on security issues. It was less than a generation ago that the notion that Japanese military personnel might set foot again on Korean soil provoked such wrenching reactions that any bilateral defense exchanges—even during the tense conditions of the Cold War era—were ceremonial, occasional, and unpublicized. The sustained danger presented by the DPRK during the post–Cold War period (ranging from collapse to outright threats) helped create the slow, incremental deepening of a security relationship.

A second security challenge relevant to the strengthening of ties between Tokyo and Seoul and to historical reconciliation relates to the future presence of the United States in the region. I have argued elsewhere that mutual concerns about the credibility of American security commitments in the region during the Cold War led to episodic but distinct periods of cooperation between Japan and the ROK.[23] For example, during the Carter years, fears (based on Carter's plan for withdrawing troops from Korea) that the United States would abandon the region resulted in distinct improvements in political and security relations between Seoul and Tokyo from 1975 to 1979.

Although the continued engagement of the United States in Asia in the post–Cold War era has been explicitly undertaken, creeping concerns in both Tokyo and Seoul about the durability of this policy remain. This is largely because the end of bipolar Cold War competition in East Asia has made allied fears of abandonment by the United States inherent in the very structure of the system. Although the current declared policy as expressed in the Nye report and *East Asian Strategic Review 1998–1999* calls for the continued, strong engagement of the United States in the region, Tokyo and Seoul are acutely aware that the nature of conflict in the region is not ideological and global as it was in the Cold War era but secular and localized, which means that a decreased U.S. presence is virtually inevitable. There is also the awareness that, with any new administration, policy can change virtually overnight and, given the weak domestic support in the United States for expensive security pursuits in Asia, the likelihood of change from current commitments cannot be ruled out.[24] As long as concerns about U.S. commitments continue, they will help to consolidate the Japan-Korea axis.

Events over the past decade appear to support this proposition. In a striking example of the abandonment dynamic, Japanese and South Korean leaders in 1992, concerned about the coming to power in Washington of a Democratic Party administration for the first time since Carter, held an extraordinary set of meetings in Kyoto. Deliberately informal to convey a sense of intimacy, the Kyoto meetings produced joint statements pledging closer consultation and urging early on that the new administration not contemplate withdrawal from Asia.[25] Moreover, since about 1990, the two governments have held a series of successful summits that have made substantial progress toward resolving some outstanding issues in diplomatic relations. From the summit meeting between President Roh and Prime Minister Kaifu in 1990 to that between President Kim and Prime Minister Obuchi in 1998, these meetings have addressed the rights of third-generation Korean residents in Japan, colonial apologies, government compensation for atomic bomb victims *(pipokja),* comfort women, joint history projects, joint technology transfer projects, and a fisheries demarcation agreement.

Hence, if the DPRK threat is the *proximate cause* for deepening cooperation between Japan and the ROK on security in the post–Cold War era, anxieties about the future U.S. presence are a latent, more subtle driver that offers the *permissive condition* for such cooperation. This concatenation of forces not only gives rise to episodic pragmatic cooperation but also promotes over time a deeper process gradually effacing historical neuralgia as a driver of relations. In other words, the more instances of bilateral security meetings, joint naval exercises, and officer exchanges that occur, the more previously held conceptions of military relations as taboo become reconstructed and redefined as acceptable and commonplace.

Democracy

Another variable critical to the growth of relations and historical reconciliation has been democracy in South Korea. Since 1987, the ROK has seen a peaceful transition from military authoritarianism to a popularly elected civilian government, culminating with the election in 1997 of the longtime dissident Kim Dae Jung to the presidency.

Democracy has helped the bilateral relationship deal with its difficult history in several ways.[26] First, it has enabled the relationship to become increasingly institutionalized as a mature relationship. Although in the past the only regularized forum for official government exchanges was the annual joint ministerial conference, both the frequency and variety of official channels have increased exponentially (see table 1) and now resemble those of two liberal, established democracies.

This is important for historical reconciliation because the relationship as previously constituted lacked public acceptance. For example, from the 1960s through the early 1980s, business was conducted primarily through backroom deals between elites in late-night parlors in Seoul and Tokyo. These arrangements were replete with corruption and side payments that greatly benefited the participants and reinforced negative images among the general public about the shadiness of relations. For South Koreans, their tenor resurrected negative historical images of Park Chung Hee and other Korean leaders as supplicants to their former colonizer, concocting deals that were ultimately unpopular with the general public (e.g., the secret memorandum agreed upon by President Kim and Prime Minister Ohira in 1962).

However, with democratic consolidation in Korea, this mode of interaction has been replaced by institutionalized, public, and popular channels of communication at governmental and nongovernmental levels. These channels foster expansive opportunities to deliberate, debate, and reach a

Table 1. Official Japan-ROK Channels, 1965–2000

Date	Type	Established	Comments
1965–85	Joint ministerial conference	1967	Annual
	High-level foreign policy council	1984	Annual
1986–2000	Foreign ministers' meeting	1986	Annual
	Twenty-first Century Committee	1988	Occasional
	Ministry of Foreign Affairs (MOFA) Asia Bureau directors' meetings	1991	Occasional
	Trilateral assistant-secretary meetings (with the U.S.) on the DPRK	1992	Occasional
	Korea-Japan Forum	1993	Occasional
	Director-general security dialogue	1997	Annual
	Executive summit: President Kim and Prime Minister Obuchi	1998	Annual (periodic prior to this)
	Trilateral Coordination and Oversight Group	1999	Quarterly
	Hot lines	1999	Ministry of National Defense (Korea) and Japan Defense Agency
	Defense ministers' meetings	2000	Annual (periodic prior to this)
	Joint chiefs' meetings	2000	Annual ROK Joint Chiefs of Staff and Japan Joint Staff Council

consensus on policy. They promote institutional familiarity and cultural, educational, and sports exchanges that reinforce the cooperative maturing of relations. This maturation continues to expand into areas such as the environment, disaster relief, and civilian nuclear energy.[27] Perhaps most important, these channels provide an institutional foundation for relations that is increasingly difficult to uproot and that can withstand bouts of friction over troublesome history issues. This gives the relationship a transparent and domestically legitimate constitution—a "new" face—that diverges from the traditional template.

It is important to note the analytic distinctions between democratization and democratic consolidation. The latter constitutes a critical variable in the improvement of relations between Seoul and Tokyo, but it is not necessarily the case that the *process* of democratization would result in similar outcomes. Indeed, the transition to democracy from authoritarianism is often unstable and dynamic, creating new political freedoms and unlimited access to information without any regulatory mechanisms in place. This unregulated marketplace of information is ripe for abuse by those seeking to garner political support and can lead to "rally-'round-the-flag" effects directed against certain internal or external constituencies.[28] A likely target of such democratization hysteria will be historical enemies. Hence, the process of democratization may lead to a temporary worsening of historical differences between parties.

This dynamic was evident during the periods of democratization in the late 1980s and early 1990s, when there were clear instances that Japan served as a convenient whipping boy for political leaders seeking to consolidate their constituencies. The Chun Doo Hwan regime (1980–87), while on the one hand seeking to meet Nakasone's initiatives for improved bilateral relations, was on the other hand also engaged in a variety of efforts to fuel anti-Japanese sentiment (e.g., over the Yasakuni Shrine, Japan's commitment to defend waters out to a thousand nautical miles, and Hirohito's apology for the colonization) to divert attention away from the regime's military origins and to gain domestic legitimacy.[29] During the Kim Young Sam years (1993–97) as well, the use of the territorial dispute over Tokdo (Takeshima) as a ploy to gain votes prior to legislative elections in Korea was evident. These rally-'round-the-flag dynamics and the negative effects of democratization did not spin out of control, in large part because they were bound at the outer limits by a salient common external threat from North Korea as well as by the moderating influence of the common ally, the United States. These factors, admittedly sui generis, yielded a more positive path toward historical reconciliation as democratic consolidation emerged in the ROK. In other cases, however, it is, entirely conceivable that democratization could dramatically worsen historical animosities.

Development

In a similar vein, development has contributed to historical reconciliation. The ROK has witnessed tremendous economic development (in spite of the financial crisis) and has grown to occupy its own place on the international stage. As the country embraces democracy and progresses toward economic prosperity, its enhanced international prestige (reflected in events such as the Seoul Olympics in 1988, UN membership in 1991, OECD membership in 1996, and the World Cup with Japan in 2002) fosters a growing self-confidence among Koreans that reduces national insecurities and xenophobia and nurtures a less petty, less emotional attitude in dealings with Japan. As generations of Koreans, in the South or in a unified entity, come to live in a democratic and developed society, they will cultivate norms of compromise, nonviolence, and respect for opposing viewpoints that will become externalized in their attitudes toward Japan. In addition, future Korean leaders with no direct experience of the occupation are less apt to carry the historical and emotional baggage borne by their predecessors and more apt to engage in rational and logical dialogue.

Democracy and development also transform Japanese images of its neighbor. Yesterday's media coverage condemned the ROK's martial law brutalities, political repression, and human rights abuses (particularly Kim Dae Jung's kidnapping in 1973 by government intelligence operatives); today's reports praise Korean political liberalization, economic development, and the Seoul Olympics. In the last instance, the Japanese vicariously relived their own development experience of the 1960s as they watched Seoul in 1988 enter the world stage as Tokyo had done in 1964. These sorts of development watersheds gradually influence the Japanese government and general public to hold more positive images of Korea and Koreans. One manifestation of this was the *Kankoku boomu* (Korea boom), in which the popularity of the Korean language, food, and music surged in Japan in the late 1980s.[30] In a study on the Korean minority in Japan, additional ways in which perceptions are changing were noted: "A new image is emerging for Koreans in Japan. This new image is vibrant, dynamic, and self-confident, backed not only by growing economic power but by changing cultural attitudes."[31]

Norms of compromise, coupled with generational changes and growing Korean self-confidence, can prevent emotional animosity from clouding realpolitik concerns. One example of this was the long-standing (until recently) Korean ban on the import of Japanese popular culture. Older generations supported this policy as a hedge against Japanese "cultural imperialism"; younger generations were less afraid. An opinion poll taken in 1994 found that over 50 percent supported doing away with the antiquated policy, and an additional 23.7 percent saw the importing of Japanese pop culture as enhancing Korea. Moreover, of those who continued to support the ban, most cited reasons of economic competition rather than of history.[32] Commentary by one observer of the relationship illustrates this more magnanimous and self-critical transformation taking place in the views of the younger educated Koreans:

> [M]any Koreans argue that the ban [on the import of Japanese culture] should be lifted only if Japan shows "satisfactory" evidence of contrition for its colonial-era behaviour. . . . But it is hard to see how allowing in Japanese consumer brands such as Sony and Panasonic can contribute to progress on these issues, while lifting the ban on Japanese movies won't. The so-far-unresolved colonial-era wrangles—and Japanese foot-dragging on them—are indeed a serious matter, but Koreans ought to realize that countering one unreasonable policy with another is no solution. . . . [M]aking difficult choices is what growing up is all about. If Koreans have demonstrated anything . . . it is that they have the maturity and confidence to chart their own destiny. The ball is now in South Korea's court. . . . Get rid of a senseless and defunct policy and at the same time convince the Japanese and the world that [Korea] is serious about forging a truly "future-oriented" diplomacy.[33]

In addition, many of the outstanding issues that provide rallying points for anti-Japan mobilization in Korean domestic politics are being dealt with. For example, apologies for the colonization, which have been made by Emperor Akihito (1990) and prime ministers Hosokawa (1993),

Murayama (1994), and Hashimoto Ryutaro (1996), increasingly aim to placate Korean complaints about Japan's lack of repentance.[34] Agreements on expanded alien resident rights for the *chae-il kyop'o* community (the Korean minority in Japan) in 1991, as well as attempts to minimize friction over the comfort women issue offer other examples of efforts to shed rational light on historical disputes.[35] In a significant step aimed at dealing with the past, the two governments agreed in 1996 and 1997 to establish binational joint history committees.[36] As ministry officials conceded, these new perceptions and actions contrast starkly with the polemics of the past over historically tainted issues.[37]

The Net Effect

The net effect of these long-term material trends in security, economics, and development is a process of deep change and historical reconciliation. What might start out as purely pragmatic, discrete instances of cooperation despite historical animosity over time become so practiced and routine that they become embedded in the preexisting negative templates and actually start to transform them. The resulting process of identity change includes steps toward historical reconciliation.

This process of identity change was evident at the October 1998 summit meeting between Kim Dae Jung and Obuchi Keizo. The events noticed by the popular press—the colonial apology, the fishery zones agreement, the commitment to joint naval exercises, and the joint action plan[38]—were undoubtedly all unprecedented accomplishments, largely driven by material factors, be they economic or security related. But more significant in the context of this chapter were the little things that went largely unnoticed. In speeches before the Diet, Kim Dae Jung mentioned that Koreans were as responsible as the Japanese for putting the history issue to rest and moving forward. The two leaders called "infantile" the fixation on fifty years of enmity between Japan and South Korea at the expense of fifteen hundred years of exchanges and cooperation. Japan praised Korea's successful road to democracy, while Korea lauded Japan's peace constitution and commitment to overseas assistance.[39] These attempts to reconstruct history, to emphasize the positive interaction over the negative, to express admiration for the other's accomplishments were not present in past interactions. They are not driven by material needs per se. Instead, they are subtle but important manifestations of changing templates and of the transformation of identity.

The Lessons for Reconciliation between Japan and North Korea

The record of the interaction between Seoul and Tokyo has very clear implications for Japan's current relations with North Korea. Normalization talks, of which there have been basically four iterations, constitute the primary arena in which the issue of historical reconciliation has been addressed. Efforts at improving relations took place during the détente years (1971–74), when a train of Japanese officials went to Pyongyang (most notably Minobe Ryokichi, the governor of Tokyo, in 1971), the Japanese Diet established a League for Promotion of Friendship with North Korea, and memorandum trade agreements were signed. In the early 1980s, additional high-level initiatives were made through personal emissaries of Prime Minister Nakasone Yasuhiro. At the end of the Cold War, a delegation led by Kanemaru Shin, who was then the leader of the Liberal Democratic Party (LDP), returned from Pyongyang in 1990 with grand aspirations for normalization that led to talks in 1991–92.[40]

The fourth and current period began with the resumption of preliminary normalization dialogue between Tokyo and Pyongyang in December 1999.[41] Two sets of talks (foreign ministry and Red Cross) took place in Beijing, with the latter producing a "humanitarian cooperation agreement" in which the two sides agreed to resume home visits for Japanese spouses of DPRK citizens. The two delegations also undertook to advise their respective governments to address in prompt fashion each side's key humanitarian concern—for Japan, the abduction of citizens by the DPRK; for Pyongyang, the provision of food aid.

Formal normalization talks opened in April 2000;[42] however, any hopes of success were quickly dashed as both sides laid out their terms of negotiation. Kojiro Takano, Japan's ambassador to the Korean Peninsula Energy Development Organization and the chief negotiator to the talks, and Foreign Minister Yohei Kono emphasized the importance of resolving the abduction issue. Their DPRK counterparts firmly entrenched themselves in an immovable negotiating position, demanding apologies for the colonization and between $5 and $10 billion in material compensation while dismissing Japanese counterdemands that the ballistic missile threat and abduction issues be addressed.

After a four-month hiatus, Japan offered token amounts of aid through international channels to help jump-start another round of normalization dialogue. The aid was offered after the normalization talks, but the pattern of what Bob Manning has termed, in the context of exchanges between the United States and the DPRK, "food-for-meetings"—either in advance or retroactively—was clearly set in the exchanges between Japan and the DPRK. Talks resumed in August 2000 with some encouraging signs: agreements in principle on schedules for the return of cultural assets. Most important, the talks also appeared to produce an implicit acceptance by the DPRK of a formula on the difficult issue of compensation. Following the model of the 1965 pact with South Korea, Japan proposed to offer not historical compensation but "economic aid" (North Korea could call it whatever it wanted to its domestic audience). The North Koreans did not reject this idea outright, which gave optimists the impression that they may be amenable to the formula. In addition, optimists hoped that the aid package to come with normalization would then prompt the North Koreans to resolve the abductions issue in some political fashion.

Pursuant to the meetings, confidence in Japan was bolstered in September by a third round of homecomings for Japanese wives residing in North Korea—arguably, a new bargaining chip for the North (i.e., politically important for Japan and relatively costless for the DPRK). Premier Mori Yoshiro and Kim Yong-nam agreed to meet at the UN Millennium summit in New York (before the North's much publicized problems at Frankfurt airport). Japanese investors expressed interest in Hyundai projects in North Korea (the tourism complex on Mount Kumgang and the industrial park in Kaesong). And as a new turn in the path to normalization, pro–North Korean residents in Japan were allowed to visit relatives in the South for the first time and resident associations in Japan representing the two Koreas began talks. However, just as momentum appeared to be building with a string of positive outcomes, another round of talks in late October brought the process to a screeching halt as the North rejected out of hand Japanese attempts to elaborate on the proposals made in August.

Japan approached the October 2000 round of normalization talks determined to achieve a breakthrough. Prime Minister Mori (at the advice of Kim Dae Jung) sent a personal letter, which was revealed on October 6, to Kim Jong Il requesting summit talks. In advance of the talks, Tokyo announced a contribution of five hundred thousand tons of rice to the North (a fivefold increase over past contributions). Having greased the wheels, Japanese negotiators then proposed to provide a purported $9 billion (60 percent in grant aid and 40 percent in loans) as a quid pro quo for North Korean moderation of the missile threat and satisfactory resolution of the abduction of Japanese nationals, which would lay the groundwork for the political normalization of relations. Japan hoped to end the year 2000 with some progress; Pyongyang's continued intransigence dashed all such aspirations. At issue was Japan's proposal of a normalization settlement formula similar to the 1965 pact with South Korea, in which economic aid and loans were offered in lieu of and explicitly termed colonial compensation. The Japanese negotiators did not expect their counterparts to accept this idea outright, but there were indications based on the previous round of negotiations that Pyongyang would show a "positive attitude." Instead, the North responded that such attempts to sidestep any statement of colonial repentance were logically inconsistent with the notion of opening a new era of cooperation (and, in no uncertain terms, criticized the South for "selling out" in its 1965 settlement). The disappointment among Japanese officials at this outcome was palpable—as one official put it, "We have exhausted what we have in our pockets." No further talks occurred until Prime Minister Koizumi's trip to Pyongyang in 2002.

Assessing the History Problem

The last round of normalization talks made explicit the material quid pro quos that were in play for the two sides: Tokyo wants satisfactory resolution of the abduction issue and some assurances on DPRK missiles. It is willing to provide occasional disbursements of food aid as goodwill gestures to bring the North to the table. Pyongyang seeks a large influx of funds with a normalization settlement and as a goodwill gesture is willing to grant temporary homeland visits for wives. With regard to historical reconciliation, the implicit working assumption and aspirations of those involved in the negotiations are that (1) a normalization settlement will include substantial economic funds as a means of materially redressing historical claims, but will not be explicitly labeled as such, (2) there will be a political statement by Japan expressing regret about the past, and (3) although this settlement will not "solve" the history problem, it will be the first step toward historical reconciliation between the two sides.

This is certainly a justifiable agenda on the Japanese side, but the problem with such a formula for resolving history is that in many respects the solution may be *beyond* Japanese control. As the preceding analysis shows, the development of relations between Japan and the ROK may offer one of the best examples of historical reconciliation in the region (e.g., in contrast to relations between Japan and China), and if the factors responsible in the ROK case are at all generalizable, this augurs extremely poorly for achieving similar results in the DPRK case. None of the factors—democracy, development, or leadership—is present in the North Korea case. This assessment does not deny that a normalization settlement may still occur between Tokyo and Pyongyang, but it does indicate that under current conditions historical reconciliation will not occur in spite of any material agreement. Hence a normalization settlement would result in a situation similar to that pertaining in 1965, when material incentives (security and economics) pressed a settlement, but perceptions and attitudes remained highly antagonistic.

Moreover, North Korea's thaw in relations with the United States in 1999–2000 and with the ROK have, counterintuitively, *increased* the history-based invectives against Japan. For example, in spite of the positive atmosphere after the June 2000 inter-Korean summit and the exchange visits between Marshall Jo Myong Nok and Secretary of State Madeleine Albright in the fall of 2000—all of which Japan supported—one cannot help thinking that the Japanese were a bit uneasy with the emerging constellation of relations. Because DPRK rhetoric on the United States and Seoul moderated greatly during this period, the result was that Japan became the target of propaganda with laser-beam intensity.

The likelihood of this situation's being rectified is low. One can assume that the DPRK is undergoing significant internal adjustment as the images of Seoul and Washington are probably undergoing a process of rapid reconstruction. To effect a similar transformation in its perceptions of Japan would appear to be difficult, particularly if the DPRK considers that, to maintain its identity and pursue its national purpose, it must continue to regard Japan as an adversary. From the Japanese perspective, this then begs three questions: why press for normalization if Japan will still remain demonized in DPRK rhetoric; why provide huge sums of money to address the history issue when an integral part of historical reconciliation requires unforeseeable changes in the regime and in the development of the DPRK; and why press for normalization if residual historical enmity ensures that a settlement will provide little in terms of a window on the North Koreans' intentions?[43]

Implications of the Argument for Other Cases

What lessons can be gleaned more generally from the process of historical reconciliation between Japan and the two Koreas?

1. The changes in the relationship between Japan and South Korea show that historical reconciliation in Asia more generally can be induced by the right combination of *material imperatives* for cooperation. For Japan and the Republic of Korea, these imperatives were security, democracy, and development. In other cases, the factors may be different. The important point is that the imperatives are material and not merely emotional. If the desire to contend with history had no material basis whatsoever, the animosity would truly be eternal, driven by emotional rather than rational causes.
2. While a necessary condition for historical reconciliation is an appropriately worded apology at the appropriate official level, it is clearly *not* a sufficient condition. The larger material incentives drive change.
3. Historical reconciliation is a two-way street. A necessary (but not sufficient) condition is the proffering of formal acts of contrition and evidence of attitudinal changes on the part of the aggressor. Such acts, however, produce no reconciliation without a willingness on the part of the victim to accept the apology and move on. In South Korea this willingness was to a great extent a function of material factors such as democracy and development that fed a self-confidence and proactive

nationalism that preferred to look forward rather than to dwell on the past. In North Korea no such factors are readily apparent.

4. Pushing too fast for some formula for historical reconciliation can be counterproductive. In the past, this haste has often taken the form of the victim's leveraging history against material compensation. However, without the requisite larger changes in domestic society (i.e., the willingness to look forward rather than to dwell on the past), such formulae usually result in a backlash from the general public. A good example of this was the attempt during the Chun era in the ROK to leverage history against a $4 billion loan agreement and a poorly worded apology from Emperor Hirohito, the net effect of which fanned more historical and emotional flames in the ROK than it extinguished.
5. Building institutional links in bilateral and multilateral contexts is extremely useful. Creating as much public accountability and transparency in interactions as possible provides a rational foundation for historical, emotion-laden relationships.
6. Domestic legitimacy is key. This is related to points 3 and 5, above. Implicit in the reconciliation between Japan and South Korea, but critical to any form of historical reconciliation, is a domestic environment in the former aggressor's state that supports the notion that it is politically legitimate (and not traitorous) for leaders to advocate atonement. Even more important, perhaps, it must be politically legitimate in the victim's state for individuals and leaders to advocate reconciliation.
7. Regional precedent is useful. In the Asia-Pacific region, the precedents of Japan and South Korea, South Korea and China, and Australia and Turkey might offer examples that such reconciliations are not beyond the realm of possibility. In Europe, the example would be the rapprochement between Germany and France.

Reconciliation between Japan and China

Problems and Prospects

Daqing Yang

IN 1959, HOTTA YOSHIE SENSED A COMING CRISIS between Japan and China, a crisis "of a nature that can't be imagined today."

> What type of crisis am I foreseeing in the future? It is difficult to put it in concrete terms. But, first, both Japan and China are strong countries in today's world, if we exclude the U.S. and U.S.S.R. Second, the younger generations —the generation after "liberation" in China and the postwar generation in Japan—lack concrete understanding of the other country. . . . It is obvious that Japan and China must always have friendly relations. After the diplomatic normalization, this must also be the case. Needless to say, it is not that once diplomatic relations are restored everything will be fine. Rather, the crisis I foresee is probably after the diplomatic normalization.[1]

Hotta, a prize-winning Japanese novelist, made similar observations on several occasions in 1958 and 1959, a time of strained relations between Japan and the People's Republic of China (PRC). Their relationship had deteriorated after Kishi Nobusuke became prime minister in 1957, and the Nagasaki flag incident in 1958 brought the limited contact between the two countries to a grinding halt.[2] Hotta stopped writing for six months and devoted his time to reading everything he could find on the relations between Japan and China in modern times. The crisis Hotta had in mind had to do with the recent history of Japan's aggression in China. He wrote this particular passage after reading reports by former officers of the imperial Japanese army who had visited China in the early 1950s. Hotta was appalled by the apparent lack of self-awareness in their writings.

Hotta was in Shanghai when Japan surrendered in 1945, an event that transformed his life and literary career. After returning to Japan at the beginning of 1947, he wrote a number of works of historical fiction on the subject of Japan's wars in Asia, including a novel published in the early 1950s about the infamous Rape of Nanjing. It may come as a surprise today that Hotta was addressing what we would call the "history problem" long before it erupted into the open in relations between Japan and China. Events in the past decade or so have, however, largely vindicated Hotta's remarkable insight.

In this chapter I first sketch the history problem and its attributed sources, drawing largely from recently published works. Then I discuss measures—both immediate and long term—that are necessary in order to overcome the problem and to bring about reconciliation between Japan and China.

The Problem with History

A reminder that there is indeed a history problem in the relations between Japan and China is probably unnecessary here. The visit of President Jiang Zemin of China to Japan in late 1998, during which he pressed for a written apology from the Japanese government for Japanese aggression against China, was perhaps the most vivid example of the past's casting a shadow on the highest level of intergovernmental relations. At present, the Chinese government considers the "history problem" to be one of the major "sensitive political issues between China and Japan," together with issues such as Taiwan, the Diaoyu (Senkaku) Islands, and security relations between the United States and Japan. Listed by the Chinese foreign ministry as a category separate from "war reparations" and "chemical weapons abandoned by Japan in China," the "history problem" seems to China to be above all an issue of attitude, albeit one with real implications:

> The history question of how to understand and deal with *(renshi he duidai)* Japanese militarist aggression in China was already a focal point in the 1972 negotiation over Chinese-Japanese diplomatic normalization. It was clearly spelled out in the Sino-Japanese Joint Communiqué and Sino-Japanese Treaty

> of Peace and Friendship, and has become the political foundation of China-Japan relations. The Chinese side always advocates "history not forgotten is a guide to the future," and is willing to look to the future and develop [a] lasting friendship between the two peoples on the basis of respecting history. . . . On the other hand, an extremely small right-wing force in Japan from time to time denies and whitewashes the history of aggression, and creates disturbances in China-Japan relations. We carried out [a] timely, necessary struggle against them, and urged [the] Japanese government to fulfill the pledges made on the history question with concrete actions, to strictly restrain the extremely small right-wing force, and to educate its people with correct views of history.[3]

Although the history issue is not mentioned on its website, the Japanese government recognizes that it is facing a problem with issues of the past, and not just with China. In speeches at the Chinese government Diplomatic Institute, for instance, the then Japanese ambassador Tanino Sakutarô devoted considerable attention to the subject, which received slightly more attention than he gave to the Taiwan question:

> Regarding the so-called history problem: first of all, during a certain period in the past, Japan embarked on the mistaken path of militarism, and caused much harm to the peoples of Asia beginning with China; secondly, the Japanese government has apologized *(shazai)*, expressing the opinion of most Japanese people, who believe that Japan's conduct was regrettable *(môshiwakenaikoto shita)*. Moreover, it is clear that, upon sincere consideration of its previous national policies, Japan has chosen the righteous path of peace and prosperity in the postwar period.[4]

Here, Tanino's admission of a problematic past is straightforward. Unlike the Chinese, however, he was reluctant to accept that the history problem still exists, let alone that Japan has not done enough to settle the issues of the past—whether in terms of apology or compensation. These caveats aside, it is obvious that both governments recognize that the historical Japanese aggression has now become a major issue in their bilateral relations.

Impact of the Problem

Since the early 1980s, evidence of Japanese attempts to discount incidents of historical aggression, such as exculpatory statements made by Japanese politicians and reports of the alleged whitewashing of Japanese textbooks, has prompted fierce condemnation from Chinese (and other Asian) governments and fairly consistently occasioned the resignation of the Japanese officials involved. Chinese protests and repeated demands that Japan repent have reinforced the sense of indignation in Japan over what is perceived as Chinese interference in Japan's domestic affairs.[5] In 1987 events took a particularly nasty turn. Against the background of economic problems, the dispute over the Kôkaryô Dormitory in Kyoto (when the Osaka Higher Court decided that the dormitory was owned not by the PRC but by the government of the Republic of China—i.e., Taiwan), and the increase in Japan's defense spending, Chinese leader Deng Xiaoping brought up the history issue, telling a visiting Japanese delegation that "Japan is the country historically most indebted to China." Although China did not ask for reparations in 1972, it was now dissatisfied, Deng intimated, with the state of affairs between the two countries. Deng's linking of the history issue with current bilateral issues caused an uproar in Japan.[6] In addition to such government-level clashes, the conflict over history took a populist turn. Since the mid-1980s students in China have staged demonstrations over such sensitive issues as visits to the Yasukuni Shrine by cabinet members. Chinese victims of Japanese wartime atrocities in China—including the Nanjing Massacre, bacteriological warfare, the sexual slavery of the "comfort women," and forced labor—filed lawsuits against the Japanese government or corporations, demanding apologies and compensation. In early 2000, a widely publicized assembly by Japanese right-wingers convened to refute the occurrence of the Nanjing Massacre not only provoked official protests from China but also led to attacks on Japanese government websites, allegedly by Chinese hackers.

An unfortunate effect of the heightened awareness of the disagreement has been a deterioration in each country's perceptions of the other. Opinion polls taken in the late 1990s indicated an increased public awareness in China of Japan's past aggression there. By 1996, the results of a nationwide poll indicated that the phrase "Nanjing Massacre" topped the list of terms the Chinese would commonly associate with Japan (84 percent), followed by "Japan's aggression to China" (81 percent). The Japanese national flag, to 96.6 percent of those Chinese surveyed, reminded them of Japan's war against China. Ninety-three percent of those surveyed considered "Japan's attitude toward the history of aggression" to be the biggest obstacle to developing relations between China and Japan. The "Diaoyu Islands problem" and the possibility of "Japanese politicians reviving militarism" were mentioned by about 75 percent of the respondents. Eighty-five percent of those surveyed considered that it is the "proper resolution of the history problem" that will determine future friendly relations between the two countries.[7] Even taking into consideration the methodological bias and timing of the polls, it is quite obvious that the history problem has contributed to the growing Chinese distrust of Japan.

In Japan, recent polls have indicated record lows (since diplomatic normalization in 1972) in the numbers of Japanese who regard China favorably. Although there are many causes for this other than the history problem—generally polls in Japan avoided direct questions about the issue of history—there is almost certainly some correlation. If the newspaper editorials after Jiang's visit in 1998 were any indication, the Japanese seem to be wearying of China's obsession with the past and some feel it to be downright offensive. In an on-camera interview, one popular Japanese TV talk show host bluntly told the Chinese ambassador to Japan that the leading cause for the worsening of the Japanese attitude toward China is China's incessant demand for apologies from Japan.[8]

The history problem is not just a matter of emotions, as it can have real effects on other aspects of the relationship. Calls for boycotting Japanese goods to stop Japan's "economic aggression" will continue to be heard in China as long as they resonate with those boycotts in the prewar era that are portrayed in history books as patriotic acts. The label of "Chinese collaborators" *(hanjian)* can be applied to those working for a Japanese company or simply buying a Japanese product. In Japan there are suggestions that Official Development Aid (ODA) to China should be reduced, as some 1.8 trillion yen of Japanese taxpayers' money paid out since 1978 seems to have done little to cultivate Chinese goodwill, let alone forgiveness for Japan's past wrongs. After all, as one Japanese foreign ministry official put it, "the main source of Japan's economic aid to China is the tax paid from their income, with their sweat, by the Japanese of the postwar generation that had absolutely nothing to do with the mistaken policy committed in Japan's relations in China for a time in the Showa era."[9] There is, however, some speculation that a reduction in aid will only confirm China's perception that economic assistance is a measure of Japan's remorse.

The history problem has implications for the foreign policy options of both governments. Many analysts have pointed out that the problem has become a constraint on Japanese foreign policy, especially in Japan's relationship with China. As political scientist Ijiri Hidenori put it, "The history of the past is not fully settled in Chinese-Japanese relations, thus creating a structure with China on the higher moral ground and Japan on the lower. The friction and conflict that burst out are temporarily contained but not fundamentally resolved, so . . . the vicious cycle" continues.[10] To many Chinese, this lack of resolution provides justification enough to strengthen China economically and militarily. *Luo hou jiu yao ai da* (if you are backward, you will be beaten) is now commonly offered as the lesson from China's recent history of humiliation at the hands of foreign aggressors. Moreover, the history problem has affected other highly contentious political issues between China and Japan, such as territorial disputes over the Diaoyu (Senkaku) islands and the issue of Taiwan. China attributes the roots of the continued separation of Taiwan from the so-called motherland to Japan's military aggression against China in 1895. Chinese activists from Hong Kong and elsewhere justified their action in the Defend Diaoyu Islands Movement in terms of recovering territory lost to Japanese aggression.[11]

When all these trends are added together, the future scenario for the region can look bleak, if not alarming. In an article in the influential journal *Foreign Affairs*, Nicholas Kristof, who had reported for the *New York Times* both in China and in Japan, described virulent anti-Japanese sentiment among China's youth and went on to note that "at the heart of the tension in Asia lies Japan's failure to apologize meaningfully for its wartime brutality." As he put it, "the danger remains that Japan will recover its nerve before it fully confronts the past."[12] This may sound too alarmist. Historical animosities between nations or ethnic groups do not in themselves lead to a military conflict, but they do make it more likely under certain circumstances because they can easily serve as convenient justifications for bellicose actions; they will also make such conflict more deadly when it occurs.

Sources of the Problem

Most political scientists as well as journalists see the 1982 textbook controversy in Japan as the event that first brought history to the fore as a serious problem in relations between Japan and China.[13] After all, Tokyo and

Beijing seemed to have put the history problem behind them when they issued their joint communiqué in 1972: the Japanese side indicated that it was "keenly aware of Japan's responsibility for causing enormous damages in the past to the Chinese people through war and deeply reproache[d] itself"; the government of the PRC declared that "in the interest of the friendship between the peoples of China and Japan, [the PRC] renounces its demand for war reparations from Japan."[14]

As this chapter's opening quotation from Hotta Yoshie shows, not everyone believed that the scars of war could be easily healed by the normalization of governmental relations. As Hotta saw it, the problem has deeper roots in individual human psychology as well as in the collective identities of each nation. Hotta characterized the trauma of war as "probably the essence of the drama that emerges from interethnic interactions. Therefore, it is also connected to the core of national culture in various countries."[15]

The late British historian Arnold Toynbee claimed that of all foreign invasions of China in modern times, Japan's was the longest and most extensive.[16] The Chinese consider Japan's aggression to have begun earlier than 1931, reaching back before the war that ended in 1945 to the First Sino-Japanese War, in 1894–95, which had led to a large indemnity, the loss of Taiwan, and other humiliating concessions. In the restrained language of another British historian, Ian Nish, the half century between 1895 and 1945 was one of "Japan's unremitting pressure on the heartland of China with only minor interruptions."[17] It was against such a background that Hotta sensed the magnitude of the crisis between the two countries. One may indeed wonder: Which comes more naturally, animosity or forgiveness, after a major conflict? Do historical animosities simply fade away with time or do they, without proper redress and reconciliation, persist? On what basis can we expect real pain to fade away when many survivors are still alive? In this sense, perhaps it was the relative silence and avoidance of the historical issues on *both* sides before the early 1980s that should be considered "unnatural."

Traumatic experience alone does not, however, become collective memory naturally. Traumatic memories are often nurtured, re-created, and even passed on from one generation to another. In the process, they can be intensified, distorted, and even falsified, if not always consciously.[18] More important for our discussion here is that for history issues to erupt into the open, they need a certain conducive environment as well as other enabling factors.

If there seems to be a general consensus that a deep historical fault line exists between Japan and China, there is considerable disagreement as to whose fault it is. Current explanations seem to break down into three major groups, although they are by no means mutually exclusive.

"China Plays the History Card." Many Japanese and Western observers see the current history problem as primarily the result of the Chinese government's manipulation of the past for political and economic gains over Japan. To many outside observers, the Chinese government had not always taken the history problem seriously, an indication that the recent Chinese protest lacks sincerity. For instance, Jiang's insistence on getting an apology in 1998 contrasts sharply with the PRC's magnanimity during the previous decades. Indeed, there were plenty of occasions when the Chinese leaders seemed ready to let bygones be bygones. For instance, when meeting with Japanese Diet members in 1954, Chinese premier Zhou Enlai noted:

> The history of the past sixty years of Sino-Japanese relations was not good. However, it is a thing of the past, and we must turn it into a thing of the past. This is because friendship exists between the peoples of China and Japan. Compared to the history of a few thousand years, the history of sixty years is not worth bringing up. Our times have been unfortunate, because we have only been living in these sixty years. However, our ancestors weren't like this. Moreover, we cannot let such history influence our children and grandchildren.[19]

Writing shortly after the 1982 textbook controversy, Chalmers Johnson was among the first to express doubt "that the Chinese government was truly interested in Japanese school textbooks, but there can be no doubt that it found in the textbook controversy a convenient lever to try to bring the Japanese government to heel, in which it was largely successful."[20] By exposing old historical wounds, this view goes, China expected to extract massive yen loans and other concessions and to moderate Japan's criticism of China.[21] Some also see Beijing's use of the history issue as a strategy to drive a wedge between Japan and the United States. What else can explain Jiang Zemin's stopover in Pearl Harbor on his way to the United States in 1997? There is some truth to another argument that the Chinese government uses history not simply (or primarily) as a card against Japan but also (or chiefly) as part of the patriotic education of the Chinese people. It is common wisdom that such patriotism—largely in the form of anti-Japanese nationalism—is intrinsically linked to the government's legitimacy in China. This should not be too much of a shock, since even the post-1949 Chinese national anthem has its origin in the war against Japanese invasion in the 1930s. The post-1979 China, with renewed emphasis on "learning from the recent history of humiliation at the hands of foreign aggressors," simply intensified that attitude.

Given the nature of the regime, with its largely state-controlled news media, it is only natural that protest from China over history issues often seems orchestrated. The China-plays-the-history-card interpretation is not so much wrong as only half right. By making state manipulation the main culprit, it tends to overestimate Beijing's role, for better or worse. In the 1980s it was Chinese students who staged demonstrations over Japanese actions such as visits to the Yasukuni Shrine by cabinet members. In the 1990s, it was activists outside the government who initiated signature campaigns demanding apologies and compensation from Japan. What we now witness in China is a societywide phenomenon highlighting the Japanese aggression in China and China's war of resistance. Public media such as feature films, television, and magazines are saturated with stories about the war and Japanese atrocities. Not all these developments were ordered from above, even if the government may be said to have fostered the overall atmosphere. The rise of ethnic nationalism in China, therefore, parallels a global phenomenon that redefines collective identity in narrower and more exclusive terms. Moreover, this government-centered interpretation does not explain why overseas Chinese, including those in Japan, were often more vociferous in condemning Japanese militarism and raising issues of reparations.[22]

"Japan Has Not Faced the Past." Perhaps not surprisingly, the Chinese government has insisted that China does not have any responsibility for this problem in bilateral relations. Support for this line of argument can be found in the fact that China is not the only country having problems with Japan over history: Japan faces war-related problems with other countries, in Asia and beyond, and also with private citizens in the United States and Europe. Likewise, it was the Korean victims and their support groups

who first brought up the issue of the "comfort women" and pressed ahead with legal suits over wartime labor.

Also giving some credence to Chinese claims is a vocal band of hawkish right-wing Japanese politicians, including even cabinet members on occasion. The Chinese government no longer has to rely on "erroneous newspaper reports" from Japan, as some alleged to be the case in the 1982 textbook controversy, having since then translated some of the leading works by nationalist-revisionist politicians and historians and made them available, on a *neibu* (internal, or domestic, circulation) basis. In this sense, if the Chinese government is playing any card at all, it is often some Japanese politicians who provide the card.[23] Conservative Diet members openly called for Japanese politicians to pay official tribute to the Yasukuni Shrine and to set up a Historical Research Committee. In particular, they sought to repudiate Prime Minister Hosokawa's 1993 apology for Japan's war of aggression, which was widely praised in China and elsewhere in Asia. Five million Japanese and a quarter of the members of the Diet had signed a petition opposing the 1995 Diet resolution on the fiftieth anniversary of the end of World War II, which was originally intended to demonstrate Japan's repentance. Members of the ruling Liberal Democratic Party (LDP) and the Liberal Party tend to think that Japan has made enough apologies to Asia.[24] Many scholars have attributed much of Japan's difficulty in coming to terms with its militarist past to the remarkable continuity between wartime and postwar Japanese politics, an effect of the Cold War confrontation between the United States and China. This attribution is by no means limited to the ideological left. Even politicians such as Ozawa Ichirô have recognized that part of the problem lies with Japan:

> We have to admit that our government has not made much effort to settle the past. Nor was public feeling sufficiently harsh to prevent the reemergence of politicians associated with Japan's past aggression. We must be strict with ourselves as we look back on our history, even if we start doing so only today.[25]

Outside political circles, the intellectual world, too, is divided over the evaluation of Japan's war record.[26] As the journalist Ian Buruma put it, "despite their second-rank intellectual status, the Nanjing Massacre revisionists cannot be dismissed as unsavory crackpots, for unlike those who argue that the Holocaust never happened, they are not confined to an extreme fringe. They have a large audience and are supported by powerful right-wing politicians."[27]

Yet, to focus on these trends in Japan is to ignore the many significant improvements since the early 1980s, such as, for example, textbook coverage and the greater general awareness of Japan's role as a victimizer as well as a victim in the war. An opinion poll conducted by *Nihon keizai shimbun* in 1997 revealed that 47.6 percent of the respondents agreed that Japan had not clearly or adequately apologized to Asia for the war, whereas 40.4 percent thought that Japan had done all that was possible.[28] Some gestures of conciliation may be noted. Following the visit of Prime Minister Murayama (a Social Democrat) to the Marco Polo Bridge memorial, Hashimoto Ryûtarô, the LDP leader (and former president of the Association of War-Bereaved Families in Japan), made the first visit of a Japanese prime minister since World War II to the northeast region of China. Another LDP politician, Nonaka Hiromu, while an acting LDP secretary-general, made an unprecedented visit to the Nanjing Massacre Museum in May 1998. Whatever the motivations behind these visits, the fact that they did take place despite apparent internal opposition within the ruling party should be appreciated. To a large extent, the recent surge in nationalistic noises is often a backlash against the progress that has been made. Resolution of the history issues may still encounter considerable domestic resistance in Japan, but the country as a whole is clearly moving ahead, even if it is often a matter of one step back for every two steps forward.

Bilateral Dynamics and International Setting. Analysis that focuses on one country, while important and revealing, often runs the risk of leading to finger pointing and thus furthering mutual animosity. An understanding of the history problem in relations between China and Japan must move beyond internal factors to consider bilateral dynamics and international trends.

Changes in bilateral relations as well as in each country's strategic priorities are perhaps the most important forces in bringing the history problem to the forefront. Before the 1972 normalization, it was often Japanese visitors to China who brought up the issues of wartime atrocities such as the Nanjing Massacre. Even though the problem of war reparations was an issue during the negotiations in 1972, and there was already a recognition that the term used in place of an apology by Prime Minister Tanaka Kakuei was inadequate (largely an effect of an interpretation error), both countries were ready to compromise in order to attend to more pressing issues, such as dealing with the Soviet threat. The trend continued until the end of the 1970s, when the two countries signed a Peace and Friendship Treaty. The fact that history did not become a problem in bilateral relations at this time, however, does not mean that it did not, as some argue, exist. In some sense, the relative tranquility then might have sown the seeds for the trouble today.

In the 1990s, the disappearance of the Soviet threat removed a bond between Japan and China that had been in place since the early 1970s. Moreover, the overall mutual perception had changed considerably in the preceding decade as a result of many issues not directly related to the history problem. The bloodshed in Tiananmen Square in 1989 incurred strong disapproval of China among the Japanese.[29] Much of the deterioration in attitude was caused by a mutually reinforcing dynamic. The talk of the "China threat," especially after the 1994 World Bank report on Chinese economic prospects, gained currency at a time when Japan was experiencing its worst postwar economic recession. China's increasing military budget, its nuclear test in 1995, and the strengthening of the alliance between the United States and Japan all contributed.[30] Perhaps the most obvious example of the interactive dynamics is that of a Chinese book, *China That Can Say No,* which caused a sensation in 1997. Regarded as an indication of rising Chinese nationalism, it was itself a copycat of *Japan That Can Say No,* a nationalist bestseller published in the late 1980s by the Japanese author (and future governor of Tokyo) Ishihara Shintarô.

Generational change has certainly contributed to this phenomenon. Not only have most of the populations of both China and Japan been born and educated after the war but also, as the result of their education, their memories of the war have become more openly pluralistic. Moreover, bilateral relations in the past decade have suffered from the passing of the so-called well-diggers—individuals on both sides who managed to establish a degree of trust between the two countries. Until the early 1980s, there had been a remarkable continuity of Chinese officials responsible for Japanese affairs. One observer noted that, "as a result of their long experience and their language competence, they have become thoroughly familiar with the intricacies of Japan's political and economic operations. They have also cultivated shared policy interests as well as deepening personal relationships with their Japanese counterparts in business circles."[31] This generation shift came at a time when the roles of mass media in the bilateral relations between the two countries as well as channels of popular contacts had increased. There now seems to be a greater linkage between domestic and foreign policy in both countries, making the emotional issue of history even more explosive and difficult to manage.

To some, the history problem also reflects a deeper difference between China and Japan that is camouflaged by the popular idea that the two countries share a common culture. With apparent sincerity, some Japanese and even some Chinese people believe that cultural misunderstanding has exacerbated the history problem between the two countries. While the Japanese prefer to be ambiguous, some argue, the Chinese style is more direct. While Japanese consider that death absolves all traces of guilt, thus making visits to Yasukuni Shrine an innocent expression of respect for the dead, the Chinese see death as a symbol of eternal evil.[32] Some of these differences are no doubt real and have an effect on mutual perceptions.

Although there are no doubt many idiosyncrasies in their bilateral relations, the history problem that exists between China and Japan also reflects a global interest in redressing historical injustice associated with World War II. Whether we speak of the manipulation of the "victim consciousness" or of "historical amnesia" or of historical settlement, the post–Cold War world has been witnessing the return of what some call "history wars."[33] Not a few Chinese have taken advantage of this global development to advance their demands for compensation for wartime sufferings. As the process of globalization quickens its pace, national identity has often been used to stem the tide of global trends, leading some to predict a clash of civilizations or at least of nationalisms. Whether or not it was the end of the Cold War that unfroze old issues, the emergence of history issues in relations between Japan and China is far from being an isolated phenomenon.

Prospects for Reconciliation

Traditional theories of international affairs based on the realist view of power politics are not very well equipped to deal with emotional issues such as historical animosities. By leaving out "vast areas of human feelings and great tides of political psychology," as one critic pointed out, realists in fact contradict the very principle of pragmatism, which, "in its true sense, means taking all the facts into account."[34] In an anthology of essays on reconciliation, it is perhaps only natural to ask what we mean by the term *reconciliation.* The purpose is not to engage in a game of semantics but to spell out in concrete terms what goals are likely to be achieved under different time frames.

Defined in the simplest form as restoration of friendship, harmony, and trust after a traumatic experience, reconciliation is a mutual, consensual process.[35] The question becomes: How are we to bring about reconciliation and historical justice? Or, in the parlance of political psychologists, how are we to develop respectful and "rehumanized" relationships among former adversaries? What are the necessary constituents and objective conditions for working through a problematic relationship? Historians might add: Is it still possible to build shared historical understanding among different national and ethnic communities? If not, how can we make sure that societies with different and even conflicting collective memories live side by side peacefully? In recent years we have witnessed many endeavors around the world to wrestle with the challenge of reckoning with past wrongs. Many of these take place in the so-called transitional societies—incomplete and fledgling democracies such as South Africa or Argentina. As the philosopher David A. Crocker put it, reconciliation poses ethical, legal, and policy challenges, as well as challenges in strategy and tactics. Crocker set forth eight different "morally urgent goals" in confronting past wrongs, of which reconciliation is but one. Others include truth, a public platform for victims, compensation, and punishment.[36]

While addressing past wrongs between nation-states often poses problems different from those incurred in addressing wrongs within a society or state, many of the issues identified by Crocker will apply to the relationship between Japan and China. According to Crocker, reconciliation can range from "thin"—formerly hostile parties continue to coexist without taking active revenge—to "thick"—which entails "forgiveness, mercy, a shared comprehensive vision, mutual healing, or harmony." In this sense, China and Japan can be said to have achieved a degree of "thin reconciliation." The challenge now is to prevent the erosion of earlier accomplishments and to prepare conditions for "thick reconciliation." One thing is obvious: If the current history problem between Japan and China has multiple causes, its solution also needs to be pursued on several fronts.

Political Leadership and National Interest

Why do Japan and China need historical reconciliation? This question may appear superfluous, but we cannot take the answers for granted, nor can we simply assume that others will readily accept our rationalization. In fact, one of the very first important steps to be taken by political and intellectual leaders in both countries is to think through this question in the context of the countries' overall relations and to articulate answers in such a way that they are acceptable to the public. Although moral and ethical persuasions are necessary, political pragmatism is even more important here.[37] There are serious limitations to their analysis, but realists do have a point when they argue that "[g]overnment has the obligation to maximize [the] national interest and welfare of its people, while diplomacy is to achieve the greatest welfare of the two peoples through the compromise of respective national interests. A government should not be allowed to sacrifice national interest and people's welfare at any cost by dragging elements of the past into diplomacy."[38] Of course, the keyword here is "any cost," since whether one likes it or not, the past is very much imbedded in the present and those who remain blind to this fact do so at their own risk.

Still, as many observers have pointed out, the relationship between China and Japan is entering a new phase, characterized by "competition and coexistence." Often a source of friction in itself, the attitude toward the past is but one aspect in an overall relationship that includes a broad range of economic, security, and political issues. These issues include many areas of misunderstanding and potential conflict between the two countries that could come to the fore in the future. Therefore, both governments should commit themselves to preventing the overall relationship from descending into outright rivalry and confrontation. They should also seek to create an atmosphere in which the history problem can be tackled. Leaving it to its own fate is no solution.

China, with its population of 1.3 billion, still faces enormous challenges in managing social transformation and pursuing prosperity. At the very least, its government and opinion leaders have a responsibility to prevent understandable grievances over the past wrongs of foreign aggression from becoming the justification for a new anti-foreign ultranationalism that would damage the country's own long-term interests. From the perspective of domestic governance, the rising temperature of emotions over the history problem is not always good news for the Chinese government, as it might find itself in the predicament that the Chinese call "mounting a tiger and not being able to get off." In the past few years, there has been some open discussion in China of the need for a new approach to relations with Japan. This is itself an unprecedented phenomenon. Emphasized in this discussion have been the importance of maintaining good neighborly relations with Japan and the need for a better understanding of postwar Japan as well as a better appreciation of public sentiment there.[39] One Chinese scholar has even argued that the Chinese government should accept the "irreconcilability of the history problem" and take measures to contain the problem within a realistic framework.[40]

Since Jiang Zemin's ill-fated visit to Japan in 1988, there have been indications that the Chinese leadership has taken particular care on a number of occasions to emphasize the positive side of the relationship between the two countries and to assign much less prominence to the history problem. During his visit to Japan in October 2000, Premier Zhu Rongji took great care not to offend Japanese public sentiment without forfeiting the history issue. Earlier that year, Jiang met with five thousand Japanese visitors and emphasized the importance of developing nongovernmental friendly relations between the two countries.[41]

On the Japanese side, there is a growing recognition that, in order to build a relationship of mutual trust with its Asian neighbors, Japan should resolve the history issue. Many Japanese politicians not identified with the left or with the Chinese position on the issue have made remarkable efforts to cope with the history question in recent years. For instance, one politician who has thought hard on this subject and proposed remedies for it is Ozawa Ichirô, a former LDP leader and the leading proponent of the vision of Japan as a "normal country." Writing in the 1980s, Ozawa declared, "'History' is not an issue we can avoid. How are we to approach the history issue? We must reflect soberly on our history, examine it in good faith, and apply its lesson to our principles and behavior, our present actions, and our future plans. We cannot deny the part aggression has played in our history in Asia."[42]

More recently, in a foreign policy speech delivered in Japan on January 23, 2001, Foreign Minister Kono Yohei mentioned as one of his goals the promotion of cooperation and understanding between Japan and China, similar to that between France and Germany. In this regard, he specifically reminded his audience that "between Japan and China there is a history problem of war(s) in the first half of the twentieth century, which we can never forget."[43] Japanese statesmen should be taking the initiative by building domestic support, if not consensus, on the need to resolve the history problem. As Mike Mochizuki correctly notes,

> Only by going through this experience could the Japanese lay to rest the international suspicion and even the self-perception that they were by nature or by culture an intrinsically dangerous people—a nation that could not be trusted with responsibilities for international security or even with leadership in East Asia.[44]

This is no easy task, especially when it comes to monetary matters. The issue of compensation is a complex one, involving legal as well as political, not to mention financial, considerations. The Chinese government has reiterated the policy of not asking for war reparations. At the same time, Beijing has begun to encourage efforts by private citizens to seek compensation. "To safeguard the legitimate interest and protect the interests of its people," China has adopted a policy of asking Japan to deal with those interests "seriously and properly."[45] Writing in early 1995, one Japanese scholar on China suggested that, in addition to government compensation, business and private volunteers should join forces to provide such compensation.[46] There is some indication that business leaders in Japan have come to realize the need to settle historical issues from the war era. The recent settlement of the Hanaoka Incident between former Chinese forced laborers and the Japanese construction giant Kajima Corporation is rightfully considered a "great postwar milestone." Even though it involved some compromises that did not satisfy everyone, that settlement between former perpetrators and victims will go a long way toward healing the wounds of the past and bringing about some closure to a painful wound.[47] As long as the current legal system in Japan cannot adequately address the issue of individual compensation for World War II–era victims in a timely fashion, the private sector and farsighted leaders should play a greater role. As Ônuma Yasuaki, who is an expert in international law at Tokyo University, has pointed out, even though it is no easy task for Japan to establish a collective fund, which may reach as high as tens of billions of yen given the current economic recession, it is in Japan's long-term interest to settle these compensation matters with its Asian neighbors.[48]

In fact, there are instances in which the two governments have managed to cooperate and address the legacies of World War II with some success. The disposal of the chemical weapons abandoned in China by the former Japanese Imperial Army, a rather concrete issue of history, has been proceeding for nearly a decade. The Japanese government has announced that it will continue to address this issue in good faith, in view of the promulgation of the Chemical Weapons Convention in April 1997. According to the Chinese government, "Japan acknowledges a large quantity of chemical weapons abandoned in China and adequately recognizes its seriousness and urgency, and expressed regret over its continued harm to the Chinese people."[49] By and large, both the Chinese and Japanese governments have handled this matter well, and it is the only history issue that is featured on the websites of both foreign ministries.

Perhaps the silver lining in the recent clashes over the history issue between the two governments is that both sides are taking the issue more seriously and realistically. Political and civic leaders, in particular, need to recognize that the relationship between Japan and China is too important and too multifaceted to be dominated by a single issue, however popular and emotional it may be, and that questions regarding past aggressions are too important and deep rooted to be simply dismissed or wished away with the passing of the war generation. The next task is to create a mechanism, at the relevant levels of government and society, to prevent future eruptions over the issue and to pave the way for its resolution in the long run.

Popular Perceptions and Cultural Diplomacy

In different ways, governments in both Tokyo and Beijing must take popular opinion into consideration in formulating policies. Needless to say, the influence of government on the media differs a great deal in Japan and China, but in both countries the media nevertheless play an enormously important role in shaping popular perceptions.

There seems to be a strong correlation between actions of the Chinese media and public perceptions of Japan. A large majority of the respondents to a poll taken in China in 1996, for instance, indicated that their main source of information on Japan came from Chinese media—news (86 percent), books and magazines (83 percent), and films and television (70 percent); 57 percent also learned from films and television programs produced in Japan.[50] Clearly, the content of Japan-related programs matters. Familiarity with certain Japanese singers or actresses, for instance, may not necessarily improve China's understanding of postwar Japanese society. The Chinese government and its opinion leaders need to work together with their Japanese counterparts to facilitate a better understanding. Japanese works that seriously consider the war and the Japanese invasion of China, including artistic pieces such as the musical *Li Kôran* (*Li Xianglan* in Chinese) and the television series *Daichi no ko* (Children of the Earth), should be introduced to a wide audience in China. Indeed, there is a need to think in terms of a new cultural diplomacy for both Japan and China.

A better understanding between the two countries is important in itself, but also it will help put the history problem into a proper context. A two-track approach is needed here: Whereas progress toward historical reconciliation must be considered an essential part of the confidence building between nations, such progress can also benefit greatly from confidence building and understanding acquired in other areas, such as cultural exchanges, human interactions, and business transactions—not that these activities cannot generate new conflicts. Even though harsh in its criticism, the Chinese government has not abandoned its emphasis on the distinction between the Japanese people and Japanese militarism on the issue of war responsibility. (One problem is that such an official line may not always sound convincing to the public.) Although in recent years the Japanese atrocities of wartime have come to dominate Chinese publications on the period, there have been historical and artistic works on the activities of those Japanese who were opposed to the war. Even as dark an era as World War II has positive legacies for relations between Japan and China. For instance, in the early 1980s both countries reported the story of Nie Rongzen, a general in the Eighth Route Army and minister of defense for the PRC, whose return of a Japanese orphan girl to the Japanese during the war led to a dramatic reunion and made headlines in both countries. So did the many stories of "abandoned women and children" *(zanryû koji)* that tended to emphasize the decency of common people in China. Even though Jiang Zemin's visit to Japan has been cast in a largely negative light in Japan and overseas because of his insistence on a written apology, he also visited Sendai, where the well-known Chinese writer Lu Xun had studied medicine under his teacher (*sensei* in Japanese, *xiansheng* in Chinese) Fujino almost a century ago. By using a symbol that is familiar to all Chinese students, Jiang tried to convey a message of genuine friendship between the peoples of Japan and China, but his effort was largely ignored in the media.[51]

Chinese society today is in the process of profound transformation that presents many problems but also new opportunities for greater international interaction than would have been thinkable only a decade ago.[52] The proliferation of Internet use in China as well as in Japan, for instance, creates the danger of the dissemination of inflammatory materials, but it also enables individuals to obtain quality information that would otherwise be inaccessible and to establish "bridges" across national borders. Popular perceptions are affected by interaction between individuals. At the grassroots level, many Japanese have made repeated trips to China to repair damage to the city wall in Nanjing, to plant trees, and to engage in other activities to atone for wartime excesses there. Increasing contact between Chinese and Japanese people, through study, work, tourism, and intermarriage, whatever new problems it may create, does promise better understanding based on real experience rather than on a second-hand, one-dimensional view of the other's society. In this regard, the recent beginning of Chinese group tourism to Japan can be considered a significant development.

Few countries today think themselves as much misunderstood by others as does Japan. Polls taken by Japan's Prime Minister's Office in recent years indicate that over 60 percent of the Japanese feel that their country is *not* doing a good job of conveying Japanese views to the world. Recent speeches by Ambassador Tanino and Foreign Minister Kono at Chinese government and party institutes is one indication that Japan is moving to correct this problem. Even though not all of their explanations are going to be readily accepted by the Chinese, a more candid exchange of views will at least help narrow the perception gap.

In addition, existing bilateral official and semiofficial institutional dialogues need to be revived and invigorated. At the same time, grassroots exchanges, especially among the younger generation (of which the Japan-China Student Conference is a good example), must be expanded. At such bilateral meetings, the presence of well-prepared teachers and historians from both sides will help to prevent the discussion of history issues from degenerating into one-sided lecturing. It is an encouraging sign that both the Chinese and the Japanese governments are already taking steps in this direction. Jiang Zemin's invitation to five thousand young Japanese people to visit China is one such indication. The Discussion Panel on Economic Assistance to China in the Twenty-first Century, for instance, recently recommended that the Japanese government apply some ODA funds for cultural exchanges with China.[53]

Government support and expanded social interactions can improve the relationship and understanding between Japan and China, helping to prevent occasional clashes from spinning out of control and providing a psychological basis for dealing with history issues that are often emotional and divisive.

Historical Scholarship and Public Education

What can historians, both inside and outside academia, do to advance the process of reconciliation? Historians perform a critically important psychological task in conflict resolution by reviewing and reinterpreting the most disputed points of modern history. Although historians today recognize that there is no single, objectively true version of the past that can be accepted by everyone regardless of national background, they can nonetheless help to create a less distorted picture of the past by marshalling and interpreting evidence according to accepted standards of scholarship. Furthermore, historians participate in a community of knowledge that transcends national borders. In an article published in 1988, Barry Buzan suggested that a resolution of Japan's history issues depends on three conditions: it must be factually sound, it must be acceptable to the Japanese, and it must be acceptable to other nations.[54] This formula is still applicable today.

First of all, historians need to realize that the history of modern relations between Japan and China consists of both positive and negative legacies. Just as the thousand years of interaction before the nineteenth century were not all peaceful and friendly, the half century from the end of the nineteenth century was not simply a history of Japanese aggression. With regard to the issues in contention—Japan's aggression and the atrocities perpetrated in China—historians can work to narrow their differences. Many Japanese would claim that the aggression against China began with Japan's invasion of northeastern China (Manchuria) in 1931 and was an aberration from, rather than a continuation of, policies from the Meiji era —an interpretation that implies excluding Japan's occupation of Taiwan in 1895 from the history problem between Japan and China. A reexamination of the First Sino-Japanese War of 1894–95 as well as its postwar ramifications for both countries would shed light on when Japanese aggression actually began. As regards war atrocities, historians on both sides must move beyond a deterministic causal explanation to take circumstances into consideration as well. On the issue of the scale of specific Japanese atrocities, both Chinese and Japanese historians must strive to reach the most accurate conclusions possible on the basis of credible evidence, but they must also recognize that complete agreement over precise numbers will be impossible. As a starting point for a useful dialogue on the history of aggression, Chinese historians must make an extra effort to see the universalistic implications of human tragedies, while Japanese historians must acknowledge the particularistic aspects of Japan's aggression and atrocities in the historical context.[55]

Second, since preexisting stereotypes shape mutual perceptions in the present, historians in Japan and China face the task of probing deeper into the histories of their own countries. As one American author has noted, "the importance of searching history for the deeply rooted and often obscure sources of ethnic and sectarian conflict cannot be overemphasized."[56] Contrary to the myth that there was continuous peace and friendship before the modern era, ill feelings between China and Japan had already existed long before the end of the nineteenth century. Therefore, even taking into consideration the alleged Japanese war atrocities in China, the fact that someone as well informed about Japan as Guo Moruo could in 1938 characterize the Japanese people as "only half civilized" is an indication of a deep-rooted bias. For many Japanese, the psychological struggle since the beginning of the Meiji era with the dual identity of being part of Asia and yet yearning to emulate the advanced West has often resulted in a sense of superiority vis-à-vis fellow Asians.[57] These preexisting prejudices have only made the scars of war more difficult to heal.

Third, efforts toward developing a shared history between Japan and China can benefit from a multilateral setting, similar to the multilateral economic and security dialogues in the region. There is much merit in internationalizing the dialogue between Chinese and Japanese historians and educators. Some efforts are already under way, such as the collaborative research undertaken by Japan, China, and the United States on the Second Sino-Japanese War, waged between 1931 and 1945. European and American historians would certainly be welcome to participate in this endeavor, but historians from South Korea who have been working on similar issues with Japanese counterparts have a particularly significant role to play. The dialogue between Japan and the Republic of Korea over history has been going on for some time, and although progress is elusive, the experience has proved invaluable.[58] An analysis of the rivalry between China and Japan in northeast Asia, which led to the First Sino-Japanese War, from a Korean perspective, for instance, can yield insights often missing from a consideration of the subject from a purely Japanese or Chinese perspective.[59] Much more can be done, and on more than an ad hoc basis. Institutionally, participation in multilateral research or dialogue can be a valuable opportunity for socialization into international norms and practices on writing history. Information about similar endeavors in other parts of the world should be made available to both Chinese and Japanese educators as well as to general readers. Conceptually, historians of the conflict between Japan and China should seek to transcend nationalism, which is, after all, the source of most interethnic conflict. The permanent solution to the history problem, if there is one, is the cultivation of a global citizenship. This requires an understanding of history based on humanist principles and values.

A yet more challenging task facing historians and educators is to disseminate their research to the wider public and to use it in educating the younger generation in both countries.[60] At the very least, scholarly opinions based on historical research must be respected and given the chance to reach a wider audience. There has been some progress in this regard in China, but much remains to be done. For example, since the 1980s, works by Chinese historians have raised doubts about the authenticity of the infamous Tanaka Memorial, long considered in China and the West as the master plan for Japan's conquest of the world. Sooner or later, such findings will percolate into the popular domain.

Over the past two decades, Japanese history textbooks have been subject to close scrutiny by domestic critics as well as by Japan's Asian neighbors. Such scrutiny has in turn made some Japanese resentful about what they consider to be foreign interference in Japan's domestic affairs. They are also quick to point out the exaggerations and inaccuracies in textbooks used in Korea and China. The current debates in Japan over the inclusion of references to the wartime sexual slavery instigated by the Japanese military and to other excesses show that education will always remain a highly contested area.

Given the deeply entrenched institutional difference between these countries, and given that the government-appointed committees in China actually write history textbooks (as was also the case in Japan until 1945), the possibility of authoring a common textbook in East Asia—as has been done in the European Union—is unrealistic. An initial step might be to develop a common reference book, either a teacher's manual or a dictionary of history for teachers.[61] In the meantime, teachers from Japan and China need to better understand the content as well as the methodology of history education in the other country. Even if China cannot abandon state-commissioned textbooks in the near future, it might consider also using an international textbook. The involvement of international institutions such as the Georg Eckert Institute for International Textbook Research or UNESCO could be helpful in breaking deadlocks in Japanese-Chinese discussions of this very sensitive subject.[62]

Democratic Values and Reconciliation

One of the difficulties in managing relations between Japan and China, including managing the problems of history, has often been attributed to the different social systems in the two countries. "Lack of understanding of the different institutions and systems of the two countries," as Ambassador Tanino put it, has contributed to the many problems in their current relations.[63] Put more directly, the question is whether democracy is a precondition for historical reconciliation between nation-states. If democracies are said to be the guarantee of lasting peace, as advocates of "democratic peace" insist, are they also the prerequisite for resolving past wrongs? After President Jiang Zemin's visit to Japan in 1998, the *Economist* magazine opined that "to treat this Chinese leadership as fitting recipients of an apology would frankly be pretty stomach-churning." Japan would do "the world and itself a service" by refusing to apologize.[64] Although the *Economist*'s commentary seems to ignore the fact that two wrongs don't make a right, the broader implication is worth contemplating: Will the history problem have to wait until China becomes a free-market, liberal democracy like Japan?

There is much truth in the argument that the "voluntaristic and multidimensional essence of reconciliation presupposes a democratic context."[65] For one thing, nongovernmental dialogue—crucial in forging ties among the people—in a country lacking any autonomous society is going to have little real lasting meaning.[66] More important, the freedom to criticize one's own government and a willingness to subject one's own past record to the same standard of judgment that one applies to the history of other nations are crucial elements in overcoming a historical bias against a foreign adversary. China has a long way to go in both regards. It is worth noting, however, that there is a growing movement among the Chinese to reexamine the painful history of political persecution in China, such as the anti-rightist campaign of the late 1950s and the Cultural Revolution, even though discussion of these issues still runs into considerable resistance. For example, Li Shengzhi, a respected intellectual and a former vice president of the Chinese Academy of Social Sciences, wrote a critique of political conditions in China in which he linked the much publicized brutality of the Japanese military in wartime with the only partially acknowledged brutal abuses within China after 1949.[67] The recognition of the violations of human dignity in China's own past not only strengthens the moral claim to condemn Japan's wartime aggressions in China but also holds the promise of overcoming historical animosities between Japan and China: Without relativizing the past wrongs committed by a foreign aggressor, it is nonetheless important to view them ultimately as part of the common human experience, instead of as intrinsic traits of one particular people.

Two qualifications should be made here, however. First, past successes suggest that efforts toward reconciliation do not have to wait for full democracy to blossom on both sides. When Chancellor Willy Brandt of West Germany made the widely praised gesture of falling to his knees before the memorial to those who died in the Warsaw ghetto, the Berlin Wall was still in place.[68] As Ann Phillips has pointed out, West Germany's accord with Poland as a result of Brandt's effort laid the groundwork for a smoother process of reconciliation in the postcommunist era (as compared with the case of the Czech Republic, whose reconciliation with Germany over World War II remains at best incomplete).[69] A case can be made that a democracy has a greater moral and ethical obligation to take the initiative in righting past wrongs. Simply labeling present-day China as authoritarian or as a dictatorship will distort one's understanding of the changing relations between state and society as well as of the dynamics of a restive population in the country.

Second, institutions of democracy alone are no panacea for dealing with issues of nationalism, which lies at the root of historical animosities between nation-states and ethnic groups. As one Japanese observer has admitted, even if Japan and China came to possess similar political values (liberalism), their "sharing political values alone will not lead automatically to reconciliation."[70] Not all democracies have come clean on the issue of past wrongs. As we can see from recent examples in Europe, membership in the democracy club does not shield a country from problems with its past, whether domestic or external. Among the few valid points made by nationalists in Japan are that not many of the former European colonial powers have apologized adequately, if at all, for their past transgressions in the colonies and that even some democratically elected officials in Europe can appear to justify certain aspects of Nazi policy.

In a democracy such as Japan, where issues of the past have been the subject of intense debate, there is concern that democratic values and practices are under threat. It is not just ironic, but in fact alarming, that some Japanese who cite the lack of academic freedom in China as the main obstacle to solving the history problem try to silence criticism with-in Japan by accusing the critics of being "masochistic" and of "serving the interest of the enemy country." Nishio Kanji, a leading exponent of the self-styled "liberalist view of history," openly calls for "eradicating *(bokumetsu)* the stupid

Apology Faction (its existence equals the behavior of helping the enemy *[riteki kôi]*) in Japan." Such language is chillingly reminiscent of the vocabulary used by the wartime militarist regime against internal dissent.[71] In this sense, democratic values are as important as, if not more important than, the mere existence of democratic institutions. In postwar Japan, democratic values such as antimilitarism, peace, respect for individual dignity, and freedom of speech should be further strengthened against ultranationalist elements in society and their new intellectual patrons.

Needless to say, these are also the values that should be promoted in China and elsewhere. If China continues to open up to the outside world and if Chinese society gains more autonomy from the state apparatus, more radical and nationalistic voices may well gain greater influence and inspire future ultranationalist demagogues. Indeed, a tendency in this direction is already evident in some Chinese Internet chat rooms. Nevertheless, even if greater openness in China in the short run unleashes more extreme ultranationalistic forces, in the long run, greater openness and critical examination of the country's own history—by a robust intelligentsia and through rigorous journalism—will help put past crimes into perspective, which is a major step toward true reconciliation. Ultimately, then, while China and Japan differ considerably in their social systems, *both* countries face the same question about how to define their greatness. A democratic and open society, self-confident and yet fully cognizant of its past wrongs, is as much a goal for China as it is for Japan.

■ ■ ■

To summarize, the history problem between Japan and China has not been invented out of thin air but has real historical roots. At the same time, the current problem is not only about the past; its emergence as one of the most sensitive issues between China and Japan in recent years says much about the present domestic conditions in both countries and the dynamics of their bilateral relations. Rooted in the way in which each country defines its national identity, the history problem is entangled with other aspects of international relations.

In order to resolve the problem and to bring about a true reconciliation between Japan and China, it is helpful to think in terms of levels of state and society, as well as of short-term and long-term solutions. In the short run, management by both governments as well as by nongovernmental institutions is required to steer the often-volatile relationship away from emotional ruptures. Both governments need to accept that it is in their interest to contain the problem. The news media as well as intellectuals and academics who write for the general public, too, must do their part and refrain from fanning the flames of conflict. These measures in themselves will not eliminate the source of the history problem but will at least help prevent the situation from deteriorating. To stop this endless wrangling between the two countries over the history problem, it is necessary, as one Chinese scholar who lives in Japan has suggested, to create a mechanism that "identifies the source of fire and prevents it." Gradually, mid- and long-term efforts will be needed to push the bilateral relations onto a track on which "Japan will not forget the history while China will not constantly talk about history."[72] In order to bring about a lasting understanding and reconciliation, China and Japan need between them a multilevel framework for honest exchanges among historians, educators, and opinion leaders on issues of war and trauma. In the long run, the resolution of the history problem requires nothing less than changes in both societies, in their education systems in particular. Developing both a healthy national pride and a global identity is as important for China as it is for Japan.

Governments can play useful roles as facilitators and perhaps monitors, but reconciliation must go deeper and take place between societies if it is to last. The road to true reconciliation between Japan and China will be a long and tortuous one. International geopolitical calculations as well as domestic constraints will influence this process. Although this chapter has dealt largely with the levels of state and society, reconciliation ultimately takes place at an individual level. Here the history of relations between Japan and China offers some hope.

In January 1932, a few months after Japan's Kwantung Army launched an invasion and occupied the northeastern provinces of China, the Japanese military provoked a minor war of distraction in Shanghai that escalated into a short but bloody conflict with heavy casualties on both sides. A Japanese doctor in Shanghai found a wounded pigeon in a war-ravaged section of the city. He took it back to Japan, but the pigeon died despite his efforts to save it. The doctor built a pagoda in commemoration and asked

Lu Xun, the distinguished Chinese writer and critic, who was living in Shanghai, to write a poem. Lu Xun's poem, "Ti Sanyi ta," written in mid-1933, ended with these words:

> *Du jing jiebo xiongdi zai, xiangfeng yixiao min enchou*
> (Enduring all the calamity brothers have survived /
> With a smile they bury the hatred).

One of the greatest Chinese writers of the twentieth century, Lu Xun still commands much respect in present-day China. An outspoken critic of the ills of Chinese society, he strove to introduce foreign literature and art into China; his works are still part of the Chinese school curriculum. Lu Xun had many friends and even admirers in Japan, but he was firmly opposed to Japan's military encroachment on China. He died before China and Japan became engulfed in a full-scale war. Hotta Yoshie, the Japanese writer cited at the beginning of this chapter, was very much touched by Lu Xun's works and became interested in China as a result. Hotta arrived in Shanghai in early 1945, nine years after Lu Xun's death. The two men never met in person, yet in reading their works today one senses a meeting of their spirits that transcends the bitter conflict between the two countries. Such a spiritual meeting between the Chinese and the Japanese is needed more than ever today.

4

Overcoming the Difficult Past

Rectification of the 2-28 Incident and the Politics of Reconciliation in Taiwan

Masahiro Wakabayashi

THE ALLIED VICTORY IN THE PACIFIC THEATER of World War II in 1945 brought an end to Japan's colonial rule of Taiwan, which had begun in 1895. The island became the "Taiwan Province" of the Republic of China. After the Chinese Communist Party won the civil war in 1949, the Chinese Nationalists (the Kuomintang, or KMT) transferred the government of the Republic of China to Taiwan, which continued to oppose the People's Republic of China, established by the Communist Party. For fifty years thereafter, the KMT monopolized political power and enforced authoritarian rule in Taiwan. However, it began moving toward democracy in the autumn of 1986, when it allowed the establishment of the first opposition party, the Democratic Progressive Party (DPP). Martial law, which had been enforced since May 1949, was lifted in the summer of 1987. In 1991 and 1992 national elections were held for all the seats in the legislature. Up to this point, the legislature had been the province of the so-called Ten-Thousand-Year Parliament, which was dominated by members who had held seats since they were elected on the Chinese mainland during the civil war against the Chinese Communist Party in the 1940s. Taiwan's transition to democracy was confirmed in March 1996, when citizens for the first time in history cast their votes to elect the president directly. In short, Taiwan's democratic transition began just before the end of the Cold War and while Russia and Eastern Europe were also moving toward democracy. Then, in the spring of 2000, Chen Shuibian of the DPP was elected president. Chen's victory put an end to the KMT's half century of rule on the island; the long-awaited transfer of power occurred on the eve of the twenty-first century.

By definition, an authoritarian regime is a political regime that lacks positive justification for restricting political freedom and public participation in politics. Hence, it is necessary for the regime to use draconian force to maintain its power. This is why a movement toward democracy often brings into the open previously buried incidents of oppression and gives rise to the issue of "overcoming the difficult past." The democratization drive in Taiwan was no exception.

In Taiwan, the issue centered on two particular events. One was the incident that occurred in 1947 in the days following the end of Japanese colonial rule, known as the February 28 Incident (referred to hereafter as the 2-28 Incident). The other was the so-called White Terror campaign, which began in 1949, and in which the government oppressed its political opponents and their sympathizers (or those deemed sympathizers by the secret police).[1]

The 2-28 Incident

The 2-28 Incident was a popular uprising that occurred against the backdrop of socioeconomic confusion resulting from the poor administration of the Taiwan Provincial Governor's Office, which had requisitioned the Japanese government offices and assets. Contributing to the incident was the friction between the Taiwanese and the Mainlanders, who came to Taiwan with Governor Chen Yi.

On February 27, 1947, in the city of Taipei, the public clashed with authorities when investigators of the Taipei City Monopoly Bureau quarreled with a woman over black market cigarettes and a bystander was shot by one of the investigators and later died. The following day, protesting demonstrators stormed the governor's office and were met with bullets from the military police guard. The ensuing riots in the city quickly spread throughout the island, and the government lost control of areas where there were no military bases. Meanwhile, influential members of the Taiwanese community formed the Committee to Settle the 2-28 Incident in

Taipei and other cities around Taiwan to bring the chaos under control and at the same time to pressure Governor Chen Yi to reform the administration. Chen Yi, while buying time by offering a superficial compromise, secretly asked the chairman of the KMT government in Nanjing, Chiang Kai-shek (Jiang Jieshi), for military reinforcements. In response to Chen's request and to contain the uprising that had spread throughout the island, two battalions of the Fourth Gendarme Regiment landed at Keelung harbor on March 8 and were followed by the Twenty-first Army Division the next day. Immediately, the troops began quashing the uprising. On the streets of the main cities, such as Keelung and Taipei, the KMT soldiers killed and injured a large number of people, including innocent bystanders and student volunteers working to maintain order. Even before that, on March 6, troops stationed in Kaohsiung (Gaoxiong) Port under the command of Peng Mengji rolled into Kaohsiung City and clashed with citizens, inflicting heavy casualties at the Kaohsiung station, the city council building, Kaohsiung Junior High School, and other centers.

Many of the Taiwanese elite, including intellectuals and influential figures, were detained and then summarily executed. Many others, who were ordered to report to the military police at the time, never returned and remain missing to this day. People never seen again include those directly involved in the incident (for example, members of the Committee to Settle the 2-28 Incident) and those with absolutely no direct involvement but with a previous history of openly criticizing Chen Yi. One U.S. scholar has pointed out that the military massacre, although seemingly indiscriminate, had a clear pattern of exterminating Taiwanese intellectuals and the elite.[2]

The military action restored government control in approximately two weeks, after which it was suspended. But in the ensuing "purge," people involved in the settlement committee were hunted down and weapons were confiscated in a thorough campaign of reprisals across the island, leading to further arrests, incarcerations, and executions. There are several estimates of the eventual number of victims of the incident, but no confirmed figures are as yet available. The Research Subcommittee set up under the 2-28 Incident Taskforce of the Administrative Yuan (discussed below) gave no definite figure in its published report but estimated the death toll at somewhere between eighteen and twenty-eight thousand people.[3] This represents between 0.28 and 0.43 percent of Taiwan's total population of approximately 6,437,000 people in 1947.[4]

The Nanjing government handled the situation in Taiwan as if it were a rebellion against the state, resorting to measures far harsher than needed to restore order. The approach sent a strong shock wave through Taiwanese society. Victims and their bereaved families, unless they were public servants (and most of those were Mainlanders at the time), received no compensation.[5] Thereafter Taiwan slid into the period of the White Terror, characterized by extended martial law. The shocking incident became a taboo topic and left those affected by it with no concrete measure of relief from the government, effects that protracted the anguish of Taiwanese society, leaving a deep scar that time alone cannot heal.

The incident and the government's handling of it have had two notable effects on politics in Taiwan. The first is that it deprived Taiwanese society of a political voice. Many elite Taiwanese—those who would normally represent the voice of society—were slaughtered, and the excessive, cruel oppression planted a deep-rooted fear of politics among the people. The bereaved families of victims were dealt not just a psychological but also a financial blow. Unable to find or even to confirm the death of their loved ones or to speak out to clear their names, these families suffered from the indifference of society and the harassment of the secret police force that was established under martial law. The anger provoked by the 2-28 Incident, given no possible means of expression, was buried but was not extinguished.

The second effect is that the incident marked the historical acknowledgment of the ethnic conflict between the Mainlanders and the Taiwanese, the most significant social cleavage in postwar Taiwanese society. In terms of ethnopolitics, the incident can be seen as the politicization of ethnicity. Friction between the two ethnic groups already existed because the Taiwanese elite were excluded from the process of requisitioning the assets of the colonial Japanese authorities and prevented from working in the government on the grounds that they had been "enslaved" by the Japanese. Untutored in Mandarin and unable in the immediate postwar years to gain greater fluency in the language, the Taiwanese elite were effectively silenced in terms of public debate by a ban on the use of Japanese in the mass media.

During the course of the 2-28 Incident, some Taiwanese expressed their antipathy toward the Mainlanders in acts of violence, for example, by beating any person identified as a Mainlander in the streets. Hence, rather than being simply a case of abusive state power, the incident was clearly also an ethnic clash between the Mainlanders and the Taiwanese.[6] Further, when the Nanjing government moved to Taiwan in 1949, Mainlanders dominated key positions in national politics, running party, military, and media organizations, including the Ten-Thousand-Year Parliament. This led to an ethnicity-based dual structure among the political elite, with national politics run by the Mainlanders and regional politics, which were open to election, managed by the Taiwanese.[7] The KMT government systematically enforced policies of "Chinese assimilation," requiring, for instance, the use throughout the school system of Mandarin as the national language. Consequently, the status of Taiwan's native culture was diminished and it became increasingly peripheral.[8]

Because of this sense of ethnic injustice, the process of overcoming the difficult past in regard to the 2-28 Incident has played a significant part in the development of a new national identity and attitude toward politics in Taiwan. Although the settlement is promoting human rights by pressing the state to redress its past misdeeds, the goal must include the pursuit of ethnic reconciliation between the Mainlanders and the Taiwanese. Therefore, the speed and extent of progress in overcoming the difficult past are defined by the need for compromise not only to achieve the transition to democracy but also to reconcile the Taiwanese majority with the Mainlanders, a powerful minority.[9] The political empowerment of the Taiwanese, a result of the increase in public offices available through elections, is contributing to an ideological empowerment, as the KMT version of Chinese nationalism recedes and Taiwanese nationalism emerges. How fast and to what extent "the difficult past" will be "overcome" will be determined to a considerable extent by the progress and limitations of such empowerment.

The rise of Taiwanese nationalism during the democratization process has brought about a political system in which the parties range between the ideological poles of Taiwanese and Chinese nationalism. Taiwan's politics, especially electoral politics, has taken on some of the character of identity politics and is often tainted by populist appeals to nationalism.[10]

We can assume that this development has to some extent influenced the process of overcoming the difficult past and ethnic reconciliation.

Rectification of the 2-28 Incident

Rectification of the 2-28 Incident started in February 1987, when more than forty organizations, including human rights groups, cultural organizations, the Presbyterian Church, and groups supportive of DPP parliamentary members, gathered to form the 2-28 Peace Promotion Society at the initiative of the Taiwan Association for Human Rights. The group held a news conference on February 13 and issued the "2-28 Peace Day" declaration, holding that "achieving peace between the ruler and the ruled, or the Taiwanese and Mainlanders" is the "foundation for the survival of Taiwan." The society also demanded that the government designate February 28 as the "day of [social] peace," "disclose the truth [about the 2-28 Incident], and exonerate the falsely accused."[11] Subsequently the group held memorial services and demonstrations (with riot police conspicuously in attendance) across Taiwan in cities such as Tainan, Taipei, Kaohsiung, and Zhanghua.[12]

The society expanded its activities in 1988 and 1989. Taiwanese legislators from both the ruling and the opposition camps seeking clarification of the government's stance on reviewing the incident and calling for the establishment of a committee to investigate it were met with a lukewarm response. When President Chiang Ching-kuo (Jiang Jingguo) died while in office in January 1988, the vice president, Lee Teng-hui (Li Denghui), who is Taiwanese, took over the post until the end of President Chiang Ching-kuo's term. At his first media conference, the new president said, "it is absurd for people under forty [who were born after it had occurred] to discuss the 2-28 Incident." This comment attracted strong criticism from the 2-28 Peace Promotion Society. (Lee, however, may not have been quite as confident of the "absurdity" as he sounded: the following day, he dispatched his second daughter, a scholar at Academia Sinica, the central research institute, to the institute's historian, Lai Tse-han, who at the time had just begun delving into the 2-28 Incident, to hear his opinion.) In March of the same year, Premier Yu Guohua (the director-general of the Administrative Yuan and a Mainlander) said before the Legislative

Yuan that the government would raise no objections to an academic study of the 2-28 Incident, but that the wounds had already healed. Then at the end of the year he generated some criticism when he told visiting scholars that the emperor of the Qing dynasty did not apologize to the people of Han even though Manchurians killed a large number of Han people when they entered the Chinese mainland. In the same vein, in February of the following year, Qiu Chuanghuan, the governor of Taiwan Province and a Taiwanese, told the parliament that 2-28 was an unfortunate incident, but that the matter had already become history and did not deserve any further examination. (Yet, in the autumn of the previous year, the Taiwan provincial government's Historical Research Commission had launched a hearing with people involved in the incident.)

Despite such sentiments, the expansion of political freedom steadily built up social pressure for a reexamination of the incident. In August 1989, *The City of Sadness,* a film directed by Hou Xiaoxian and depicting Taiwan in the days before and immediately after the 2-28 Incident, won an award at the Venice Film Festival, making this incident in Taiwan's modern history known to the rest of the world. The film was released across the island in the fall and attracted large audiences. By now it was clear that the incident was no longer a taboo subject for open discussion. Taiwan's first 2-28 Incident monument was erected in the southern city of Jiayi (the city in which armed civilians had clashed violently with KMT troops), where an independent politician with political views close to those of the DPP served as mayor at the time. On February 27, 1990, in the Legislative Yuan, a legislator proposed a minute of silence in memory of the victims of the incident. The attending cabinet ministers did not observe the silence, but this was the first sign that the Taiwanese state organ was changing its attitude toward the incident.

The next month Lee Teng-hui won a full term, which allowed him to serve as president until May 1996, and the administration shifted its stance gradually. In response to popular pressure, Lee proposed a scheme of democratization in which amending the constitution of the Republic of China would be the central method. That year a description of the incident was included for the first time in a high school history textbook, although the reference was limited to only fifty-eight characters. The Administrative Yuan (equivalent to the cabinet) set up a task force to investigate the 2-28 Incident, and five scholars, including Lai Tse-han, formed a research subcommittee that was to submit a report in one year.

In April 1989, the Presbyterian Church had issued an apology, saying that it had failed to provide support and acts of compassion to the bereaved families of the 2-28 Incident victims during the period of martial law.[13] In December 1990, the Presbyterian Church held the first memorial service for victims of the 2-28 Incident. Prime Minister Hao Pei-tsun (He Bocun), a Mainlander, and his cabinet members attended. Taiwan's Presbyterian Church was divided into the "National-language" (that is, Mandarin) group and the "Taiwanese-language" group, depending on which language was used for the sermon. The memorial service brought these two groups together, with a clergyman from the National-language group delivering a sermon in Taiwanese, and a clergyman from the Taiwanese-language group delivering a sermon in Mandarin.

In 1991, the bereaved families broke their long silence. In March, seven people representing the families met with Lee Teng-hui and submitted a five-point request, demanding that the government

1. disclose the truth of the incident with fairness and impartiality;
2. offer a formal apology to the victims of the incident;
3. pay compensation to the bereaved families;
4. erect a 2-28 Incident monument in the city center of Taipei; and
5. establish a 2-28 Incident Memorial Foundation to engage in activities contributing to the eradication of ethnic confrontation between Mainlanders and Taiwanese and to the promotion of democracy.[14]

While refraining from showing all-out support, Lee Teng-hui said that the time was ripe for a solution, and that he himself "was almost shot down" when he went to Taipei City at that time.[15] Ensuing government action progressed largely in line with the five-point request. Associations of victims' families were set up across the island. In August, the Federation of 2-28 Victims' Families Organizations was established.[16] In November, the Administrative Yuan expressed its intention to erect a monument for the 2-28 Incident, and in February of the following year, it established a special committee within the Yuan to pursue the matter.

The report on the incident by the Research Subcommittee of the Administrative Yuan was published in February 1992. Lai Tse-han, one of the authors of the report, said that the subcommittee had access to only

70 percent of the reference documents owing to the reluctance of the defense department to make such materials available.[17] Some people criticized the subcommittee because they believed that the researchers had managed to uncover only 60 percent of the truth,[18] but the publication of the "report" had a decisive effect in raising the handling of the incident from social debate to policy making.

On February 21, 1992, several drafts of acts on the 2-28 Incident were published. Wu Zi and seventeen other KMT legislators submitted a draft act on the handling of the incident; another twenty KMT members, led by Hong Zhaonan, proposed an act on compensation; and nineteen DPP members led by Xie Changting drafted an act on reparations.[19] These drafts were submitted to the joint committee on internal and judicial affairs. At the time, the Legislative Yuan was still the Ten-Thousand-Year Parliament, dominated by legislators who had not been re-elected since they had arrived from the Mainland. All three drafts were submitted by members elected through the "supplementary elections," the procedure by which regular regional elections have been held in Taiwan since 1972.

The joint committee halted its first round of deliberations on March 18 and did not convene for the second round until almost a year later, on March 10, 1993, following national elections for all the seats in the Legislative Yuan. The "ten-thousand-year legislators," mostly Mainlanders, bowed out of the political arena, and the prime minister, Hao Pei-tsun, the leader of the Mainlander camp opposing Lee Teng-hui, was replaced by Lian Zhan, a Taiwanese. The balance of power between the Mainlanders and the Taiwanese in Taiwan politics was clearly shifting.

On June 10 of the same year, the Administrative Yuan adopted its own draft act on the handling of the 2-28 Incident, and, on June 16, it submitted it to the Legislative Yuan's joint committee on internal and judicial affairs. The DPP took the upper hand in the committee deliberations, leading to the approval, on June 21, of a draft act that was closest to that submitted by Xie Changting.[20] The draft stated that

- the act was to "provide reparation in relation to the 2-28 Incident, promote public understanding about the truth of the incident, heal the wounds of history, and encourage reconciliation between ethnic groups";
- a committee on reparation issues should be established in the Administrative Yuan;

- the government should issue an apology, prosecute those responsible for the incident, and declare February 28 a public holiday;
- victims should be given reparation, have their names cleared, and be granted a special pardon, according to the findings of the Reparation Committee;
- government offices should be obliged to respond to the committee's requests for materials related to the incident; and
- a memorial foundation should be established to enlighten society about the incident.

However, the ensuing deliberations went far from smoothly. It was not until June 1994 that the committee's draft was tabled in a plenary session of the Legislative Yuan, only to be left pending until the next session. When the draft was submitted to a plenary session in January 1995, the ruling KMT used its majority power to overturn the committee's proposals one after another. On March 23, amid fierce protest from DPP legislators, the parliament passed the Act on the Settlement and Compensation for the 2-28 Incident (the 2-28 Act).[21] The 2-28 Act differed from the committee's draft in several respects:

- In the description of the objectives, the term *reparation* was replaced with *compensation.* In other words, rather than have the state award reparations to victims, a government-funded foundation would be compensating for the suffering of victims, with the maximum compensation being NT $6 million.
- Rather than establish a special committee within the Administrative Yuan, the government would fund and establish a memorial foundation with duties that included those designated in the Reparation Committee's draft.
- The act did not include a clause about the prosecution of those involved in the incident, citing difficulty in identifying them after so many years and the expiration of the statute of limitations. A government apology was included, but the act designated February 28 only as a memorial day, not as a public holiday.
- Victims would be given compensation, have their names cleared, and be granted a special pardon, according to the findings of a study by the 2-28 Incident Memorial Foundation.

- Government offices would be obliged to respond to the foundation's requests for material related to the incident.
- The 2-28 Incident Memorial Foundation would be established to enlighten society about the incident.

The 2-28 Act was proclaimed by the president on April 7 and enacted on October 7.

On February 28, 1995, a monument for the 2-28 Incident was unveiled at the New Park in the heart of Taipei. In the unveiling ceremony, President Lee Teng-hui, as the head of state, expressed an apology, but somewhat indirectly. (The KMT, in contrast, offered no apology.)

> I am among those who experienced the 2-28 Incident. I have long felt a deep remorse over this historical tragedy, which broke out when it did not have to and spread when it did not have to. This unfortunate incident deprived our society of a large number of intellectuals, disregarded the dignity of many human lives, hindered harmony between citizens and the government, suppressed people's interest in public affairs, delayed the progress of this society, and caused immeasurable damage to the overall development of our state. Today, the bereaved families of those who fell victim to the incident are witnessing the unveiling of the 2-28 monument on the ground of the Taiwan island, depicting historical justice and calling for ethnic harmony. You are also hearing that I, as the head of state, acknowledge the mistakes made by the government and offer the most sincere apology. With this apology, I am convinced that your ragged heart filled with animosity will be transformed into a heart of peace and harmony, appeasing the mind of all people in Taiwan. It is to my deepest regret that some of the bereaved families have already passed away and could not witness the completion of this monument.[22]

Because of a dispute over the wording of the inscription, the unveiling ceremony went ahead with no inscription on the plaque. At issue was the identification and description of the actions of those, such as Chiang Kai-shek and Peng Mengji, responsible for the suppression, and the description of the massacre by the military. The duty of preparing the inscription was later handed over to the 2-28 Incident Memorial Foundation. A consensus was reached just before the fiftieth anniversary of the incident in 1997, when the agreed text was inscribed on the plaque. However, it was removed on the afternoon of the same day by dissatisfied members of an organization of victims' families, which held that the inscription obscured both the responsibility of those involved and the cruelty of the incident itself.[23] In spring 1999, the government of Taipei City quietly reinstalled the plaque with the original inscription, which remains on the monument to this day.[24] (A translation of the inscription is included at the end of this chapter.) Ma Yingjiu, the mayor of Taipei, a Mainlander and member of the KMT who won the election in 1998 and in 2002, insists that the Mainlanders should not be burdened with the "original sin" of the 2-28 Incident; his predecessor, Chen Shuibian, a Taiwanese, a member of the DPP and currently the president of Taiwan, supports the possibility of changing the inscription in the future.[25]

The 2-28 Incident Memorial Foundation, defined in the 2-28 Act, was established in October 1995 and started accepting compensation applications from victims and their families in December. Initially, the application period was set to end two years from the day the act went into effect. However, it has been extended twice, and the third deadline was October 6, 2002. As of December 25, 2002, compensation totaling NT $6,688 million had been granted in 2,226 cases.[26]

In a related development, the New Park in Taipei City was renamed the 2-28 Peace Park on February 28, 1996. In the park a building formerly occupied by the Taipei broadcasting office and thus one of the sites associated with the incident was turned into the Taipei 2-28 Memorial Museum, which opened on the anniversary of the incident, in 1997. Also in 1997, the 2-28 Act was revised to declare February 28 a national holiday. Postage stamps commemorating the incident (showing the image of the monument, NT $19 per stamp) were also issued.[27]

In June 1997, the Administrative Yuan approved a plan to grant presidential pardons to victims of the incident, to clear their names and exonerate them. Although the President's Office also approved this policy,[28] these measures have yet to be implemented, due to a delay in specifying the beneficiaries.

Rectification of the White Terror

The White Terror campaign, orchestrated by the martial-law enforcement body, the Taiwan Garrison Command headquarters, and the secret police, refers, strictly speaking, to the severe crackdown on Communist

Party members that began in the early 1950s. The name is also sometimes used to refer to the entire history of political oppression under martial law. According to an official estimate, 29,407 people were arrested, and approximately 15 percent of those arrested were executed over the course of the thirty-eight years from 1949 to 1987.

The waning sense of taboo surrounding the 2-28 Incident helped to pave the way for open discussions about the White Terror. So too did Lee Teng-hui's constitutional reforms, which significantly expanded political freedom. The Antisubversion Act, which had been very instrumental in "producing" political prisoners out of dissidents, was abolished in May 1991. An article in the criminal code that permitted authorities to charge people with rioting when they were simply speaking out was amended in May 1992. These measures put the White Terror on the country's social agenda as one of the elements of Taiwan's difficult past that, like the 2-28 Incident, needed to be overcome.

The Act on the Restoration of Rights Undermined during the Martial Law Period was declared in January 1995, prior to the 2-28 Act, and stipulated the restoration of rights and qualifications of those who had been convicted of political crimes or had had their qualifications as public servants, lawyers, and so on suspended under the law. The enactment of the 2-28 Act led to another act, the Compensation Act for Improper Trial [of] Cases of Sedition and Spies during the Martial Law Period, which was proclaimed in June and enforced in December.[29] This act was revised slightly in November 2000 to expand its scope and now includes victims of the left-wing suppression that occurred just before martial law was imposed, as well as victims of the 1979 "Formosa Incident."[30] In addition, a foundation modeled after the 2-28 Incident Memorial Foundation was set up to handle compensation for unjust convictions on sedition and spying charges during martial law. The foundation began its work in April 1999[31] and by May 20, 2002, had handled 4,714 cases. The deadline for applications was set as December 16, 2002.[32]

Ethnic Reconciliation

There are three main observations to be made about the process of reconciliation and how the government in Taiwan handled the need to make amends for policies and actions that had caused considerable harm and anguish to people from all walks of life.

The first is that the review of the 2-28 Incident opened just as Taiwan began its move toward democracy and reached a tentative conclusion as Taiwan completed that task. During this period, a smooth transition was a matter of the highest priority for the political elites, and especially for the KMT, which did all it could to prevent the process of overcoming the difficult past from generating political tensions that might hinder the democratization process. President Lee Teng-hui, who helped to shape both the transition to democracy and the process of rectifying the 2-28 Incident, made some coldhearted remarks at his first press conference as the president in early 1988, and his apology, as head of state, to bereaved families at the unveiling ceremony for the 2-28 monument in February 28, 1995, was rather equivocal.[33] These public statements illustrate clearly the extent to which the KMT leadership needed to exhibit prudence in dealing with this problem.

Overcoming the difficult past has been not only a human rights movement intended to rectify past abuse of state power but also an element of the identity politics that developed along with democratization. The settlement of painful historical issues occurred within the limits prescribed by the compromise reached between the Taiwanese, who were empowered by the expansion of election-based politics, and the Mainlanders, the minority that still enjoys significant influence over the military, the mass media, and other centers of power.

The second observation to be made is that the measures taken by the government merely provided for the victims and did not seek to prosecute the victimizers. A large sum of money was paid out for compensation, not for reparation. A monument was erected. A memorial day was declared. The head of state offered a formal apology. Yet those, including Peng Mengji, responsible for the excessive military crackdown, were never forced to admit their responsibility publicly, let alone have criminal charges brought against them.[34] In the official report by the Administrative Yuan as well as in the inscription on the 2-28 monument, references to Chiang Kai-shek's responsibility as the supreme leader were extremely measured. In fact, the idolization of Chiang Kai-shek in state symbols, though waning, has never been officially suspended. The aggressors might have been prosecuted more strongly if the parliament had passed the DPP-initiated draft act on compensation for the 2-28 Incident victims, prepared by the Legislative Yuan's joint committee on internal and judicial affairs, and if the Compensation Committee had been established in the Administrative Yuan.

In other words, overcoming the difficult past was successful only in putting an end to its political ramifications, not in overcoming the problem in a deeper sense. Much remains to be done to foster an understanding of the difficult past that would establish genuine mutual respect between the two ethnic groups.

The third observation is that progress in rectifying the 2-28 Incident has led to a general reflection on the abuse of power by the KMT regime during the White Terror in the 1950s and during the whole period under martial law and has resulted in exoneration and compensation for victims and their families. Although the political context of the rectification process has been heavily tainted with identity and nationalist politics, other aspects of the process have not been colored by ethnic antagonisms. Thus, for instance, although some victims of the White Terror were Mainlanders, and although some former political prisoners have become proponents of the reunification of China and vocal opponents of Taiwanese nationalism and of Lee Teng-hui's so-called Taiwanization policy, rectification measures were nonetheless extended to all the victims of the White Terror. Chen Shuibian, the president of Taiwan, has publicly pledged to incorporate into the political system measures for the protection of human rights, among them the adoption of the UN principles regarding human rights and the establishment of a government commission on human rights. These promises deserve more international attention.

To what extent has the process of overcoming the difficult past furthered the goal of achieving ethnic reconciliation in Taiwan? It seems fair to say that, having removed the biggest historical impediment to ethnic reconciliation, the process has so far achieved some success. As a result of liberalization measures and the active civil campaign to reexamine the 2-28 Incident, people in Taiwan have quickly begun to regard the victims and their families with sympathy and respect. In addition, government measures since the 1990s have helped substantially to ease the resentment of the Taiwanese majority toward the state and its past misdeeds. This can be seen as a reflection of the mutual understanding between the Taiwanese and the Mainlanders that has developed as a result of their common experience in living on the same island for half a century, and as a reflection of reconciliation fostered by the public debate that has been stimulated by political liberalization and democratization.

The diminishing intensity of feeling regarding historical abuses can also be attributed to the fact that the generation—both Taiwanese and Mainlander—with direct experience of the 2-28 Incident and the White Terror is now retiring from leading roles in society. Among the younger, postwar, generation, the social and cultural distance between Taiwanese and Mainlanders is becoming narrower. Furthermore, to the extent that the ethnic antipathy between the Taiwanese and the Mainlanders was inspired and shaped by the Cold War, fading memories of the Cold War should be accompanied by fading ethnic hostility.

The democratic transition, however, has also brought about a structured rivalry between Taiwanese and Chinese nationalism in Taiwan's politics. On the one hand, political elites and opinion leaders seem to have reached some consensus on the multicultural nature of society and to have agreed on the necessity of mutual respect for each ethnic group. But on the other hand, politicized issues tend to be interpreted from the viewpoint of national identity (Chinese vs. Taiwanese), and electoral campaigns tend to be partisan, with ethnonationalistic rhetoric spouted both in the north, with its relatively high population of Mainlanders, and in the south, where the Taiwanese population is dominant. If this polarization continues, the hard-earned ethnic reconciliation will be damaged and with it the prospect for democratic consolidation.

Two events illustrate this situation. In the three months immediately after the March 2000 election, ethnic conflict might easily have erupted. On the night of March 18, after the historic victory of the DPP's Chen Shuibian was announced, a large number of supporters of Song Chuyu (James Soong), believing that the defeat of Song and of Lian Zhan (the KMT candidate for the presidency) was caused by Lee Teng-hui's alleged secret support for Chen Shuibian, gathered in front of the KMT's headquarters in central Taipei and demanded that Lee step down as the chairman of the KMT. The bulk of the crowd consisted of Mainlanders from the northern part of the island. There was a strong and swift reaction, mainly from the southern part of the island, the stronghold of the DPP and of Taiwanese nationalist activists. Some of the DPP branch offices there began to organize counterdemonstrations by mobilizing DPP supporters and moving north toward the central area of Taipei. Lin Yixiong, then the party chairman of the DPP, promptly and strongly urged every party branch not to organize any counterdemonstrations in Taipei. His order was very effective. Song Chuyu declared that he would organize a new political party of his own on March 22, Lee Teng-hui resigned his party chairmanship on March 24, and the crowd, which had unlawfully occupied a section of the city for several days, quickly dispersed.[35]

Then, on the morning of May 27, only one week after the inauguration of the new president, when former president Lee Teng-hui attended an athletic meeting in the town where he lived, a retired officer who was a Mainlander threw red ink at Lee, accusing him of destroying the party and the state. As Lee Teng-hui enjoys great popularity among the Taiwanese, any overt insult to him could have aroused ethnic tensions. The former president expressed neither outrage nor a word of blame for the offender but, after changing his clothes, played golf with his friends as scheduled. Legislators of the DPP and the opposition took the event seriously and appealed to the public to understand the importance of "ethnic harmony" on the island. As a result of these measured responses, the event did not provoke any serious consequences and the tension subsided.[36]

That Lee and his supporters reacted so mildly to these events does not mean that they did not fight back politically. The next summer (2001), Lee's supporters organized a new political party, the Taiwan Solidarity Union (TSU), and put up candidates throughout Taiwan for the Legislative Yuan election. Lee vigorously backed those candidates during the campaign and the TSU won thirteen seats in the Legislative Yuan.[37] In a sense, Lee Teng-hui did react to the insult, but he did so within the democratic system by using the framework of party politics.

That these events occurred within the first few months of the first democratic transfer of power in Taiwan, shows us, on the one hand, that there still remains much to be done in overcoming the difficult past and, on the other hand, that Taiwan's democratic system, however far from mature, has already become capable of dealing with such critical situations. A careful and thoughtful performance by the political elites in upholding democratic principles when handling crucial issues is indispensable if the seeds of historical reconciliation are to take root in society.

■ ■ ■

The Inscription on the February 28 Commemorative Plaque

In 1945, when news of Japan's surrender reached Taiwan, the populace rejoiced, congratulating one another for having finally escaped the injustices of colonial rule. Unexpectedly, Chen Yi, chief executive officer of the Taiwan provincial government, responsible for the takeover and administration of Taiwan but ignorant of public sentiment, governed in a partisan manner, discriminating against the Taiwanese. Combined with bureaucratic corruption, production and distribution imbalances, soaring prices, and severe unemployment, popular dissatisfaction was soon pushed to the boiling point. On February 27, 1947, while confiscating smuggled cigarettes on Yen Ping North Road in Taipei City, Monopoly Bureau personnel injured a female vendor and mistakenly killed a bystander, inciting popular outrage. The next day, crowds in Taipei demonstrated in protest, marching to the Office of the Chief Executive to demand punishment of the killers. To their surprise, the demonstrators were met with gunfire, which killed and injured several participants, thereby igniting a fury of widespread public protest. In order to resolve the conflict and extinguish pent-up resentment toward the government, local Taiwanese leaders organized a settlement committee to mediate the dispute and even presented demands for political reform. Contrary to expectations, Chen Yi, haughty and obstinate by nature, entered into public negotiations while at the same time treating these leaders as rebels and requesting military assistance directly from Nanjing. Chiang Kai-shek, chairman of the Nationalist government, upon hearing reports from Taipei, immediately dispatched military troops to Taiwan. On March 8, the Twenty-first Army Division, under the command of Liu Yu-chin, landed at Keelung, and on March 10, martial law was declared throughout the island. In the course of suppressing local resistance and pacifying the countryside, K'o Yuan-fen, chief of staff of the Garrison Command, Shin Hung-hsi, commander of the Keelung Strategic Area, Peng Mengji, commander of the Gaoxiong Strategic Area, and Chang Mu-t'ao, chief of the Military Police Corps, implicated numerous innocent citizens. Within months, the number of those killed, injured, and missing exceeded ten thousand; residents of Keelung, Taipei, Chiayi, and Gaoxiong suffered the greatest losses. This event is known today as the February 28 Incident. During the subsequent half century, under the shadow of long-term martial law, both officials and private citizens have maintained a discreet silence, not daring to mention this taboo subject. Nevertheless, long-suppressed injustice eventually had to be rectified, and the problems of antagonism originating from native place differences and controversy over unification or independence needed to be solved. After the lifting of martial law in 1987, many sectors of the populace truly felt that peace and harmony would be impossible unless these grave afflictions were first cured. Thereupon, an official investigation of the February 28 Incident was undertaken, the head of the state made a public apology, victims and their families were compensated, and a memorial to the incident was erected. However, full recovery from this devastating social wound yet awaits the joint efforts of the entire nation. By engraving this plaque, we seek to comfort the souls of the deceased, to soothe the suffering and resentment of countless victims and their families, and to evoke this event as a lesson to all our compatriots. From this day forth, let us unite as one with mutual trust, treating one another with love and sincerity while dissolving all enmity and revenge, in the hope of establishing eternal peace. May Heaven bless this beloved island and grant her everlasting life.

Erected this 28th day of February, in the year nineteen hundred and ninety-seven, by the Memorial Foundation of the February 28 Incident.

5

Cambodia

Unable to Confront the Past

Nayan Chanda

THERE WAS A TIME WHEN THE NAME CAMBODIA evoked images of Angkor Wat and of an island of peace in an Indochina in flames. The name now conjures up images of bleached skulls in the killing fields, refugees, and endless violence. If there is one country that needs to heal its wounds, it is Cambodia. The nation has been ravaged by three decades of war and genocide. Under the Khmer Rouge, nearly a quarter of its seven million people died from disease, malnutrition, and outright execution. Religion, money, market, and education were abolished. With the exception of those who managed to flee the country, the entire surviving population has either experienced inhuman suffering and the trauma of seeing loved ones die or been forced to participate in the orgy of violence. The country's minority populations, especially the Vietnamese, have suffered disproportionately, and Cambodia's historic conflict with neighboring Vietnam has exploded into open war.

Yet, more than twenty years after falling from power, no Khmer Rouge leader has been tried in a court, far less punished for his role in the genocide. Nobody has even apologized.[1] Victims and many perpetrators and their family members carry on living with their trauma and nightmares, still not knowing why they had to go through this ordeal. The country's Vietnamese minority, who were targeted for slaughter by the Khmer Rouge first, continue to live in fear. Relations with Vietnam, whose intervention ended the genocide, remain strained amid unresolved border disputes, accusations of territorial encroachment, and mistreatment of the Vietnamese minority. Cambodia thus needs a three-way reconciliation: between the victims and their oppressors, between the minority Vietnamese and the Khmers, and between Cambodia and Vietnam.

In the following pages I argue that none of these reconciliations is likely to take place soon. The possibility of an international court trying the Khmer Rouge is slim and, even if a trial were to be held, not all of the responsible leaders would be tried and the outcome might still fall short of fair. The miasma of suspicion and unproven allegations about the roles of different politicians that hangs over the country may not be dispelled any time soon. The dynamics of Cambodia's internal politics also makes it difficult to achieve reconciliation with Vietnam or to heal the wounds of the Vietnamese residents.

Healing the Wounds of History

Cambodia's descent to hell was swift, but it has taken a long time for the country to crawl back to some plateau of normality. While the clandestine use of Cambodian territory by the Vietnamese communists and the secret bombing of the eastern part of the country by the United States were dragging the "island of peace" toward a greater war, it took the coup d'état of March 1970, which ousted the head of state, Prince Norodom Sihanouk, to trigger a civil war and bring direct foreign intervention. When the Vietnam War ended in 1975, Cambodia was plunged anew into an inferno by the victorious Khmer Rouge. It took intervention by the Vietnamese army to end, in 1979, the brutal rule by Pol Pot's Khmer Rouge, but that marked only the beginning of another phase of war. Backed by an international alliance opposing the Vietnamese-installed regime, the murderous Khmer Rouge got a new lease on life as partners in a war of resistance. Their former victims were forced to join hands with them in an uneasy alliance to oppose the regime in Phnom Penh. The same international constellation that encouraged the war of resistance eventually brought the parties to the negotiating table. An international peace accord signed in 1991 and a UN-mandated election in 1993 still failed, however, to bring total peace. Civil war sputtered on until 1998, when the Khmer Rouge resistance finally collapsed amid bloodletting and the disintegration of the movement. The late 1990s saw the revival of talk of a tribunal to try the surviving leaders for genocide and crimes against humanity.

Superficially, Cambodia has already achieved a remarkable degree of reconciliation. Barring a few revenge killings of Khmer Rouge cadres in villages immediately after the collapse of the regime in 1979, the country has been relatively free of retribution. In the two decades thereafter, the anti-Vietnamese resistance led by the Khmer Rouge along the Thai border resulted in an odd reconciliation of Khmers of all hues. Despite deep antipathy toward the Khmer Rouge, the noncommunist Cambodian parties, pushed by the Association of Southeast Asian Nations (ASEAN), China, and the West, forged a tactical cooperation with Pol Pot's forces. Over time, a similar accommodation was reached inside the country between Khmer Rouge defectors and the regime installed by the Vietnamese. In the mid-1990s, numerous former Khmer Rouge cadres and military officers defected and were absorbed into the Phnom Penh government. In towns and villages in Cambodia, many soldiers and officers of the Pol Pot regime now live among the people they once brutalized, although frequently their past is unknown to the villagers or even to their own wives and children.[2] Despite this apparently peaceful coexistence of victims and their abusers, Cambodia is far from putting its past behind it. People still abhor contact with these former Khmer Rouge, and the latter, in turn, live in perpetual fear of retribution. Anger against both the Khmer Rouge and, ironically, the Vietnamese still lurks beneath the surface and can erupt into violence at any time. As Youk Chhang, the director of the Documentation Center for Cambodia, has noted, "We all—Cambodians and the international community—will continue to point fingers at each other for the rest of our lives and for many generations to come if we fail to establish an independent tribunal."[3]

Roadblocks on the Path of Justice

While the need to start the healing process is self-evident, the first step—an accounting of the past—has been the most difficult to undertake. The most obvious cause has been the absence of the necessary peace and stability to attempt such healing. The time it has taken to end the civil war and the compromises made have blurred the lines between the perpetrators and their victims. Six specific domestic and external factors can be identified as hindering the process of reconciliation so far.

First, the way Khmer Rouge rule was ended by Vietnamese military intervention brought with it seeds of a new conflict. The war crimes tribunal that was held by the Vietnamese-backed government in 1979 and the sentencing of Khmer Rouge leaders Pol Pot and his brother-in-law Ieng Sary in absentia did not have any legitimacy. Set up by a foreign-installed government, it was not a tribunal that could establish justice. The purpose of the trial was political: to discredit the Khmer Rouge, who still sat at the United Nations and challenged the Phnom Penh government. Even the death sentence passed by that tribunal on Ieng Sary, the third in command in the Khmer Rouge leadership, was commuted in 1996 by the government in Phnom Penh in order to facilitate reconciliation. This amnesty would emerge in 2001 as a major obstacle to setting up a tribunal, the details of which are discussed below.

Second, Cambodia's deeply anchored Buddhist tradition, abhorring violence and accepting karma (fate resulting from a past life's action) as determining one's life, explains why there have not been many revenge killings by survivors. As Cambodia's patriarch, the Venerable Tep Vong, put it, "A trial of the Khmer Rouge cannot be accepted by Buddhism because Buddhists educate people not to take revenge. I ask all to be united together and to have national reconciliation."[4] Indeed, many, believing that such killers will face divine punishment, do not want to enter a cycle of violence by seeking retribution. There is also a reluctance to punish perpetrators who were ordinary folk and young children forced to commit barbaric acts under the threat of being killed themselves. This forgiveness has not, however, had the expected healing effect, as it has been a one-sided gesture. It has not been reciprocated by the sincere apology that Buddhist teaching calls for.[5]

Third, many Cambodians are loath to reexamine the past or reopen old wounds, fearing that such action could bring new division to the country. Cambodia's current leaders, including the constitutional king, Norodom Sihanouk, believe that a trial of the Khmer Rouge might re-ignite a civil war.[6] Given that the Khmer Rouge leadership has been totally discredited and its supporters dispersed and demoralized, talk of a new civil war is a political argument rather than a realistic threat.

Fourth, the decade-long Vietnamese occupation that followed the ouster of the Khmer Rouge from power muddied the situation. The fact that the Pol Pot regime could not be removed by the Cambodians themselves and that its overthrow was effected by occupation by Vietnam, a historical enemy, created a new dynamic. In this situation, justice—a prerequisite for reconciliation—could not be attempted. Despite Vietnam's role in ending the mass killings, the regime that was subsequently installed never gained legitimacy. In the people's eyes, the distinction between the ruthless Khmer Rouge and their less ruthless but authoritarian Hanoi-backed successors became blurred as the foreign-backed civil war continued, with Vietnamese troops holding sway over the country.

Fifth, the long-drawn-out war of resistance and the international balance of forces favoring the Khmer Rouge meant that the Phnom Penh regime could obtain peace only by making a deal with the Khmer Rouge. Speaking in January 2001 about peace in Cambodia, Prime Minister Hun Sen chastised the international community: "I only wish to recall that the recent calls for prosecution and punishment of the former Khmer Rouge leaders for their past crimes come strangely from those who had actively pardoned, fed, and supported them and installed them in the seat of peace negotiations in 1991."[7] There is no question that the legitimacy the world had accorded the Khmer Rouge since 1979 further blurred the distinction between the abusers and the abused. To start with, there were no paragons of virtue. Some of the stalwarts of the Phnom Penh regime, including Hun Sen himself (although no record has been found linking him to atrocities), were former Khmer Rouge cadres who had broken ranks early. The numbers of former Khmer Rouge within the government have continued to swell in the past few years as many, including some with serious records of abuse, have been granted amnesty and have been absorbed into the administration and the army. As the composition of the government has changed with the incorporation of new defectors (some even holding high rank in the military), the government's reluctance to hold a tribunal has intensified.

Ironically, in 1996 a violent split within the Khmer Rouge created the possibility of bringing Pol Pot to trial. However, by the same token, the chance that opened up for the government to make a deal with one faction undermined that possibility. The Khmer Rouge leader Ieng Sary and his associates defected to the government on condition of receiving a royal pardon for the 1979 sentence mentioned earlier. Hun Sen publicly argued that Ieng Sary should not be brought before a tribunal because he had made a "significant contribution to national reconciliation" by leading 70 percent of the former guerrilla forces to the government side, resulting in the elimination of the Khmer Rouge military organization. Sary's trial, Hun Sen warned, could restart hostilities. The details of this will be discussed later.

Sixth, the establishment of an international tribunal that would reveal the records of the fallen Khmer Rouge regime was strongly opposed by a permanent member of the UN Security Council—China.[8] Apart from its long-standing opposition to international intervention in any country, China has cause to worry about its own reputation being damaged by revelations of its role in the Khmer Rouge government. For instance, photographic records found in the archives of the Tuol Sleng interrogation center and recent interviews with former prison guards conducted by the Documentation Center of Cambodia show Chinese martial arts experts training the guards. Not only were the guards taught how to capture the suspects, but also, according to the testimony of a guard, Chinese experts accompanied them to the field to supervise them in action.[9] From the very beginning of the Khmer Rouge insurgency, China has been, along with Vietnam (at least until 1973), its principal foreign supporter. Beijing's dogged support for the Khmer Rouge in its struggle to regain power from 1979 through 1991 was aimed at thwarting Vietnamese ambition and strengthening China's own position in the region. The same objective has led China to switch its support to the Hun Sen government, once despised as a "Vietnamese puppet." Erasing the memory of its support for the Khmer Rouge while seeking to bolster its position as an ally of the current government has become an essential element of Chinese policy. Thus the issue of justice and reconciliation in Cambodia has become entangled with China's strategic ambition in Cambodia specifically and in Southeast Asia generally.

Pressing for a Tribunal

A combination of external pressures and growing demands within the country did, however, lead the government to change its approach to the tribunal. The fact that by 1998 three senior Khmer Rouge leaders responsible for serious crimes were in government custody and the rest of the surviving leaders had surrendered and were living freely in the country made the tribunal a real possibility. Although there is no accurate way of judging the national mood, there is enough anecdotal evidence to suggest that public demand for a trial has grown. Rithy Panh, a leading Cambodian documentary filmmaker who has traveled extensively throughout the country, quotes a thirty-year-old peasant: "The Khmer Rouge should be put on trial. If they aren't, people like me will be tempted to take revenge." Panh's own view is that Cambodians "should face up to our history so that our relatives and friends didn't die in vain. Mourning will not be possible unless moral and political responsibility for the Cambodian genocide is established. We owe a debt to the dead and we have an obligation to our children."[10] In January 2001, both chambers of the Cambodian parliament passed a law to set up a special court to try the senior leaders of the Khmer Rouge. To the world, especially to Cambodians unaware of the backroom maneuvers, the new law provided a glimmer of hope that the process of national reconciliation was beginning. As we will see later, this was yet another obstacle rather than a step toward an accounting of the past.

Another necessary condition for a fair trial has been fulfilled by a private organization. Founded in 1995, the privately funded Documentation Center of Cambodia has amassed half a million pages of documents from the Khmer Rouge period, including 5,922 pages that directly implicate a dozen former Khmer Rouge leaders who are living freely in Cambodia. A closer examination of the situation suggests, however, that a fair trial may still be beyond the reach of Cambodia. And a verdict reached by tainted judges, albeit with the international community in attendance, may achieve little to heal Cambodian wounds.

This pessimism about the prospects for a fair trial has to be understood against the backdrop of the troubled birth of a tribunal. From the outset, the government has been more concerned with its own survival than with national reconciliation. After all, in the beginning, the regime was still fighting the Khmer Rouge. If the "People's Court" tribunal to try the Khmer Rouge in 1979 was a mere political act, thirteen years later it was political considerations again that dictated the government's interest in setting up an international court. The government calculated that the threat to try the Khmer Rouge would help to isolate the group, which was still opposing the government. In a letter to UN secretary-general Kofi Annan, dated June 21, 1997, First Prime Minister Prince Norodom Ranariddh and Second Prime Minister Hun Sen called for help. They urged the United Nations to bring to justice those persons responsible for the genocide. Holding that "Cambodia does not have the resources or expertise to conduct this very important procedure," they cited the ad hoc tribunals in the former Yugoslavia and in Rwanda and requested that "similar assistance be given to Cambodia." In response, the United Nations set up a Group of Experts to evaluate how the organization could assist in establishing a tribunal.[11]

In July 1997, within weeks of their letter to the UN secretary-general, Hun Sen deposed co–prime minister Ranariddh in a violent exercise of power in Phnom Penh. Soon thereafter he negotiated the surrender of a section of the Khmer Rouge led by Ieng Sary. This inevitably altered the political landscape. By the time the UN Group of Experts recommended an international tribunal in 1998, Hun Sen had changed his mind, saying that there was no need for an international tribunal, which would impinge on Cambodian sovereignty. Besides, he argued, the Cambodian courts were "fully competent" to conduct trials of former Khmer Rouge officials. The Hun Sen government also stressed that any decision to bring Khmer Rouge leaders to justice must take into account Cambodia's need for peace and national reconciliation. He argued that a trial would prevent reconciliation as it might cause panic among former members of the Khmer Rouge and lead to a renewal of guerrilla warfare.

Even if one were to accept Hun Sen's concerns at face value, the record of his government raises suspicion about the real motives behind his objection. In the decade that the government has been in power, it has not been able to establish either the rule of law or an impartial judiciary. Worse, the frequent use of extrajudicial killing and intimidation has shorn the regime of the moral authority it needs to hold a fair trial. The government's volte-face in 1998 was thus greeted with suspicion. Having cut off assistance after the Hun Sen coup in 1997, in which opposition party activists were executed in cold blood, the U.S. Congress was more adamant than ever about the need for an international court. The American government was also keen to establish a precedent in bringing gross human rights abusers to trial in a special international court. Kofi Annan and the United Nations, too, were pressing the Hun Sen government to deliver on its earlier promise. A compromise was eventually reached with the United Nations in July 2000, creating a court with some foreign and a majority of Cambodian judges. In January 2001 a draft law to establish an Extraordinary Chambers to try the senior leaders of Democratic Kampuchea and the individuals "most responsible for the crimes" was published.

Doubts about Fair Trial

This compromise did address the concern about preserving Cambodia's sovereignty, but a legal ruling was devised to prevent partisanship. Under the law passed by the Cambodian parliament, a decision to block any prosecution would have to be agreed on by a "supermajority"—that is, a majority of Cambodian judges and at least one foreign judge. On August 10, 2001, Cambodia passed the Law on the Establishment of the Extraordinary Chambers in the Courts of Cambodia for the Prosecution of Crimes Committed during the Period of Democratic Kampuchea. It would be based within the Courts of Cambodia with international participation.

Although the passage of the law may have appeared to be the beginning of the long-overdue process of bringing those responsible to justice, it soon became evident that the law provided less than met the eye. The fact remains that the Cambodian judiciary is both untrained and thoroughly politicized and, by the government's own admission, corrupt as well. According to Justice Ministry records, more than half of Cambodia's 120 judges haven't finished high school. Only 15 have law degrees, mostly from former Soviet bloc countries.[12] The government recently ordered the re-arrest of criminals who were reportedly set free by corrupt judges. In fact, the culture that has developed in Cambodia, in which powerful men commit crimes with impunity, is an additional reason to set up a credible tribunal. Holding leaders accountable for crimes they committed, even in the name of the state, would be a first step toward building a civil society. Other concerns involve the competence of the small cadre of judges, few, if any, of whom have the expertise in international law required by the special court. The method of selecting the judges is also questionable as the selecting body is packed with people from the ruling party. Opposition leader Sam Rainsy's volte-face over the tribunal law that he himself voted for in the parliament is an indication of the trouble ahead. Three months after the passage of the bill he said, "The trial that is envisaged now can only be flawed because it is going to be held in Cambodia, where the leaders are themselves former Khmer Rouge and their conception of justice is shaped by a legacy of dictatorship and violence."[13]

Most important, the way in which the law was passed and some of the provisions of the law have raised serious doubts about the possibility of establishing an impartial, nonpolitical tribunal governed by acceptable international norms. Right from the moment Cambodia rushed to pass the draft law in parliament in January, the United Nations, whose blessing and funding were essential, raised its objection. Other concerns center on the ambiguity of the definitions of "serious crimes" for which leaders could be prosecuted. There is a strong possibility that Cambodian and international prosecutors would disagree on who should be brought up for trial. Observers have pointed out that the law does not clarify or make provision for a case when a supermajority is not reached or when the judges vote on conviction or acquittal. There is a possibility that the government would argue that a verdict of guilty can be reached only if a supermajority votes for it. In such a situation the Cambodian judges, who are in the majority, would have the de facto power to acquit any suspect they did not want to see convicted. In a letter written on January 9, 2001, the UN undersecretary-general for legal affairs, Hans Corell, demanded that the phrase originally agreed to by Cambodia "that no amnesty shall be a bar to prosecution" be reinstated.[14] That clause could ensure that Ieng Sary, who had been granted amnesty by the king, could be tried. However, there was doubt that Cambodia could adopt a phrase that ran against the constitutional prerogative of the king to grant amnesty.

There is also concern that the government will interfere with the working of the tribunal. The prime minister has repeatedly said that he opposes the trial of Ieng Sary, with whom he struck a deal in 1998. Government leaders who earlier claimed that the Khmer Rouge was a spent force now raise the specter of the Khmer Rouge's restarting the war if the leaders who are now living free are brought to trial. Many observers in Phnom Penh view this argument as a red herring. Both Cambodian and foreign visitors to the Khmer Rouge zones report that, although some Khmer Rouge cadres are worried about a tribunal, the rank and file wish to see their chiefs brought to justice. In any case, there is no desire among the vast majority of the former Khmer Rouge to return to the jungle to fight a guerrilla war.

Although it has been reported that Khmer Rouge leader Khieu Samphan has written to Hun Sen about his willingness to appear before the court if called, doubts persists that the process could produce anything more than a show trial. There is suspicion that the government will not only avoid bringing the top leaders to trial but also drag out the process and end up trying at most the two notorious leaders who are in custody —Ta Mok and Kang Kek Ieu, alias "Duch"—if they do not die first of natural causes. The reason for the doubt is a fundamental difference in what the Cambodian government wants to see and what nongovernmental organizations and the international community wish. The latter want justice through on open trial and conviction; the more important issue for the Hun Sen government is peace and stability. The concern, real or feigned, about the restarting of war, however, dovetails with the inclination of the ruling Cambodian People's Party (CPP) to avoid scrutiny of its own ranks. Its desire to be on the best terms with China for both ideological and political reasons is also believed to be an important factor. Since the 1997 coup giving the CPP a dominant role, China has emerged as a major supporter of the party, offering significant loans and grant aid. Private Chinese investment in Cambodia was reported to have tripled from 1997 to 1998 and increased by another 40 percent in 1999, making China Cambodia's second largest source of investment. China's wish to prevent international involvement in a trial was delivered bluntly by Foreign Minister Tang Jiaxuan of China to a delegation of Cambodian lawmakers during a visit to Beijing. According to Son Chhay, the chairman of the National Assembly's industry commission, "It was a clear message from [Tang] that this is a Cambodian problem and outsiders should not interfere."[15] Since the autumn of 2000, and starting with the president and party secretary-general, Jiang Zemin, Cambodia has seen a procession of senior Chinese officials visiting the country. Although the Chinese leaders have avoided public comment, they have, according to well-placed sources, privately argued against a tribunal.[16] There is a strong suspicion that the Cambodian government is trying to have its cake and eat it too. On the one hand, it is trying to placate Western countries by passing a law on the tribunal, and, on the other hand, it has diluted the process originally agreed on with the United Nations and is trying to delay its implementation to please China. Chinese aid and its foreign policy goal in Cambodia being so intertwined, Hun Sen's public pleading for Chinese aid and investment can only raise concern about the nature of the tribunal.[17] With the United States, Japan, and Australia pressing for it, the holding of an internationally accepted tribunal has emerged as a test for the foreign policy orientation of the Cambodian government, caught between China and the West. At this writing, in early January 2003, the prospect for a tribunal looks brighter than at any time in the recent past. In late December 2002 the UN General Assembly passed a resolution asking the United Nations to restart negotiations to establish such a court. The prospect had dimmed when, on February 8, 2002, the UN secretary-general withdrew from negotiations with the Cambodian government, saying that the law to set up extraordinary courts as passed by Cambodia "would not guarantee the international standards of justice required for the United Nations to continue to work towards [the courts'] establishment."

At the heart of the dispute over the tribunal is which document, the Cambodian law or the agreement between the government and the United Nations, would govern the conduct of the Extraordinary Chambers. In brief, the debate centers on the issue of ultimate authority. That question clearly was not at stake when, on June 21, 1997, co–prime ministers Hun Sen and Ranariddh requested the secretary-general's assistance in bringing to justice persons responsible for genocide and crimes against humanity. On March 15, 1999, an Expert Group appointed by the secretary-general proposed that an international court be established. We noted earlier the strong Chinese opposition to the notion immediately after the UN proposal. Two months later, Hun Sen, now the sole prime minister, modified the request. The focus was now to be on a national court with the participation of foreign judges and prosecutors. More important, ignoring the United Nations' insistence that the two sides agree on the terms of the extraordinary court before passing the law, Cambodia passed a draft law without first reaching a controlling agreement (i.e., an agreement on the way the law would be implemented) with the United Nations. Explaining the reasons for UN pullout, Hans Corell, the chief legal counsel for the United Nations, said:

> The United Nations cannot be bound by a national law. In addition, it has been our consistent position that the law would have to conform to the contents of the agreement. The question of Cambodia's sovereignty is not at issue here, since the matter required an agreement to be implemented under the principle of *pacte sunt servande.* Binding character of a contractual agreement obviously presupposes that an agreement has actually been concluded by the parties and that the agreement reached is not affected by any ground of invalidity.[18]

Reducing the agreement to the status of a technical, administrative document subordinate to the law would, Corell said, "deprive it of its substantive role of ensuring that international standards of justice, necessary for the continued participation of the United Nations." Cambodia clearly saw the agreement with the United Nations as a mere technicality, the main purpose of which was to secure funding for setting up the tribunal. The United Nations also found the law not up to international standards. A senior UN official said that to have been associated with the court as it was being proposed by Cambodia would have brought embarrassment to the United Nations. Further, the United Nations concluded from the pace at which the arrangements for the tribunal had moved that the government lacked any sense of urgency, especially when that delay extended the time before which aged Khmer Rouge leaders could be brought to justice. "We fear that this lack of urgency could continue and affect the work of the Extraordinary Chambers, which would be vulnerable to delay," Corell said.[19]

Stunned by the UN decision in February 2002 to pull out of the negotiations, the Cambodian government called for the resumption of negotiations. Even some Western countries, especially the United States, were unhappy at the UN move and, led by Japan, lobbied for the resumption of talks to set up a mixed tribunal. The UN secretary-general refused to budge, saying that his good offices had failed and that the United Nations would resume only after receiving a detailed mandate from the Security Council or the General Assembly. Given China's adamant opposition to the idea, a Security Council mandate was out of the question. In December, the General Assembly did pronounce itself in favor of a fresh effort, but it is unlikely to offer the direct political and financial support required for a tribunal with international standards.

Dealing with the Past

Holding a tribunal for the Khmer Rouge leadership would be judging the past—not just of Cambodia's fallen rulers but also of the current government and of the foreign powers with strong ties to the past. The question that naturally arises is: In this political climate, would a tribunal be able to establish the truth? Would it be able to question the role of foreign backers such as China in the Khmer Rouge's genocidal rule, or even of the Vietnamese communist leadership in the early years of the Khmer Rouge revolution? In fact, Khmer Rouge leaders have argued that, for a trial to be fair, it has to cover not just the period of their rule but also the periods before and after. "The true justice has to find out who was behind the killers," one Khmer Rouge participant argued, darkly pointing to machinations of external players such as Hanoi. "The Khmer Rouge problem is an international problem that has many interactions like 'small-shrimp soup'"—a Cambodian metaphor that suggests complex interaction among various players. By the end of 2002, when the prospect of a tribunal had brightened, Ta Mok, the notorious Khmer Rouge leader known as "the Butcher," even darkly threatened to expose unidentified Western countries for their backing of the genocidal government. In a statement issued from jail he said, "It was the Western countries that gave us the recognition and support to go ahead and we proceeded primarily because of the help of these developed Western countries. The truth will be revealed during the trial and the world will be shocked to know the truth behind the Khmer Rouge regime."[20]

This attempt by the Khmer Rouge to widen the circle of responsibility is obviously designed to stave off the possibility of convening a tribunal. None of the powers involved in the Cambodian conflict (including the United States, whose former secretary of state Henry Kissinger has been mentioned as being responsible for the secret bombing of Cambodia, which is believed to have provoked the Khmer Rouge brutality) would be interested in being dragged into a tribunal. In the highly charged early years of its rule, in 1979–80, the Phnom Penh government accused China of backing the Khmer Rouge in exterminating the Cambodians so that the country could be populated by Chinese. That theory was accepted by many Cambodians, who refused to believe that any Khmer could do what Pol Pot and his party did to the population. Since then, however, the wind has turned and it is now Vietnam that is frequently seen as the source of all trouble. The Khmer Rouge has started calling the Vietnamese "genocidal" and blames them for the mass graves. Pol Pot claimed that it was Vietnamese agents within the party who were responsible for the massacres. After Pol Pot was ousted from leadership, he in turn was accused by his comrades of being a Vietnamese agent. In Cambodian eyes Vietnam remains an aggressor and is frequently blamed by politicians for many of the country's problems.

Some believe that, given the complexity of Cambodia's recent history and the role played by different political groups and foreign powers in the making of the Cambodian tragedy, a South African–style Truth and Reconciliation Commission (TRC) would be more appropriate than a divisive tribunal. The TRC set up under the chairmanship of Archbishop Desmond Tutu called on victims of the South African apartheid regime to come forward to recount their experiences, and the perpetrators were given the opportunity to confess to their crimes and seek pardon. Those who refused to come forward could be prosecuted in the ordinary court of law. In the two-year-long proceedings the TRC heard the testimony of twenty-four hundred victims and dealt with seven thousand requests for amnesty.[21] In forums held to discuss the best means of bringing justice, some Cambodians have called for a shorter version of the South African TRC. Some have called for holding a national town-hall meeting. One suggestion has been a meeting in Phnom Penh's Olympic stadium, where, in the presence of the king and queen, the Khmer Rouge leaders would make a public confession and seek forgiveness; similar ceremonies would be held throughout the country. This, however, has been rejected as impractical and potentially fraught with security risks.

South Africa's TRC was also considered impracticable. Chea Vannath, the leader of a Cambodian nongovernmental organization, visited South

Africa to study the institution and returned convinced that it would not be applicable in Cambodia. "The parties that come before a truth and reconciliation process must reach a level of . . . trust that the process will achieve truth, then the process can move forward. Unfortunately, here in Cambodia, there is a lack of trust in society."[22] The fact is that Cambodia does not have a Bishop Tutu or a Nelson Mandela to lend credibility to such a commission. Vannath also said that, in spite of the great efforts of the TRC, it did not achieve complete reconciliation in society nor was justice done. That view, though, has been refuted by South African writers, who have argued that "reconciliation is not a single event. It is a process." They said that the TRC dealt with enormous human tension that could have exploded with disastrous consequences. As noted earlier, in Buddhist Cambodia there is no such reservoir of anger and revenge waiting to burst. But a more pertinent objection to a TRC in Cambodia is that it might establish the truth but would not punish the guilty. Finding the guilty and forcing them to bear the consequences of their actions is critically important in rendering justice to the victim. "A trial would also show to the world that Cambodia is a state ruled by law," said a Cambodian participant at a public forum held in Phnom Penh in January 2000. Another participant said, "If we provide amnesty to anyone who has killed millions of people, then all the criminals in jail must also be set free in order to have equal justice."[23] A proper tribunal would also have to address the important but emotional issue of the place of ethnic Vietnamese in Cambodia and the country's tempestuous relations with Vietnam —factors that played a major role in Khmer Rouge policies and remain critical for the long-term peace and stability of the country. But this is not the mandate of the tribunal that the National Assembly voted to set up in January 2001.

It would be the task of the special tribunal to ascertain the facts about what the Khmer Rouge did and why. However, I suspect that the tribunal, if it takes place, will not go beyond establishing the facts of killing and torture committed by the Khmer Rouge leaders. It is unlikely that the tribunal would delve into the reasons behind the Khmer Rouge's murderous policies or cause a national soul searching. Yet this is precisely what is required not only to heal the wounds of the victims and survivors but also to prevent the recurrence of similar policies.

Unlike the problems that exist between China and Japan or between Japan and South Korea, which date back to pre–World War II years, the wound within Cambodia is much deeper. It involves not just the actions of the Khmer Rouge rulers but also a more profound question of the country's identity. Cambodia's national reconciliation remains complicated by the history of the country's troubled relations with Vietnam and by the long-standing antipathy toward the ethnic Vietnamese minority. Clearly an accounting is needed of the mass killings in the country and there is a possibility that at least some of the Khmer Rouge leaders can be tried. But beyond punishing a few, Cambodians may not be ready to look deeper into the racist anti-Vietnamese ideas that informed the Khmer Rouge policies. There is limited interest in exploring the roots of Khmer Rouge ideology because those ideas go to the very heart of Cambodia's own struggle to define an identity and forge a modern nation out of an ancient but wounded civilization.

Shorn of ideological shibboleths, the Khmer Rouge policy was essentially a chauvinistic enterprise aimed at building a strong and prosperous Cambodia to undo historic wrongs. The racist notion about the superiority of the Khmers and paranoia about "enemies of all stripes" threatening to suffocate the revolutionary regime were the main driving concerns. The regime wanted to build a strong Cambodia at breakneck speed in order to stand up to those enemies, especially Vietnam, the hereditary enemy, which had annexed its territory and through its Communist Party continued to threaten Cambodia's existence. Rapid economic growth and military strength were to be achieved through socialism and by the proven Stalinist-Maoist tool of terror. As the attempt to build a socialist utopia ran aground, the Pol Pot leadership increasingly searched for enemies in its own ranks and for their suspected foreign backers—Vietnam, the CIA, and the KGB. For the Khmer Rouge leaders, the principal obstacle to achieving their ambition turned out to be the Vietnamese. The Khmer Rouge revolution soon became consumed in fighting imaginary Vietnamese and other enemies within its own ranks. It ended up challenging Hanoi's military machine along the border with disastrous consequences.

A brief history of Vietnam's interaction with Cambodia is necessary for an understanding of the conflict that has run as a red thread through the recent history of Indochina and still hangs like a dark cloud over it. Since its heyday in the tenth century, when the Angkor empire extended over most of Thailand, Laos, and Vietnam, the country has been reduced to its current size by a steady loss of territory to Vietnam and Thailand. The most resented is the loss of the lower Mekong Delta to Vietnam in the seventeenth and eighteenth centuries.

The establishment of a French protectorate in 1863 helped to save the country from further territorial loss but created a different problem with Vietnam. The arrival of Vietnamese administrators and workers in the French protectorate did not help create amity between the two communities. The Vietnamese Communist Party led by Ho Chi Minh attracted some Cambodian nationalists but the mainstream nationalism was nurtured on an anti-Vietnamese and an anticommunist platform by the young king, Norodom Sihanouk. Sihanouk sought to forge national sentiment based on history and the racial superiority of the Khmers. Historians note that from the 1950s, "anti-Vietnamese rhetoric became a classic theme among Cambodian politicians wishing to establish their nationalistic credentials." They harped on the idea of the "lost Kampuchea Krom" (lower Cambodia, meaning the lower Mekong Delta) and exalted the quality of the Khmer blood in order to win the support of the masses who were not attracted to the idea of a Khmer nation. But the memory of the harsh and direct rule of the Vietnamese in the nineteenth century left its imprint on the Cambodian mind. One folkloric story that all Cambodian children were brought up on was that of the Master's Tea: After the conquest of a Cambodian village, the Vietnamese commander ordered three Cambodians to be buried alive up to their necks. Their heads were then used as tripods to support a pot for boiling the water for his tea. As the victims began to writhe in agony from the heat of the fire, the commander mocked their plight, saying, "Don't spill the master's tea."

The Khmer Rouge repeatedly told the population this story in order to arouse their hatred and, in 1978, in the *Livre Noir* (Black Book), published by Pol Pot's foreign ministry,[24] stated the position baldly: "Whether in the feudalist era, in the French colonialists' period, in the U.S. imperialists' period or in the Ho Chi Minh period, the Vietnamese have not changed their true nature, that is, the nature of the aggressor, annexionist, and swallower of other countries' territories." The book claimed that the Cambodian people foster "a deep national hatred" for the Vietnamese and have since the epoch of Angkor called them *yuon,* or "savage."

Reconciling History with Geography

While it is true that Cambodian people do commonly refer to the Vietnamese using the pejorative slang *yuon,* claims of "deep national hatred" among Cambodians—who have for centuries lived alongside the Vietnamese—are exaggerated. The fact is that the Khmer Rouge leaders, facing opposition to their radical policies, made Vietnam and the resident Vietnamese the scapegoat for their difficulties. According to Prince Sihanouk, there were more than four hundred thousand Vietnamese in Cambodia in 1969. After the 1970 coup, Lon Nol and his supporters eliminated or banished to South Vietnam "at least half of these Yuons." The remainder, Khieu Samphan told him, were finished off by the Khmer Rouge. In a broadcast from Phnom Penh radio on May 10, 1978, a clarion call was issued to exterminate the Vietnamese race. The Khmer Rouge provided a simple and brutal mathematical formula. "In terms of numbers, one of us must kill thirty Vietnamese." Sacrificing two million Khmers would eliminate the entire Vietnamese population, and "we would still have six million [Khmers] left."[25]

The purges and killings that ravaged the country were motivated by the desire to catch all the Vietnamese and Cambodian "traitors" hidden in the party's ranks and among the general population.[26] "The Vietnamese" became shorthand for any real or imagined enemy of the regime. David Chandler has concluded from his study of Khmer Rouge documents that the victims of the Tuol Sleng interrogation center were considered subhuman and therefore not of the same "race" as their captors. He says that prisoners, as enemies of the state, "became for all intents and purposes Vietnamese." Although most of the victims were, in fact, of the same race as their killers, Chandler says, "racist mechanisms came into play in their arrest, torture, and execution. Turning the victims into 'others,' in a racist fashion—and using words associated with animals to describe them—made them easier to mistreat and easier to kill."[27] The Khmer Rouge also called their Cambodian opponents people with a

"Khmer body [and a] Vietnamese brain"—an epithet that political opponents freely use today to describe CPP members.

In his last interview in 1997, Pol Pot was unapologetic. He said he was proud that his policies had prevented Cambodia from becoming another Kampuchea Krom. If nearly two million Cambodians died to achieve this goal, Pol Pot implied, it was worth it. His conscience, he said, was clear. It would be a mistake to generalize about public perception in Cambodia, but it is nevertheless disturbing to hear many Cambodians crediting Pol Pot with saving Cambodia from the Vietnamese. To the Khmer Rouge's delight, the twelve years of conflict that followed the Vietnamese intervention allowed the resistance forces to base their political campaign on a racist anti-Vietnamese theme and present the Hun Sen government as agents of Vietnam. It was not just a political ploy. It had fatal consequences for the Vietnamese community living in Cambodia. According to the final report of the human rights component of the United Nations Transitional Authority in Cambodia (UNTAC), between July 1992 and August 1993, 116 ethnic Vietnamese were killed and another 87 injured in Khmer Rouge attacks. Some thirty thousand ethnic Vietnamese from the fishing community fled to the Vietnamese border.[28]

Many more Vietnamese lives have been lost since the departure of UNTAC, and many Vietnamese have been uprooted from their homes. Whatever the official figures (estimates of the ethnic Vietnamese community range from two hundred thousand to five hundred thousand), twelve years after the withdrawal of the Vietnamese forces, people believe that tens of thousands of Vietnamese settlers have moved into Cambodia to grow rice or work as fisherfolk, construction workers, mechanics, plumbers, and prostitutes. In Cambodia today, for nearly everything bad—from incidents of crime and house fires to prostitution and the spread of HIV/AIDS—Vietnamese residents or Hanoi can be blamed. The stereotyping of a hardworking minority that is seen as aggressive is not uncommon in other multiethnic societies. With tension ever present just below the surface, the Vietnamese minority's alleged misdeeds and Vietnam's suspected aggressive intentions remain hot-button issues for politicians to exploit. Politicians of all stripes—from Sam Rainsy to Ranariddh—have used the popular anti-Vietnamese sentiment, especially at election time, to attack the CPP for its Vietnam connection. Not to be seen as protecting the traditional "swallower of Khmer land," as the Vietnamese are called, the government is reluctant to come to the aid of the Vietnamese community. In a suspicious fire in November 2001 some ten thousand huts in an overwhelmingly Vietnamese-occupied slum were razed to the ground. Miscreants cut loose the moorings of boats housing Vietnamese fisherfolk. Brothels in Phnom Penh, where many prostitutes are Vietnamese, are also targets for arson. There is never any redress. No one has ever been punished for killing a Vietnamese in Cambodia. What makes the race issue potentially more dangerous in Cambodia is that it is linked to a live dispute with Vietnam over land and sea borders and over the use of natural resources. The opposition's charges that Vietnam has annexed territory from Cambodia in the years since its overthrow of Pol Pot find resonance among the people and make it difficult for the government to conclude an agreement that would be acceptable to the public at large.

How, then, does one resolve this ever present tension? A tribunal for the Khmer Rouge in which their murderous, racist policies are brought out into the open would perhaps begin a process of understanding. But the reduction, if not the outright removal, of the deep-seated suspicions rooted in centuries of history is a harder task and would require sustained effort by people on all sides. Such a step would also necessitate a long-term vision and statesmanship in both Cambodia and Vietnam. Some nongovernmental organizations in Cambodia have already begun a laudable educational effort to explain the plight of the minority population, but it is a very small beginning. At the government level, a place to start would be to ban the incitement to racial violence in public rhetoric and to punish the culprits. Ultimately, however, economic development in both countries would provide a longer-lasting solution to the race issue. At the root of the issue is the basic struggle for survival by a fast-growing population with finite resources of land, forest, and water.

Thus reconciliation in Cambodia would, in the end, have to be based on economic growth combined with social and political justice. Developing Cambodian institutions, educating Cambodian people about the history of the country in the context of the region, and encouraging greater economic and cultural interaction with neighbors will go a long way toward creating the necessary conditions for reconciliation. Cambodia's joining the Association of Southeast Asian Nations is a first step in the process of regional integration. The Cambodian and Vietnamese peoples' memory may still be too raw to permit greater interaction, but as members of ASEAN they could begin by cooperating within the group. The more developed ASEAN countries can also contribute to reconciliation in Cambodia by offering educational and technical help. There is, of course, historical baggage for ASEAN as well, because some of the members were very directly involved in supporting the Khmer Rouge and the noncommunist insurgency against Phnom Penh during the decade-long civil war. ASEAN countries, too, would have to understand the need to heal the wounds of the country. Peace and stability in Cambodia will depend on creating harmony based on the awareness that for all the history that divides the two people, geography has made their fate indivisible.

Before that more difficult reconciliation can be attempted, however, the Cambodian people will have to come to terms with their own past by looking it squarely in the eye and establishing accountability. The work done by the Documentation Center for Cambodia in assembling the documentation to establish the criminal responsibility of the Khmer Rouge leaders who are still alive has laid a valuable base for launching a tribunal. The most critical question, however, remains to be answered: Will Cambodian leaders cease to be self-promoting politicians and emerge as statesmen ready to deal with the demons of the past in order to build a strong future? Summing up the feelings of many of his compatriots, the director of the center, Youk Chhang, told an audience in September 2002: "We refuse to accept a world where people who do these kinds of things remain unpunished. God may forgive the killers, but here on earth, until there is justice, until the truth is told about these crimes, our people cannot reconcile with one another. We want to live in the present, not in the past, but the past is still with us. We need to have closure."[29]

East Timor

A Nation Divided

Todung Mulya Lubis

By international law, East Timor was never considered part of the jurisdiction of Indonesia. Article 1 of United Nations Resolution 3485 (XXX) clearly declared that the annexation of East Timor by Indonesia in 1975 was a breach of international law:

> The General Assembly . . . calls upon all States to respect the inalienable right of the people of Portuguese Timor to self-determination, freedom and independence and to determine their future political status in accordance with the principle of the Charter of the United Nations and the Declaration on the Granting of Independence to Colonial Countries and Peoples.

International law guaranteed the "inalienable right" of the East Timorese people under Portuguese colonization to determine their own future, and thus East Timor could not be arbitrarily annexed.[1] Likewise, many legal experts in Indonesia were of the opinion that the East Timor annexation violated international law. Unfortunately, those legal experts remained silent on the issue. Only a handful of constitutional law experts were of the opinion that the East Timor annexation was a valid process of territorial integration based on the People's Consultative Assembly Decree no. VI/MPR/1976.[2]

The annexation of East Timor was a case of Indonesian aggression and expansionism supported by Western allies, who were consolidating their strength during the Cold War. The pretext for the invasion was a communist threat from left-leaning elements coming to power in East

Timor. The invasion commenced one day after a state visit to Jakarta by U.S. president Gerald Ford and Secretary of State Henry Kissinger in December 1975. Jose Ramos Horta, who won the Nobel Peace Prize in 1996 for his longtime advocacy of the rights of the East Timorese, said that the annexation of East Timor by Indonesia had the obvious blessing of the United States.[3] Many people, from both East Timor and elsewhere, concur,[4] though we must leave it to history to come to a final judgment.

The years from 1975 to 1999 witnessed a series of gross and systematic violations of human rights in East Timor. We do not know exactly how many people were victims of such abuses, but it has been estimated that a third of the population was killed, was wounded, or went missing.[5]

For reasons that remain uncertain, Indonesian president Bacharuddin Jusuf Habibie decided to grant East Timor a referendum on independence, which was eventually held on August 30, 1999. When an overwhelming majority voted in favor of independence, local pro-Indonesian militia, backed by the Indonesian military, went on a rampage, committing extensive human rights abuses. Following the arrival of international peacekeeping troops in September 1999, the United Nations Transitional Administration in East Timor (UNTAET) took charge in October. Overseen by UNTAET, East Timor finally realized independence on May 20, 2002.

This chapter first outlines the human rights abuses that occurred during the Indonesian occupation of East Timor, especially during the bloody concluding phase of occupation, and then examines what steps have, and have not, been taken toward reconciliation since Indonesian forces left East Timor. Reconciliation—both between Indonesia and East Timor and among the East Timorese themselves—is the bedrock on which a stable, independent East Timor must be built. Unfortunately, the conduct of the trials in Jakarta of high-level figures accused of involvement in the massacres has done little so far to further reconciliation and much to harm confidence in the United Nations and to hamper its ability to function effectively in the Indonesian archipelago.

A Pebble in the Shoe

East Timor turned into an extremely expensive economic and political burden for Indonesia. In international forums, Indonesia was frequently showered with criticism and scorn, and with regard to business relationships, East Timor was often used as a pretext to put pressure on Indonesia. Even after huge investments had been poured into East Timor (making other provinces in the eastern part of Indonesia envious of the resources and attention the province received), the de facto existence of East Timor as part of the Indonesian territory failed to convince the international community that the East Timor matter was final. Meanwhile, the people in West Timor could not help wondering why their province, which had been part of Indonesia since 1945, did not receive equal attention from the central government in terms of development spending,[6] and conditions in the provinces of Maluku and Irian Jaya were no better than those in West Timor.[7]

The authoritarian government of Indonesia under President Suharto ignored international criticism and instead pursued the systematic and unrelenting persecution of the East Timorese people. Human beings and livestock were slaughtered as part of an attempt to eliminate an entire ethnic group and its culture. Simultaneously, the bureaucracy and business in East Timor were dominated by outsiders, as were the posts of regional military chief and regional police chief and other key security offices. Meanwhile, the offices of governor, regents, and mayors were held by comprador local East Timorese. There was a mass influx of "transmigrated" people from Java, who brought their culture with them. Slowly but surely, the deliberate process of "Indonesianization" was enforced, representing a destructive form of cultural colonialism, described by Peter Carey as "the slow death of a society and culture."[8]

Even though widespread East Timorese armed resistance was suppressed, violent opposition to Indonesian military rule continued to erupt sporadically. East Timor was kept under emergency rule with the military always dominant. Eventually, the East Timorese struggle was taken up by the younger generation—a generation that had not yet been born when the invasion occurred—who opened up a Pandora's box that had been kept tightly sealed by the ruthless brutality of Indonesian commanders and their forces. The Santa Cruz incident of November 12, 1991, in which approximately two hundred unarmed youths were massacred in cold blood by Indonesian soldiers after a funeral rally, marked a major turning point in the history of East Timor's struggle for independence.[9] Because a videotape of the massacre had been smuggled out of Timor, the usual denials of atrocities could not be made by Indonesian diplomats such as Foreign Minister Ali Alatas, and international attention on East Timor increased dramatically. A world conference on human rights sponsored by the UN Commission on Human Rights and scheduled to be held in Jakarta was canceled as a result of the incident.[10]

The Indonesian government was forced to set up the State Investigation Commission (KPN) to investigate the human rights abuses committed by the military and bureaucracy at Santa Cruz. The KPN was sufficiently independent that its estimates of the number of people who died, although far below those of international observers who had witnessed the slaughter, were still significantly higher than the figures claimed by the Indonesian military. The KPN concluded that at least fifty people were killed and more than ninety injured; the military reported only nineteen deaths.[11] In addition, there were persistent and credible reports that the bodies of missing persons had been loaded onto boats and dumped far out to sea.

The precedent of the commission on the Santa Cruz incident led to pressure on the Indonesian government to establish the National Commission on Human Rights (Komnas HAM). The commission managed to produce several impressive and transparent findings along with firm recommendations.[12] Its reports pertaining to the human rights violations in East Timor, the Marsinah labor case, and the violent attack on the Indonesian Democratic Party (PDI) headquarters earned considerable respect. The government's intention to make the commission part of a slick public relations drive did not prove entirely successful.

The Santa Cruz massacre became a symbol of martyrdom that triggered more struggles by the East Timorese, leading to the loss of hundreds or even thousands more lives. With the international community continuing to focus considerable attention on East Timor, and with the Suharto regime unwilling to admit the blunder it had committed in annexing the territory, East Timor became an increasingly painful pebble in the government's shoe, hampering most Indonesian maneuvers in the international sphere.

When a financial crisis hit Indonesia at the end of 1997, the economy that many thought was solid and strong crumbled abruptly. The exchange rate plummeted from 2,500 rupiahs per U.S. dollar in June 1997 to a low of 17,000 rupiahs per dollar in January 1998. The Suharto regime could not endure a shock of this magnitude and the aging president was forced to resign in May 1998. Vice President B. J. Habibie replaced Suharto. One month after taking office, President Habibie announced a major shift in the policy on East Timor: "I'm going to give it [East Timor] an autonomy. What kind of autonomy, a special autonomy, I can't tell now, but an autonomy. Maybe like Aceh, like Yogya."[13]

It is unclear whether it was economic or political pressure from abroad that caused Habibie to propose autonomy for East Timor. But what is certain is that the Habibie administration demonstrated a markedly more sympathetic approach to the East Timorese struggle. This evolved into a pledge by Habibie to offer two options for East Timor: independence or integration. The announcement of these two options was made abruptly by Habibie on January 27, 1999, and it was rumored that the president had made the decision without consulting his aides.[14] The new policy caught everyone in Indonesia off guard, including government officials, who were unprepared to handle such a dramatic change. Meanwhile, the news was warmly welcomed by the East Timorese and the international community. Rebel leader Xanana Gusmao, who was then in prison in the Salemba jail in central Jakarta, described the situation.

> The East Timorese are joyous. After twenty-three years, Indonesia has just realized [its mistake] under international law. . . . We understand that it takes some time to recognize a blunder and requires efforts from all parties [to mend it]. However, we appreciate the decision Habibie made, we accept it happily as we have lost so much, and we believe that the truth will prevail.[15]

Following the announcement of the two options, the New York Agreement was signed on May 5, 1999, by the United Nations and the governments of Indonesia and Portugal. The agreement constituted an umbrella framework leading to a referendum that would take place in East Timor.[16] The signing of the New York Agreement was a new beginning for East Timor because it set a specific date for Timorese self-determination. Voting in the referendum would be by secret ballot conducted under international auspices. For Indonesia, the New York Agreement represented the first step toward removing the pebble from its shoe.

Bloody Referendum

The referendum was held on September 5, 1999. As expected, a huge majority voted in favor of independence from Indonesia rather than for special autonomy within Indonesia. Instead of respecting this decision, pro-Indonesian militias launched a bloody campaign designed to prevent East Timor from actually gaining independence. (These militias had been created by the Indonesian military to shore up Indonesian control of East Timor. In the buildup to the referendum, they had been reorganized for the specific purpose of undermining the pro-independence campaign.) Numerous human rights violations were committed, including murder, torture, rape, forced deportation, and arson.[17] These brutal acts took a heavy human toll. The international community criticized them as a "gross and systematic violation of human rights." Worse, the Indonesian military —whose job it was to guarantee security before, during, and after the referendum—failed to stop the abuses. In a formal statement, the National Commission on Human Rights said: "[A]t the time the lives of the East Timor people had reached a state of anarchy and acts of terrorism by both individuals and groups were widespread, witnessed openly, and allowed to occur by the security apparatus."[18]

The gross violations of human rights prompted the UN Commission on Human Rights to convene a special session in Geneva, beginning on September 23, 1999. The gathering concluded that there had been "collusion" among the military, the police, and the Timorese militias, which unleashed most of the violence. The commission adopted a resolution condemning the abuses and holding accountable the Indonesian military and police along with the militias. Moreover, the resolution demanded that an independent fact-finding commission, made up of respected human rights activists, be established immediately.

Under heavy pressure, the Indonesian government gave ground. On September 22, 1999, the Indonesian National Commission on Human Rights set up the Investigative Commission for Human Rights Violations in East Timor (KPP HAM Timtim).[19] KPP HAM was staffed by members of the National Commission and by others.[20]

The investigation conducted by KPP HAM concluded that "gross crimes against humanity" had been committed. These acts fell within the universal jurisdiction on mass genocide, slavery, rape, arson, and forced deportation,[21] the ruthless and systematic violations including breaches of due care for lives, the right of human integrity, the right to freedom, the right to travel, and property rights.

After the crackdown, human rights abuses continued, albeit sporadically, in East Timor. Several outrageous murders were perpetrated in the churches of Liquisa and Kallaco, in the Dili bishopric office, and in the residences of Bishop Bello, Bishop Meliana, Bishop Suai, and Manuel Carascalao, one of the leaders of the independence movement. Although KPP HAM gathered information from witnesses and family members, it was hard to ascertain how many people had been killed and how many were missing because so many East Timorese had been forcibly deported from the cities and the countryside.

It is hard to believe that the militias could have committed such large-scale human rights violations simultaneously throughout East Timor without the help and support of soldiers and policemen. Furthermore, there is strong evidence to suggest that the militias were in fact created, overseen, and funded (through the bureaucracy) by the Indonesian armed forces. Confessions from several former district heads in East Timor investigated by KPP HAM show that government officers had special budget allocations with which to assist the militias.[22]

Atrocities were committed "by commission" and "by omission." Although commanders and officers did not themselves carry out atrocities, they were well aware of what was taking place and did nothing to prevent it. In its final report, KPP HAM named several generals who had been involved and recommended that they be investigated and tried.[23] The "command responsibility" doctrine as cited in various international human rights documents must, argued KPP HAM, be duly applied in Indonesia.

The legal prosecution of these human rights violators, however, has not moved forward satisfactorily. The investigation process has been exhaustive, but significant question marks hang over the legal process now under way in Indonesia (as described below). There is a real danger that the question of responsibility for the atrocities will be left unresolved—thereby validating the ongoing campaign by nongovernmental organizations (NGOs) in East Timor to establish an international tribunal along the lines of the tribunals set up for Yugoslavia and Rwanda. Although trials for atrocities are in the first instance an internal affair of the Indonesian government, the conduct of such trials will significantly influence the prospects for long-term reconciliation in East Timor and between East Timor and Indonesia.[24]

A Shattered Nation?

East Timor is small—not more than 18,900 square kilometers—and is not rich in natural resources, which may explain why for centuries it had escaped the attention of its neighbors, including Indonesia. Portuguese ships arrived in East Timor around 1512, one year after they moored at Mallaca's pier (in present-day Malaysia). During the three hundred years East Timor was a Portuguese colony, its economy barely developed. Indeed, under Portuguese rule, it was a place held back in time. James Dunn, the Australian consul in Dili before East Timor was annexed by the Indonesians, found good reason to quote Lord Wallace, an Englishman who had visited the territory in 1861:

> The Portuguese government in Timor is a most miserable one. Nobody seems to care the least about the improvement of the country. . . . [A]fter three hundred years of occupation there has not been a mile of road made beyond the town, and there is not a solitary European resident anywhere in the interior. All the government officials oppress and rob the natives as much as they can, and yet there is no care tâken to render the town defensible should the Timorese attempt to attack it.[25]

By 1974, when the Portuguese were preparing to leave Timor, virtually nothing of what Wallace described had changed. The coup that deposed Salazar in Lisbon heightened tensions in East Timor as the Portuguese government lacked the resources to continue funding their colonies. The political situation in East Timor began to break down with the rise of contending political parties. The first was the Uniao Democratia Timorense (the Timorese Democratic Union, or the UDT), a relatively conservative party that sought "progressive autonomy" rather than swift autonomy. The Frente Revolutionaria de Timor-Leste Independente (the Revolutionary Front for an Independent East Timor, or Fretilin) was a more radical party, standing for the right to independence and rejecting any form of colonization.[26] Both parties had considerable strength, though Fretilin had a slightly stronger base of support. A third party, Associacao Popular Democratica Timorense (the Timorese Popular Democratic Association, or Apodeti), then entered the scene, saying that it supported integration with Indonesia. Apodeti, backed by Indonesia, added to the existing political tension, though not significantly.

With the invasion and annexation of East Timor by Indonesia, open and widespread violent conflict broke out between the pro-independence and the pro-integration groups. The UDT partly supported Fretilin and partly endorsed Apodeti.

For approximately twenty-four years, the Indonesian military and the militias repressed this political clash. Though the pro-integration group was vastly outnumbered by those demanding independence, it nevertheless grew in support as a result of East Timor's economic dependence on Indonesia and the educational system, imposed by Indonesia. By the late 1990s, nearly all East Timorese were conversant in Bahasa Indonesia, as almost all textbooks, official correspondence, and trade documents were written in that language. A new culture was being established and an old one destroyed.

Yet, when the referendum on independence was held, a clear majority opted to cut East Timor's ties with Indonesia. The military, the police, and the militias—perhaps deluded by the myths and falsehoods of their own occupation—could not accept such a bitter reality and responded instead by conducting a well-planned campaign of forced displacement and deportation.[27] This was part of an effort to delegitimize the outcome of the referendum by insisting to the international community that a large number of East Timorese would not accept independence. And judging by the number of refugees forcibly evicted to Atambua in West Timor—approximately 250,000 East Timorese—there was ostensibly reason to question the legitimacy of the referendum. But of course the refugees driven to West Timor had not all rejected independence. As KPP HAM concluded in January 2000:

> Terror and intimidation before the popular consultation [referendum] resulted in the displacement of the population to various places of refuge such as churches and the mountains. After the results of the popular consultation were announced, a large-scale forced displacement and deportation of the population occurred with logistic and transportation support from the civil military and police authorities in compliance with established plans. The

> forced displacement was the ultimate target of the various acts of violence and the scorched-earth campaign that occurred in many locations. Terror and intimidation were the means to ensure the forced displacement and deportation of the refugees and continues to be used to obstruct the return of the refugees to their homes. [Even] now, there are still refugees who are unable to return to their places of origin.[28]

Criticisms and reprimands continued to be aimed at the military and the militias, for Atambua, the refugee site in West Timor, was in fact a gigantic prison, run by the military and the militias, who were determined to prevent the East Timorese refugees from returning to their homeland in the immediate aftermath of the violence. The killing of three volunteers from the Office of the UN High Commissioner for Refugees (UNHCR) exemplified the militia's brutality in terrorizing and intimidating the refugees.[29]

Reconciliation?

The reconciliation process in the wake of the East Timor massacres and the displacement of refugees has a dual character. On the one side is the East Timorese desire to reintegrate the new country's opposing factions and to ensure the safe return of refugees from West Timor. On the other side is the issue of reconciliation between East Timor and Indonesia. Clearly, these issues are intimately connected. The extent to which both internal East Timorese scars and the divide between Indonesia and East Timor can be healed will depend on whether justice is seen to be done in the continuing trials of former military and police commanders in Jakarta. If it is not, international attention may turn again to international tribunals.

Despite problems, the repatriation of refugees from West Timor has progressed well, according to UNHCR, which is working with the Indonesian authorities. Originally, about 250,000 refugees entered West Timor. There were approximately 50,000 remaining as of June 2002, and the United Nations expected that of these, only a "hard core" of about 15,000 would still be there by the deadline for their return, set as December 31, 2002. This number would include many members of the militias who committed serious human rights abuses and others who held official posts under the Indonesian occupiers, who fear reprisals if they return.

A UN official said of the scenes in the Dili refugee transit center, "The reconciliations are amazing. They sit in little huddles and cry and hug each other." The policy of forgiveness advocated by the new East Timorese president, Xanana Gusmao, is judged by the United Nations to have been key to this process.[30] The Commission for Reception, Truth and Reconciliation in East Timor is also playing an important role in providing a truth-telling forum in which victims and perpetrators can describe past human rights abuses. Its aim is to facilitate community reconciliation in cases of relatively minor offenses for the entire period between 1974 and 1999. It is also mandated to report on its findings and to make recommendations to the government.[31]

Nevertheless, both during the period of the United Nations Transitional Administration in East Timor (UNTAET), from October 1999 through May 2002, and since the country's attainment of full independence, the legal aspect of reconciliation has been complicated by several factors. Foremost are the current UN attitude, the changed international situation after September 11, 2001, and a division within East Timor itself on the issue of independent tribunals.

The United Nations was in the vanguard of calls for an international tribunal after the postreferendum violence. Secretary-General Kofi Annan promised that "[t]hose responsible for the atrocities in East Timor will be made accountable and will be brought to justice."[32] The International Commission of Inquiry on East Timor to the Secretary-General, which conducted investigations in the closing months of 1999, came out strongly in its report of January 2000 in favor of a tribunal based on Balkan and Rwandan precedents.[33]

NGOs based in East Timor pressed consistently for such tribunals. Under UN administration, however, there were only a limited number of prosecutions in East Timor. As early as May 2001, the East Timor NGO Forum (an umbrella organization representing sixty-eight national NGOs and six international aid groups) registered its discontent with the progress of UNTAET's serious crimes unit and called for either an improvement in the situation or the creation of an international war crimes tribunal.[34] Claiming to speak on behalf of the victims' families, the forum issued a press release summarizing its views:

> "If an international court is not a priority for resolving war crimes cases in East Timor, what other court is able to ensure that the war criminals concerned do not just walk free?" asked Arsenio Bano, Executive Director of the NGO Forum, adding that future improvements in East Timor–Indonesia relations depend inter alia on how Indonesia completes its investigations into the war crimes it perpetrated in East Timor, together with its willingness to assist in the return from Indonesia of East Timorese refugees.[35]

However, the UN Security Council now seems to have no interest in an international tribunal. Attention has shifted toward Afghanistan, the Middle East, Kashmir, and Iraq and forced the East Timor issue off the international agenda. In particular, the extent of U.S. pressure on Indonesia has lessened. Although the first wave of sentences in the Jakarta trials, handed down in August 2002, elicited U.S. criticism of the prosecution after a long period of silence, the priorities of the "war on terror" have persuaded the Bush administration to lobby to reforge military relations with Indonesia, and at present this seems to override all other concerns.

China and Russia do not favor a tribunal for their own "domestic" reasons: Russia does not want to create a precedent for international scrutiny of its own actions in Chechnya; China has a similar concern in regard to Tibet. Anxieties over Indonesian disintegration and the manner in which it is handled by the international community have therefore coalesced with the post–September 11 U.S. policy to make international tribunals for East Timor a very delicate subject. The net effect is that even if the Indonesian procedures prove obviously inadequate, the international community cannot be expected to step into the breach.

The United Nations is also said to be wary of interfering with the ongoing process of normalization between East Timor and its previous master. As the Australian ambassador to the United Nations, John Dauth, puts it,

> Until [the Indonesians] have exhausted their processes and it's clear they haven't produced results, our inclination is to leave it with [them] and to urge them to do the right thing. So, while we're not going the international tribunal route at the moment, we're not ruling it out for the future.[36]

Even Kofi Annan seems not to have been openly critical of the Jakarta trials and has gone so far as to offer technical assistance to the ad hoc court holding the trials.[37] Some international pressure has nevertheless been brought to bear on Jakarta to punish those responsible and may indeed have been the crucial factor influencing the Indonesian government's decision to prosecute its own trials in Jakarta.[38]

There is skepticism among human rights groups, however, that the Jakarta trials will bring anything recognizable as justice. Major-General Adam Damiri (the former commander of East Timor and the surrounding islands), Brigadier General Tono Suratman (the former commander of troops in East Timor), and sixteen other military and government officials are on trial at the ad hoc court in Jakarta. Nevertheless, in the trials of at least seven senior figures to date, prosecutors have asked for only up to six months above the minimum sentence, the maximum sentence being death. By the summer of 2002, only seven sentences had been handed down. The police chief at the time of the massacres, Brigadier Timbul Silaen, one other police officer, and four midranking army officers have all been acquitted. The former governor of East Timor, Abilio Soares, received a three-year sentence, seven and a half years less than the prosecutors demanded; critics have complained that it is too lenient. In particular, the decision not to prosecute General Wiranto, Indonesia's military commander when violence erupted on East Timor, has brought derision from human rights groups.[39] Indeed, many of those accused of complicity in the atrocities have since enjoyed flourishing careers.[40] Commenting on the situation, Filomena dos Reis of the East Timor NGO Forum said: "The East Timorese are united in their desire for an international tribunal. Over two decades of first-hand experience with Indonesian justice tells us the current ad hoc court will not be meaningful."[41] And, in April 2002, the forum issued a press release reiterating its position: "The NGO Forum regards an international tribunal as an option that needs to be seriously considered given that to date Indonesia has not made any progress in investigating human rights offences committed by the Indonesian military in East Timor."[42]

Reacting to the statement made by the chairperson of the UN Commission on Human Rights in April 2002, giving broad UN support for the Indonesian trials,[43] a spokesman for the East Timor Action Network (ETAN) was outspoken in his criticism: "The statement ignores flaws identified by the UN High Commissioner for Human Rights in Indonesia's ad hoc human rights courts on East Timor. Any reference to the ridiculously limited mandate of the court—two months out of a twenty-four-year military occupation and only three of East Timor's thirteen districts —has been removed."[44]

The report on the Indonesian trials by the Indonesia Project of the International Crisis Group (ICG) elaborates on this assessment:

> The problem is not so much with the way the cases are being judicially conducted. Inexperienced as they are, the judges have thus far exceeded expectations, rejecting military arguments and demonstrating a willingness to use international human rights law in a way that defies a common perception of them as incompetents or political hacks. Rather the problem, as revealed in court documents obtained by ICG, is with the limited mandate of the ad hoc court and the very weak way in which the indictments have been drawn up and presented by the prosecution.[45]

Within East Timor itself, however, opinion on the right road to reconciliation is divided. The new president, Xanana Gusmao, elected with a landslide vote, has convincingly made the transition from veteran guerrilla to conciliator, internal and external—even going so far as to embrace one of his former enemies, General Prabowo Subianto of Indonesia. He favors an amnesty for the accused. Indeed, he wrote to the Jakarta court to ask it not to single out Abilio Soares, the Timorese ex-governor, for punishment when the real Indonesian orchestrators of the violence go free. Gusmao's attitude is diametrically opposed to the position of his former party, Fretilin.

■ ■ ■

Problematic as it is, reconciliation is the key to the solution of East Timor's problems. This new and tiny country cannot afford to be fragmented. All the parties involved must show the highest statesmanship if there is to be any hope for a brighter future. But before they can chart the future, a truthful account of the country's history must be established. In addition, legal action against the parties who were directly involved in the human rights abuses before and after the referendum must satisfy this imperative for historical truth. Otherwise, with no prospect of genuine healing, the wounds of the East Timorese will continue to bleed.

The chances that the Indonesian courts will satisfy these criteria obviously appear slim. The Indonesian proceedings might have been a chance to correct the misconceptions of the Indonesian public, but given the lack of interest shown by the Indonesian media and the apathy displayed by the Indonesian public, the trials may in fact harden those misconceptions:

> [F]ar more important than the verdicts is what the trials have to say about the nature of the conflict in East Timor, the role of the military, the role of unofficial armed forces, and the nature of crimes against humanity. Both prosecution and defense portray the events of 1999 as resulting from a civil conflict involving two violent East Timorese factions in which Indonesian security forces were concerned and sometimes helpless bystanders. The evidence that this was not the case is overwhelming, from reports by East Timorese human rights organizations and press accounts at the time to the Australian military intercepts leaked to the *Sydney Morning Herald.* To portray the violence as two-sided, however, dramatically weakens the case for a charge of crimes against humanity, in a situation where the ability to prove the charge was already undermined by the restricted mandate of the court. It also changes the nature of military involvement in the violence from active to passive, [as] failing to prevent violence rather than actively orchestrating it.[46]

Both prosecution and defense in the Indonesian case apparently believe, as do many Indonesians, that the United Nations falsified the result of the East Timor referendum. (The trials could, of course, have set the record straight by explaining the military's hand in events, but this does not now seem probable.) This belief seems to undermine further the reputation, already poor, of the United Nations in Indonesia. Indeed, the government forbids the United Nations Development Program to display the UN flag in Aceh, for fear that the rebels will believe that the United Nations may be taking up a political role there.[47] The low status of the United Nations in Indonesia could have dire consequences for its ability to function effectively in the context of the very serious situations in Aceh and Papua.

The international community must not abandon pressure for a solution that simultaneously ensures that justice is done and that the record is set straight. The solution for East Timor rests not with the East Timorese alone but with everyone in the civilized international community.

7

Aboriginal Reconciliation, Asian Australians, and Some Heretical Thoughts

Greg Sheridan

THE TREATMENT OF ABORIGINAL AUSTRALIANS is the single greatest historical injustice in the little more than two-hundred-year history of the modern nation of Australia. The broad story is well known but details are maddeningly elusive because many central facts were unascertainable at the time and for some of the worst events there was a deliberate decision to keep no records.

At the time Europeans began settling in Australia in 1788 there were probably three hundred thousand or more aborigines living on the continent, although this number is an estimate and reputable scholars disagree widely on the figure. A large number died from diseases generally inadvertently brought by the European colonizers. In its broad outline the tragedy of the aborigines was as close to inevitable as anything could be. In the age of great European colonies it was inevitable that Australia would be colonized. Given their long physical isolation it was inevitable that the aborigines would be particularly vulnerable to new diseases.

Moreover, given the morality attending colonization in the eighteenth century, it was inevitable that the aborigines would be dispossessed of their lands. This was even more inevitable because the aborigines were a predominantly nomadic people without established cities or systems of land title that were comprehensible to European settlers. It is quite possible, as many others have observed, that the aboriginal tragedy would have been even greater had Australia been colonized by a different European power. From the very first the British settlements in Australia were constrained in their treatment of aborigines by law, custom, and morality. Nonetheless, it is equally true that these constraints were frequently ignored.

From the first the aborigines resisted European settlement, but given the divergence in technology that existed between the two sides, it was completely inevitable that this resistance would be unsuccessful. The attempted military resistance led to numerous battles between aborigines and European settlers and especially the British authorities. However, there were also undeniably significant numbers of massacres and murders that had little or nothing to do with resistance to European settlement.

In all, most reputable scholars believe that some twenty thousand aborigines were killed by white settlers or forces operating under the authority of the British Crown, some in battle, some in massacres, many singly. This figure has naturally been subject to vigorous scrutiny and controversy. Because the needless killing of aborigines was always a crime, although nonetheless often carried out by the official forces of the colonies, some care was taken not to keep official records. Indeed, mostly there were no records of individual aborigines killed. Even so, there is ample documentary historical evidence, including many accounts in diaries, letters, and so on, of particular massacres and other killings, and of the not inconsiderable efforts of people who were morally outraged by such occurrences and tried to prevent them. There is simply no way of knowing a precise figure. But the matter has been exhaustively researched and debated. It is impossible to prove any figure, but the present writer is inclined to accept the scholarly consensus of twenty thousand, with a suspicion that, if anything, it is likely to be on the conservative side.

The needless killing of twenty thousand people is an appalling human tragedy and it is certainly the gravest breach of human rights in Australian history. It does not, however, suggest that there was ever a deliberate plan to wipe out or destroy the aboriginal race. Nor should it be allowed to obscure the fact that there were also many cases of cooperative relations between settlers and aborigines and of cross-racial friendships. Nonetheless, Australia in the eighteenth and nineteenth centuries was as subject to the generally racist attitudes of Europeans at the time as was any other settler society.

Many officials plainly believed that human rights did not apply in their fullness to aborigines in the way that they applied to Europeans. This was never a unanimous view in any of the six British colonies that in 1901 federated to become the Australian nation, but it was often a predominant view.

■ ■ ■

Part of the aboriginal tragedy was a result of the vast cultural and technological gap that existed between aboriginal society and European society. Even a polity much more firmly committed to aboriginal rights would have wrought devastation on a people whose entire culture was so radically at odds with that of the Europeans of the time. Thus the tragedy needs to be seen in the round. Aboriginal society was devastated, its culture was wrecked, the sense of purpose and accomplishment was destroyed, and traditional lands and means of providing food and shelter became impossible to sustain under the onslaught of European territorial advance. The aborigines themselves were divided into hundreds of tribal and linguistic groups and this made it more difficult for them either to offer effective resistance or to enter into meaningful negotiation.

Throughout the nineteenth century and much of the twentieth century aborigines were subject to an extraordinarily paternalistic and arbitrary regime of control by the British authorities. Unless granted a certificate of exemption from their aboriginality, they were effectively limited in where they could live and even sometimes in whom they could marry and what occupations they could follow. As a matter of law they were not paid the same wages as other Australians for carrying out the same jobs. Until well after World War II aborigines could not vote in federal elections. Mixed-blood aborigines were often distinguished from full-bloods and could be granted certificates of exemption from the regulations that applied to aborigines. But the certificates could be easily revoked.

There were always Australians who campaigned against these injustices. And there was a great variation in the aborigines' own circumstances. Much racial mixing occurred through white men taking aboriginal women as partners. There was a lot of rape and coercion, there were also consenting and supportive relationships. The large number of racially mixed people of part aboriginal descent were caught in some ways between two worlds. Many aborigines and part aborigines drifted to the cities. The authorities tried, often with disastrous consequences, to use the law to distinguish between part aborigines and full-blooded aborigines. Many tribal aborigines maintained something like a traditional existence in remote areas of Australia. Others were forced to live on reservations. The legal regimes were often flouted, but even the formal legal regimes differed greatly among the six colonies.

From the mid–twentieth century it became increasingly clear to a growing majority of Australians that the nation's treatment of its indigenous people not only had been unjust and inconsistent with its own standards but also had encompassed an immense historical tragedy. Trying to come to grips with the legacy of that tragedy has not been a happy or predominantly successful experience for the Australian nation. In 1966, a referendum was passed overwhelmingly by the Australian people to allow the national government for the first time to make laws for the benefit of aborigines. Much of the primary policy responsibility for aborigines was removed from state and territory governments and transferred to the national government. The referendum was passed in an atmosphere of great goodwill toward aborigines and of hope that it would presage a brighter future for them. It was not just a technical transfer of power but also a serious national commitment to try to do something better.

Throughout the 1970s and 1980s an increasing movement for land rights developed within Australia, and substantial tracts of land were granted to aboriginal communities for their economic and social use. There they were free to try to make whatever accommodation between traditional and modern lifestyles they felt most beneficial. This was the first serious step toward self-determination as an ideological and programmatic response for aborigines, as distinguished from the two previous doctrines of separation for full-blooded aborigines and assimilation for part aborigines, although the latter would later be replaced by a policy of assimilation for all aborigines. Much previous comment, especially in the nineteenth century, had assumed the ultimate extinction of full-blooded aborigines because of high death rates and low birth rates. Parts of this comment make gruesome reading today but it would be wrong to portray it as genocidal policy. There was no deliberate plan to wipe out aborigines;

what prevailed were the widely held assumptions that full-blooded aborigines were a "doomed race" and that part aborigines would eventually be absorbed into "White Australia."

In 1992 in a landmark case the High Court of Australia determined that the previous doctrine of *terra nullius* was invalid. *Terra nullius* had held that the land of Australia effectively belonged to no one before European settlement, that no people had legal title to the land until that title was granted by the British Crown. In this case, the Mabo case (named after Eddie Koiki Mabo, leader of the Merriam people from the Murray Islands), the High Court recognized for the first time the validity of native title. This was not only legally revolutionary; it was also a most complex judgment, in part because traditional aboriginal land ownership systems were so radically different from those of any modern society. The court, of course, did not seek to invalidate existing land title in the modern Australian nation. It found that any title of ownership granted by an Australian government automatically extinguished native title. But if specific groups of aborigines could demonstrate continuing association with particular lands, they could claim certain rights on these lands if the lands did not belong, by legal title, to someone else. In the most ideal case, aboriginal groups who could demonstrate continuing association with a piece of land not otherwise subject to land title could acquire full ownership of such land.

Australia is a vast nation with large tracts of unalienated Crown land and it is to these lands that the new judgment would primarily apply. In subsequent judgments the court also found that limited native title conferring limited rights, mainly for ceremonial and camping usage, could coexist even with modern pastoral leases, that is, that some modern pastoralists would have to share the land they leased with aboriginal groups. However, the court also found that where native title conflicted with pastoral lease, the pastoral lease would have priority, and it severely circumscribed the nature of the rights aboriginal groups could exercise in such cases.

All this, as may be imagined, was a subject of great controversy and interest in Australia. Substantial scare campaigns, which were completely dishonest, were waged to the effect that people's ownership of their suburban homes would be at risk as a result of the court's judgments. A more virulent form of this scare campaign was aimed at farmers. A more subtle scare campaign, and one with some substance, held that the nation's mineral resources could be substantially more difficult to develop because of these legal judgments.

Throughout the 1990s there was a wide-ranging, government-led campaign for formal reconciliation between the Australian nation and its indigenous peoples. This often led to great outpourings of goodwill. On one occasion, in the year 2000, nearly a quarter of a million people marched across Sydney Harbour Bridge in support of reconciliation. Similar marches, also of great size, were held in the other capital cities. However, the 1990s also produced serious policy clashes, which have become apparently insoluble and which still bedevil attempts at reconciliation.

The most important, and controversial, result of the reconciliation process was the report by the Australian Human Rights and Equal Opportunities Commission entitled *Bringing Them Home,* published in 1997. This report dealt with the phenomenon that came to be known as the "stolen generations." After interviewing more than five hundred aboriginal witnesses the commission came to the view that between 1910 and 1970 somewhere between 10 and 33 percent of aboriginal children were taken from their parents and placed in foster care or institutional care. It later became clear that this was a significant overestimate, and the generally accepted figure now is about 10 percent. It is extremely important to try to get these figures right. Even the figure of 10 percent is controversial and contested. It is based on a survey by the Australian Bureau of Statistics. But Australia, like other Western societies, has a strong cultural emphasis on victimology, an elevation of the status of victimhood. In the politically and emotionally charged atmosphere that has surrounded this issue the tendency toward significant overreporting is obvious.

The broad story of the stolen generations is generally accepted in Australia but there has been great controversy about the report's methodology and therefore about its final conclusions. The report nonetheless adduced sufficient documentary evidence to show that some states and elements of the federal government before World War II followed a bizarre eugenics policy of trying to "breed out" aboriginality. This was done by taking so-called half-caste or mixed-blood aboriginal children away from their natural parents. Much blatantly racist thinking underpinned these policies. There was an assumption by some policymakers that mixed-blood aborigines could be trained at a higher level than full-blooded aborigines and indeed could be integrated into white society. It was also explicitly held that if mixed-blood aborigines were encouraged to marry whites and prevented from marrying other aborigines, then over the course of a few generations the "stain" of aboriginality could be bred out. It was often assumed that full-blooded aborigines were simply destined to die out anyway, so that in the long run they would not pose a problem for what was ideally regarded as White Australia.

There is no doubt that this was all shockingly racist. At the same time it is also clear that, on the one hand, many of the people involved in the process, especially many of the families that welcomed aboriginal children into their homes, were well intentioned. On the other hand, there was also indiscriminate cruelty, both in the arbitrary and terrible business of actually removing children from their parents' care and in the treatment that these children often received subsequently in institutions and sometimes in private homes.

The policy was much less energetically pursued during World War II. It is clear that after World War II the wholly offensive eugenics elements of the removal of children disappeared and were replaced by a more restrictive removalist policy that was partly welfarist and generally assimilationist in its assumptions. During this period state authorities would not automatically seek to remove mixed-blood children, and the supervision of a court was needed. Removal of children, black or white, in the case of neglect or abuse was much more common then than it is now, when the emphasis is on keeping children with their natural parents for as long as possible. Thus even the more generally accepted 10 percent figure for the number of aboriginal children being removed needs to be seen as incorporating a goodly number that the authorities would have had reasonable grounds for regarding, at least from the point of view of the time, as abused or neglected.

It is certainly true that the practice of taking aboriginal children away from their parents was more capricious than that involved in taking white children away from their parents. And the aboriginal children suffered in ways that white children did not. They often ended up in institutions in which their very aboriginality was seen as a badge of shame. It is necessary to point out that the whole process involved every different human type, from the utter sadist to the truly and even heroically compassionate.

Most important, it is clear that post–World War II policy, although confused and disorderly in many ways, proceeded from a generally welfarist and assimilationist set of assumptions, rather than from the earlier, bizarre idea of "breeding out" aboriginality. The welfarist assumption was that, in problem families, defined really as more or less any family that came consistently to the notice of the authorities, child removal was a ready if not automatic option. The assimilationist assumption was that all aborigines should be assimilated into the predominant white society so that over time they, or at least their descendants, would attain the same living standards and enjoy the same opportunities as other citizens.

Not all of this was explicitly spelled out in the original report, *Bringing Them Home.* Its publication led at first to a huge public outpouring of grief, guilt, and sadness for the fate of so many aboriginal children. But the Human Rights Commission itself had made some terrible mistakes that in time contributed to a serious souring of the public attitude. First, its methodology in several key matters was faulty. The estimate that between 10 and 33 percent of aboriginal children of the period were forcibly removed was made by the commission. It turned out subsequently that only the lower figure could have any credibility, and even that only with the serious qualifications already mentioned. This sort of mistake seems perhaps nit-picking when an undeniable and gross injustice is involved, but people need to know that they are dealing with the truth. The inflation of figures, although done in good faith was, when exposed, devastating to the public credibility of the report.

A much more serious mistake was the commission's decision to describe the policy as an attempt at genocide. This foolish and grievously damaging exaggeration resulted from the commission's resorting to rhetorical maximalism on every point and, ultimately, it did the genuine victims of a genuine injustice a great deal of harm. The commission relied on the United Nations' definition of *genocide,* which can involve various means of attempting to eradicate a racial or cultural group. Thus the commission argued that, in attempting to "breed out" the aboriginality of part aborigines while assuming that full-blooded aborigines would die out eventually, Australian governments had been guilty of attempted genocide against the aborigines. There were many problems with this tortured line of reasoning. First of all, it defies common sense, something authors of government reports ought always to be careful about. Second, even in its own terms the commission did not properly distinguish between the pre–World War II vaguely eugenicist policy, which itself was not genocidal but might at least be argued to have a distant-cousin relationship with the thinking behind genocidal policies, and the post–World War II welfarist and assimilationist policy.

But there is a more general problem with the use of the word *genocide.* The term has come to have a variety of meanings in the context of attempts by the United Nations to grapple with questions of group rights and injustices done to individuals on the basis of their membership in groups, and indeed on injustices targeted at whole groups. However, to the overwhelming majority of Australians, including this author, *genocide* had always been understood to mean the attempt to kill an entire racial group, or at least the entire portion of a racial group that lives within particular borders. The culture of the United Nations has seen a proliferation of terms such as *cultural genocide* for the effective death of a particular culture. In all of this it can be argued that the United Nations and its committees are doing valuable work in attempting to deal with complex issues of justice, rights, and reparations. However, this work of the United Nations has not entered popular culture to the extent that the term *genocide* has a wide range of meanings in normal discussion in Western societies such as Australia. Moreover, insofar as the term has a popular resonance in Australian culture, it is associated with the extermination of six million Jews in World War II by the Nazi regime of Germany.

Thus it did not take long for Australian popular sentiment to react vigorously against the use of the term. The effect of the Human Rights Commission's wording was not to provoke a reevaluation of the meaning of the term in popular Australian culture. Rather, it was to discredit the work of the commission in popular Australian culture.

Australia is a mature democracy. It is a federal system with six states enshrined in the constitution. It has the full separation of judicial, legislative, and executive powers. It is governed nationally by a unique hybrid of the Westminster parliamentary system and the American federal system, with an elected Senate comprising an equal number of senators for each state. It is a wealthy and peaceful nation. It has a vast range of checks and balances of power at all levels. It has three distinct levels of government —national, state, and local. It has a rambunctious free press, compulsory school education, and a high level of tertiary education. It is one of the oldest continuous democracies in the world.

All of its citizens, regardless of race, religion, or background, enjoy absolute civic equality, including equal protection under the laws of Australian parliaments. It has perhaps the most racially neutral and nondiscriminatory immigration policy of any nation and for many years 30 percent or more of its immigrants have been from Asia, while New Zealand residents of any race enjoy free entry to Australia.

Needless to say, it has its full share of problems, policy failures, and injustices. Nonetheless, taken altogether this is an awe-inspiring record of nation building. For Australians, then, to be told that the whole story of their nation building was founded on a policy of genocide toward the indigenous population was deeply shocking. However, the liberal instincts of Australians are sufficiently well developed that even this might have been acceptable publicly if it had been true.

But because the term *genocide* is wildly inappropriate for policies toward aborigines that were certainly unjust and involved grievous and unnecessary suffering, in its developing hostility toward the Human Rights Commission's exaggerated rhetoric, the public came to believe, to some extent, that the real injustices that the commission had correctly identified might also be exaggerated. In other words, many Australians came to feel that their nation was being unreasonably slandered. This was an extremely unfortunate road for the reconciliation debate to take. As a result, over many months the Human Rights Commission's report was subject to increasingly aggressive attack. Some of this attack was itself rhetorically exaggerated, and thus rhetorical and political debate in Australia degenerated, exaggerated claims by genuine victims evoking not compassion but exaggerated responses of dismissal.

The slander of Australia by the Human Rights Commission was reminiscent of the polemical thrusts of the Left against capitalist societies during the Cold War. Capitalist societies undoubtedly did encompass many real injustices and it was right to campaign against those injustices. But the polemics often involved a grotesque moral equivalence between liberal democratic societies and the totalitarian societies of the communist bloc. Similarly, the wildly exaggerated rhetoric of genocide involves an almost equally foolish inference of moral equivalence between modern, democratic Australia and Nazi Germany. Such an equivalence recalls George Orwell's observation that to believe certain things you have to be an intellectual; no normal person could be so stupid. This kind of absurd moral equivalence not only generally leads to a conservative backlash but also demeans and distorts the reality of history. It makes the genuine, painful, necessary facing up to moral responsibility for real events much more difficult. In seeking the moral and polemical high ground, it confuses the public sphere; in seeking to inflame the heart, it darkens the mind. It is the enemy of clear thinking, which is the basis of good policy.

Similarly, the agenda on reconciliation has, since the report was published, come to rest on a series of fairly sterile symbolic demands. In recent years the ideology of indigenous peoples around the world has tended to switch from earlier demands for full and equal citizenship—what might be regarded as the assimilationist phase—to a new form of self-determination. In Australia it is hard to see what self-determination has really achieved. At the practical level it has two primary expressions. One is that on those lands that aborigines occupy as a result of land rights determinations, they are free to decide their own living and economic arrangements. The other is that the main federal government agency for aborigines, the Aboriginal and Torres Straits Islander Commission (ATSIC), has its governing body determined by elections throughout Australia in which the only voters are aborigines.

Yet the real measure of aboriginal disadvantage lies in the appalling levels of social indicators such as health generally and infant mortality in particular, specific diseases such as diabetes and glaucoma, life expectancy, educational achievement, crime and incarceration rates, domestic violence, drug abuse, unemployment, and so on. On each of these indicators aborigines fare much worse than do other Australians, whether they are other Australians born in Australia or immigrant Australians. It is impossible to trace any improvement in these indicators that has resulted either from self-determination as it is practiced on aboriginal lands or from the self-governing nature of ATSIC. Indeed, a substantial case can be made that the effort put into these endeavors has, if anything, taken attention away from the real problems. The reluctance even to discuss the problems of domestic violence is a good and often cited example. Similarly, some impressive aboriginal leaders have recently begun a debate on welfare dependence within aboriginal communities and the extremely damaging effects that prolonged dependency on passive welfare seems to have on too many aborigines.

Instead of focusing its efforts on these real problems, the aboriginal leadership seems preoccupied, especially since the report of the Human Rights Commission, with a set of symbolic issues. These have included demands for an apology and financial compensation for the stolen generations and for a treaty between aborigines and the rest of the Australian nation, as well as for increased land rights, greater UN involvement in aboriginal issues, and reserved seats for aborigines in parliament. The instinct of every decent Australian, of whatever background, is to be generous to the aborigines and to help them in any reasonable way possible. The proponents, black and white, of the symbolic agenda claim that its realization would endow aborigines with renewed pride in their aboriginality and that this in time would help to advance more practical aims.

It is the view of this writer that the government under Prime Minister John Howard should have made an apology for the stolen generations. Notwithstanding all the serious methodological problems with the report and the irresponsible rhetorical exaggeration it engaged in, the Human Rights Commission undoubtedly disclosed a major historical injustice. The numbers are unclear, the intent confused and various, and the results certainly not genocidal, but there is still no doubt that the forced removal of large numbers of aboriginal children from their natural parents without sufficient cause was a grave injustice. Mature nations apologize for the injustices in their past. Howard's insistence that the present generation of Australians should not apologize for something undertaken by a previous generation is, frankly, ridiculous. It is a direct contradiction of the international demands that have for the past sixty years been placed upon Japanese leaders to apologize for the actions of Japan during World War II. By now, however, the moral utility of an apology is much less clear. The prime minister, with the broad support of his half of the electorate, has refused to apologize. Even if an apology is eventually dragged from him, or if a successor eventually apologizes, it will not have the unifying and possibly cathartic effect that a timely apology generously given might have had. It might still be necessary but it is unlikely now to have any great positive effect.

Some of the other elements of the symbolic agenda are rejected by a majority of Australians for good reason. The idea of a treaty is not only impractical but also offensive to Australian ideas and traditions of universal democracy. Although technically a constitutional monarchy, Australia is profoundly republican in sentiment, that is to say, in a civic sense, profoundly egalitarian. The notion of citizenship as universal, nonnegotiable, and conferring both rights and obligations on all Australian citizens lies at the heart of Australian civic life and is the basis for its success as a multicultural nation with people drawn from more than 150 different national backgrounds. There have been other treaties between indigenous peoples and settler societies. They have been almost universally ignored or have had little, if any, practical consequence.

A treaty between modern Australia and a part of modern Australia involves a logical non sequitur. By definition it means that modern Australia does not include or represent aboriginal Australians. If such a treaty actually limited Australia's normal freedom of movement as a nation, it would be bitterly opposed, bitterly divisive, and almost certainly overwhelmingly rejected. If it became mere empty symbolism achieved only so that it might be achieved but with no effective normative content, it would inevitably disappoint aborigines' expectations. It would also discredit the whole business of making treaties and breed further alienation, among Australians of all backgrounds, from the political process.

The same applies to special reserved seats in parliament for aboriginal representatives. Would aborigines get to vote twice, once for aboriginal representatives and once for normal members of parliament, who presumably may be either aboriginal or nonaboriginal? Is it to be not only assumed but also declared as policy that nonaboriginal members of parliament do not represent aborigines? The notion of racially defined seats in parliament is profoundly offensive to the universal ideal of citizenship. It is wrong in principle and almost certain to be bad in practice. And it is rejected, in opinion polls, by substantial majorities of Australians.

The excessive concentration on a symbolic agenda is creating an increasingly sour taste about reconciliation. Australians are a very practical people. Australia has been called the undramatic country. It is dogmatic only in its insistence on pragmatism. If it is proud of anything in a civic sense, it is proud of being free of class distinctions and the pomp and ceremony of older societies. It is sometimes aggressively egalitarian. Australians were postideological even before modern ideologies were important. Australians were never socialists and they have never been laissez-faire capitalists. Their disinclination to get excited by politics, and certainly by political symbols or ideology, is sometimes annoying to their political and chattering classes but is a large part of their solid imperturbability and political stability. In short, grand gestures are against the Australian tradition. Empty grand gestures are particularly likely to be greeted with scorn and derision. In recent years the nation has become overwrought about reconciliation. Signs of a backlash are there. The opposition to moves such as treaties or racially determined seats in parliament is well grounded in Australian democratic tradition.

Some commentators believe that modern societies should encapsulate a variety of forms of citizenship and that indigenous people should occupy a special place with a different kind of citizenship. The present writer believes this not only is wrong in principle but would permanently consign indigenous people to a marginal status. The attempt to make indigenous people "super Australians" would end in their being "not really normal Australians." Moreover, the whole trend of such policy leads to the moral quicksand of racial classification. Australia is not, as is, say, Malaysia, composed of several fairly readily identifiable major racial groups. As already noted, its population is drawn from more than 150 national origins. Furthermore, the rates of racial intermarriage are high among virtually all Australians (higher for some than for others, obviously, but generally high across the board). Racial classification is inherently offensive and antidemocratic in any case, but in the multicultural context of contemporary Australia it is literally nonsensical. A whole offensive machinery of racial classification would need to be set up in Australia to give life to the full agenda of symbolic recognition of aborigines proposed by some.

Even seemingly innocuous symbolic proposals, such as a constitutional preamble that recognized aborigines as the first occupants of Australia, have been rejected by Australians. A proposal to incorporate such a preamble was overwhelmingly rejected at a referendum in 1998 even though it had the active support of John Howard, the conservative prime minister.

All of which is not to say that symbols and symbolism cannot play a useful part in aboriginal reconciliation. Australians are notoriously sports mad. The greatest sporting event in Australian history, and indeed in global history to the time of this writing, was the 2000 Olympic Games, held in Sydney. These games were hugely popular in Sydney and in Australia generally. For the purposes of this chapter two attributes of the games deserve attention. One was the overwhelming priority given to aboriginal themes and motifs in the opening and closing ceremonies of the games. Both ceremonies included a wide range of Australian icons and cultural expressions, but very heavy emphasis was given to aboriginal culture and images. These were seen in a wholly positive light, as representative of and distinctively Australian. The entire Australian community was happy to unite behind them.

Similarly, the Australian athlete who was chosen to light the Olympic flame, and who was in many respects the single personification of the games, was the gold medal–winning aboriginal athlete Cathy Freeman. It is impossible to overstate the goodwill that she attracted. The graciousness of her conduct was genuinely admirable. She lived up to national expectations in winning with commanding authority her chosen event, the four-hundred-meter sprint. She also displayed consistent good humor, humility, and self-confidence in her many public appearances. The whole nation fell in love with "our Cathy." Now it would be right not to apportion too much political significance to all this. Nonetheless, it is clearly valuable in many respects. Cathy Freeman represents a wholly positive role model for any young aborigine, or indeed any Australian of any background. She also represents the sense, and the reality, of opportunity in Australia. Further, and perhaps most important, she is a unifying figure, someone whom Australians of all backgrounds felt happy to claim as their own. And she was a sign that the whole Australian community was capable of feeling active affection toward aborigines and individual Australians of aboriginal background.

Similarly, it has been the case for many years now that aboriginal art occupies an honored place in the pantheon of Australian art. Hardly a single Australian gallery of consequence does not have a substantial aboriginal section, and aboriginal art has become an important part of the commercial side of Australian art. Its distinctiveness, its obvious connection to the land, and its variety have made it powerful and popular. It is also promoted, as are other elements of aboriginal culture, in schools.

These factors are of limited political import but they are of some import. The symbolism and the aboriginal motifs were well handled by the games organizers. Freed of a political agenda, Australians of all backgrounds were happy to unite across racial barriers. The same was true, of course, of immigrant Australian athletes who did well at the games. The popularity and unifying quality of aboriginal motifs in sports may owe something to the fact that those motifs have grown up, as it were, naturally, without the sense of heavy state imposition (even though Olympic sport does receive substantial government subsidy).

■ ■ ■

The most important sign of popular hostility to aborigines has been the rise of Pauline Hanson's One Nation Party. The Hanson phenomenon is worth considering at some length because it is the first serious expression of antiglobalization sentiment in contemporary Australian politics and one of the very few occasions since the dismantling of the White Australia policy in the 1960s and 1970s on which a political party basing its appeal in part on racial sentiment has had a measure of success.

Hanson herself first came to prominence as a maverick candidate for the Liberal Party, Australia's main conservative party, in the 1996 elections. Her controversial statements during that election got her expelled from the Liberal Party but it was too late for the Liberals to select another candidate and, in the great anti-Labor landslide of that year, she was elected as an independent member of parliament.

Hanson's appeals were crude and unintellectual. She frequently got basic facts mixed up, asserting in an early speech to parliament, for example, that there are 300 million Malaysians (when in fact there are about 22 million). She was incompetent, halting, and self-contradictory in media interviews. And thus her popularity grew, because it was these very defects that formed the chief emotional ballast of her support. She was the first antipolitician to win significant support in Australia. It has to be said that her support represented a measure of the disillusionment with or even alienation from the political process in a significant minority of the Australian community.

Insofar as she had economic policies, these were crudely populist and nationalist. She supported higher tariffs and greater rejection of international institutions and was generally opposed to free trade, internationalization, and globalization. An interesting pattern would emerge that, whenever she issued any detailed policies, her support declined sharply, because inevitably they were highly unrealistic. While she remained a symbol of protest she gained considerable support.

Racially Hanson seemed hostile both to most of the program for aboriginal advancement and to Asian immigration. She thus appealed to nativist white sentiment. Australia's peaceful transformation from a society that had defined itself as White Australia as recently as the 1960s to one that is now genuinely multicultural, with perhaps 7 percent of its population born in Asia, another 2 percent identifying themselves as aborigines, perhaps another 2 percent Arabs, and large populations from southern and central Europe and smaller groups from literally all over the world, is a remarkable success story of beneficial social and demographic transformation.

In many ways it was Hanson's anti-Asian statements that generated the greatest controversy. In her maiden speech to parliament she declared that Australia was in danger of being "swamped by Asians," who, according to her, live in ghettos, follow their own religion, and fail to integrate. Some Hansonite propaganda was extremely nasty. In *Pauline Hanson's The Truth,* a book issued by her associates and to which she held the copyright, the eventual extinction of the white race in Australia was predicted, with Australia to be populated by two billion Asians. All these claims are, of course, ridiculous. Asian Australians are geographically widely dispersed. Only the poorest cluster much for even the first generation, and the rate of subsequent out-settlement—that is, people moving out of the original places of settlement as they and their children become more affluent—is actually higher than it was for previous cohorts of immigrants. Similarly, the Asians who have come to Australia are religiously extremely diverse, and a large minority certainly are Christian, although only a minority of Australians of any racial background practice any religion at all. Similarly, all measures of social and economic integration—from rates of racial intermarriage through educational and professional achievement—show Asian immigrants integrating very rapidly.

Not surprisingly, Hanson also had strong opinions on aboriginal issues. She was opposed to land rights, especially the concept and practice of native title, and felt that the aboriginal agenda was a threat to farmers especially. In her own frequently inarticulate fashion she also opposed root and branch the symbolic agenda proposed by the leaders of the campaign for reconciliation. She was similarly opposed to the concept of multiculturalism.

The media can be fairly criticized for overexposing Hanson. Even though there was endless appropriate condemnatory comment about Hanson, there was also a bizarre celebrity-style coverage of her every utterance and activity. One reason for the level of media attention was the extreme slowness and insipidity of Prime Minister Howard's outright rejection of everything she stood for. Much of the political story was not just about Hanson but about Howard's apparent unwillingness to offend her supporters, although he did so eventually.

Perhaps the high point of Hanson's fortunes came in the 1998 Queensland election, when her party received 23 percent of the statewide vote. Happily, the party, like many right-wing fringe parties the world over, was subject to endless internal dispute, often concerning money, and splintering. In the 1998 national election, of more than two hundred members elected to the federal parliament, the One Nation Party accounted for just one, and its share of the vote fell to about 9 percent.

Following many internal party splits, her support in opinion polls declined to a negligible level but then recovered in subsequent state elections to hover around the 10 percent mark. In her second incarnation she was a much more sophisticated political operator, and One Nation appeared to drop almost all of its racial rhetoric. The party said little more than that it wanted complete equality for all Australians—which is also a way of opposing special measures for aborigines but certainly is not meant to imply that aborigines should be excluded from welfare or other benefits that other Australians receive. Similarly, on immigration, One Nation seemed to concentrate its fire on illegal immigrants, boat people, and criminal networks among immigrants. It also argued for a lower level of immigration overall but this is not in itself a racial policy, although of course it can appeal to people with racial motives. Most of the party's rhetorical efforts in its second incarnation were directed against tax reform and against any aspect of economic reform, free trade, or globalization that adversely affected a domestic Australian constituency. Thus One Nation seemed to be becoming a more conventional vote-hunting political party, albeit one firmly on the side of exclusionism, isolationism, nationalism, and a kind of dumbed-down, Australianized know-nothingness. Over the long term One Nation clearly poses the greatest political challenge to the National Party, which has been the mainstream party of rural conservatism in Australia for many years, operating continuously in coalition with the Liberal Party. In the 2001 Australian elections Pauline Hanson again failed to win a seat in the federal parliament and has since announced her retirement from politics. Her One Nation Party is riven by internal division and harassed by court cases and again has only one representative in the national parliament.

The most important things to note about One Nation are that it failed in its core objectives, it did not become a credible contender for government, it did not disturb the consensus for a completely racially nondiscriminatory immigration policy, and it did not even really disturb aboriginal policy, partly because Australian nationalists with even the slightest grain of common sense, or a desire to build a majority position, always want to incorporate at least some benign version of the aboriginal experience into their product. In its second incarnation the One Nation Party even went out of its way to attract some aboriginal and some Asian supporters. Although the extent of this apparent moderation can be overstated, as extremist parties go, One Nation is a relatively mild variety. It does not call, for example, for the repatriation of migrants or the exclusion of any group from any state service. It deserves thoroughgoing opposition, but bearing in mind its small minority status it ought not to be taken as an indication of a recrudescence of majority racism in Australia.

Naturally, the media coverage of One Nation in Asia tended to see it somewhat in those terms. In a sense nations tend to be forever trapped in their stereotypes, and in Asia the stereotype of Australia is of a racist, white nation. Asians who spend time in Australia—whether as tourists, businesspeople, students, scholars, or migrants—will discover that, while elements of this stereotype remain, it is not overall an accurate reflection of contemporary Australia.

■ ■ ■

The decision of One Nation to conflate the issues of aboriginal policy and Asian immigrants is perhaps more interesting than it seems.

The story of Asians in Australia is less traumatic than that of aborigines, but it may offer some clues for useful policy toward minorities in the future. Australia's history regarding Asians is as complex as its history regarding aborigines, and some of the same issues have been faced. For much of the nineteenth and twentieth centuries Australia's sense of identity was tied up with its fear and rejection of Asia. The White Australia policy itself derived not only from racial sentiment but also from a desire to create a high-wage, socially egalitarian society. There were always some Asians in Australia, but the nineteenth-century gold rushes greatly increased the number. At times in the nineteenth century such iconographic Australian settlements as Alice Springs were, in fact, substantially Chinese. The opposition to "cheap Asian labor" and the strategic fear of Asian nations, especially Japan, were high in the minds of Australian leaders. There was also sometimes gross and violent public sentiment. Although on a much smaller scale than the injustices inflicted on aborigines, there were some massacres of Asians in Australia. These generally involved small numbers and went mostly unpunished.

In the nineteenth century the state colonial legislatures passed several acts designed to prevent Chinese immigration to Australia. The very first act passed by the new national parliament after the Australian nation was founded in 1901 was the Immigration Restriction Act, which was a blatantly racist measure designed to keep Asians out. At that time the positive element of Australia's national identity was the attachment to the British Empire (though this was always contested by a minority of Australian nationalists of Irish extraction), while the main negative element of Australian identity was the rejection of Asia. Alfred Deakin, who was to serve three times as Australia's prime minister, and who was the dominant, and in many ways most liberal, leader of the time, declared during the parliamentary debate on that act that "unity of race is essential to the unity of the nation."

Although Australia welcomed large numbers of immigrants, first from Britain and Ireland and then from southern and later eastern Europe, the White Australia policy remained substantially intact until the 1960s, when it began to break down. It was finally comprehensively interred in 1972, although it was not until the late 1970s that large numbers of Asians were welcomed into Australia for the first time as permanent settlers. These were the Vietnamese, Cambodian, and Laotian boat people welcomed by the government of the Liberal prime minister Malcolm Fraser.

Since that time Australia has pursued a racially nondiscriminatory immigration policy, and as a result at least 30 percent of the immigration intake each year has come from Asia. Now perhaps 7 percent of Australians were born in Asia. Given the children they have had and the high rates of racial intermarriage, perhaps 10 or 15 percent of Australians must have some Asian connection in their extended family.

This is a social revolution in Australia, and one that has occurred, notwithstanding Pauline Hanson's One Nation Party, with virtually no violence and very little social upset of any kind. And the results have been stupendously positive for everyone involved. Most Asian groups fare better now, according to social indicators, than does the rest of the population. The academic leadership of Asian Australians at schools and universities is evident. Moreover, the presence of large numbers of Asian immigrants has added considerable dynamism to the Australian economy and underpinned growing economic and even political engagement with Asia. It has been a success in terms of the lives of the Asian immigrants and it has been a success in terms of Australian society. Moreover, Australians of all backgrounds routinely feel pride in the achievements of Asian Australians. The annual award of Australian of the Year is surprisingly popular and it has on several occasions been awarded to Asian Australians. In terms of this chapter, the most interesting thing about this success is how characteristically Australian it has been and how little symbolic accompaniment it has involved. In a sense, no one has talked much about it, which has allowed it to happen without drama or fuss. Of course, there are weaknesses in a lack of political ballast for a major social development, but it is hard to argue with the success of Asian immigration.

Asian Australians are noticeably underrepresented in Australian politics, but this seems to be cause for little complaint or activism among Asian Australian communities. Similarly, Asian Australians figure almost not at all in the great national obsession of competitive sport. But, again, this seems to be of little moment to the communities involved. Instead, the leadership of Asian Australian communities and the hundreds of thousands of individuals involved have been much more concerned with questions of real substance—above all access to a decent education. Indeed, one of the many ways in which Asian Australians have influenced the broader Australian culture is precisely in this field. In Sydney now there is a great flourishing of cram schools along the Japanese and Korean models, often enough staffed by Korean teachers, as parents try to give their students a competitive edge in education.

Of course it goes without saying that the experiences of Asian Australians and aborigines are vastly different. It would be foolish and facile to pretend that what has worked for one can simply work for the other. Nonetheless, there was probably not much less active hostility to Asians than to aborigines in much of the twentieth century in Australia. Those Asians who did live in Australia were subject to extensive racial discrimination. Yet the past generation has seen prodigious success. Insofar as this success has had a symbolic underpinning, it has been the inclusive notion of universal citizenship that has sufficed. This has provided a sense of entitlement to opportunity among Asian immigrants, an avenue of civic participation, and a sense, too, of some civic obligation. But it has also provided the wider society with a rationale for enabling and celebrating the achievements of the new immigrants.

One suspects that this is the best way for symbols to operate in Australia—essentially low key. Once the nation gets them right, or even mostly right, it can then substantially forget about them. It has been argued that some of the symbols of the Australian nation are offensive to aborigines—celebrating as the national day, for example, the day on which Europeans first "invaded" the country. Yet these symbols are at best also irrelevant for non-British immigrants and their descendants, and certainly for Asian Australians. Citizenship entitles immigrants to take pride in the achievements of the past and also to shoulder a share of ownership for the mistakes of the past. In any event, these symbols are themselves changing and are likely to be changed more in the future. In 1998 Australia in a referendum decided by a narrow margin not to become a republic just yet. But polls show a substantial majority of Australians wanting a republic. The main disagreement is over how and when that republic should be established and precisely what form it should take. The formal change to a republic will even more clearly emphasize the universality and democratic nature of Australia's civic symbols, and those symbols will be about the future more than the past. Whatever experience a community has had historically, it can have full access to the inclusiveness of the symbols for the future.

As I observed earlier, the experience of aborigines and Asian Australians is vastly different. Yet it is defeatist and ultimately patronizing to believe that only aborigines are incapable of taking advantage of the opportunities of modern Australia. Obviously, all Australians of goodwill want aborigines to enjoy more success in their lives. Recent experience is not satisfactory for Australia as a nation. It may be that the grand symbolic approach is not well suited to ameliorating this kind of social disadvantage. Apart from anything else, it tends to dramatize and emphasize victimhood and separateness. That it is a fashionable approach among UN committees is hardly a convincing recommendation.

In this case, too, it is difficult to see UN involvement as producing much of a positive nature. Rather, it contributes to the backlash that the overly symbolic agenda seems to entail. None of this is to deny the tremendous injustices aborigines have endured in the past and continue to endure today. Any deliberate injustice by the state must be addressed by law. Similarly, the conduct of individuals is regulated by law. But the civic imperative for addressing these injustices resides fully, and most effectively, in the notion of a universal citizenship that is applicable to all Australians. Aboriginal Australians, in their civic identity, are above all Australians and must be given the full rights and respect that belong to all Australians. It is easy to see what has failed. It is difficult to know what can succeed. But the liberal notions of equality, of a lack of hierarchy of descent, of the absolute divorce of ethnicity from citizenship have offered the best way forward for the most people. Their better application, not their partial abnegation, is needed in the future.

Conclusion

Yoichi Funabashi

Obstacles to Reconciliation

As the seven preceding chapters in this volume have shown all too clearly, numerous obstacles stand in the way of developing and implementing a policy of reconciliation between victims and victimizers. Some of these impediments to reconciliation are specific to a particular case. Others, however, have wider relevance and thus may help us to identify common problems and dynamics.

For example, progress toward inter-Korean reconciliation cannot proceed until the parties address such crucial questions as, Who was responsible for starting the Korean War? Who were the victimized and who were the victimizers? How should the responsibility be borne? Lee See-Young, a former South Korean ambassador to the United Nations, has noted that the conservatives and the opposition party in the Republic of Korea (ROK) claim that Kim Jong Il ought to apologize to the South Koreans if he should decide to visit Seoul.[1] They do not really believe that Kim would deliver such a message; they are merely playing to the public sentiment in the ROK, where a chronic lack of process in addressing the legacy of pain left by the Korean War has prevented old wounds from healing. On the other side, probably no one in the North Korean leadership carries a sense of guilt over the war. Some certainly must believe that what they did was the right thing. This lack of guilt is even more prevalent among the younger generations in both the North and the South, who consider past events to be the responsibility of their fathers and grandfathers. Such a refusal to address, or even to acknowledge, difficult and painful issues plagues not only the inter-Korean case but also many other situations.

Other obstacles to reconciliation can depend on factors such as whether the parties are states or ethnic groups. Interstate reconciliation (as in the cases of Japan and the ROK and Japan and China) and intrastate reconciliation (as in the cases of Cambodia, Taiwan, and Australia's aborigines) differ greatly in background and context, and an awareness of such differences is essential when pursuing reconciliatory measures. "One difference," Marianne Heiberg has noted,

> is the length of conflict or war. If you take the twentieth century as an example, the average duration of an interstate war was about three years. If you take a look at civil wars or intrastate conflicts, they were likely to be anywhere between ten to fifteen years. Civil wars are extremely difficult to put an end to. Interstate wars, once they are over, have such rituals as surrender and conclusion of peace treaties so as to reach a final end. This is not necessarily the case with civil wars. It is not as simple as that. Additionally, interstate wars, at least theoretically, must adhere to such international laws as the Geneva Convention and ensure the protection of noncombatants. Such practice does not necessarily apply to civil wars. They are neighbor-versus-neighbor fights and are thus more prone to extreme violence, people resorting to hand-to-hand killing, and other brutalities.[2]

I am confident, however, that although the conclusions below are drawn from international conlicts, they are also applicable to interethnic and intersocietal reconciliation.

Whether interstate or intrastate, individual processes of reconciliation can be influenced, both positively and negatively, by the examples of other cases. Thus, for instance, the process of reconciliation between the ROK and Japan will help shape that between North Korea and Japan, and vice versa. The problems to be overcome are to some extent similar: How can the normalization of relations be achieved? How should the apology issues be dealt with? What of the matter of compensation? Yet, while success in resolving issues in the negotiations between Japan and the ROK will facilitate discussion of similar issues by Japan and North Korea, it is crucial not to forget the very real differences between the two relationships. The abduction and nuclear issues complicating reconciliation with the North are entirely absent from Japan's relations with the South. We must always be careful not to conflate or confuse the Japan-ROK process with the Japan-DPRK process.

In Cambodia and East Timor, measures have been taken to create reconciliation schemes that borrow from South Africa's Truth and Reconciliation Commission (TRC). These countries faced difficulties not only in devising strategies for implementation but also in coming up with a working conceptualization of the meaning of "truth" and "justice," which are critical components in the construction of a new process of reconciliation. In the case of East Timor, political disagreements over the best system for ensuring justice have occurred between and within East Timor and Indonesia. Furthermore, the United Nations' approach to the establishment of a TRC has not worked well to date. In South Africa's case, the TRC was grounded in a concept of "restorative justice," according to which a crime (especially a large-scale, well-organized crime involving human rights violations) is not committed in isolation but is normally freighted with historical antecedents.

This notion of restorative justice is poles apart from the idea of "retributive justice." Retributive justice uses punishment of the individual as a deterrent. However, this approach to obtaining justice does not promote reconciliation in cases that involve groups with deep-seated historical motivation for violent action. Placing the individual perpetrators on trial will not allow a society to come to grips with the true nature of the underlying problems. What is needed is not so much obtaining reconciliation between individuals as implementing a reconciliation process that encompasses the whole community affected.

Implementing Reconciliation

Such examples of the formidable problems confronting policymakers who would seek to foster reconciliation can easily be multiplied. Fortunately, however, the chapters in this book also offer lessons on how such obstacles can be overcome and on the forces and dynamics that can be recruited by a policymaker in an effort to pursue reconciliation.

Richard Solomon has pinpointed three such lessons. First, reconciliation requires a "ripening of opportunity." It is very difficult to accomplish reconciliation between victims and victimizers when the latter still grasp the reins of political power. In such cases, time must pass before reconciliation can occur. Take the case of Tiananmen Square: it will be difficult for China to confront this issue squarely as long as the current leadership continues to hold political power.

Second, there is a crucial need for leadership in reconciliation efforts; strong political will is particularly important. In some instances, national leadership needs to be spurred by external pressure to take action. A case in point is postwar Germany: the United States and European nations had to apply pressure to get Germany to face up to its Holocaust experience. In the final analysis, however, the leadership will need to act on internal forces and exercise its own political will in pursuing a policy of reconciliation.

Third, reconciliation is a process that must proceed through four phases: truth, memorialization, compensation, and accountability. Once this has happened, the curtain may be drawn, both intellectually and emotionally, on the issue in the sense that justice will be seen to have been achieved. Such an outcome is indispensable to success.[3]

With Solomon's observations in mind, let me offer the following ideas on reconciliation and its policy implementation.

1. Human Rights Violations Are a Universal Human Experience

Large-scale, serious human rights violations of the kind that underlie the historical issues presented in this volume occur in all societies. It is a mistake to seek the causes of our historical problems in the supposed ethnic "traits" implied in such expressions as "Japanese culture is essentially such-and-such" or "the Chinese (or Koreans) are generally so-and-so." In considering these issues, furthermore, we must not cast them in terms of a kind of original sin; that is, we must avoid characterizing any ethnic group or country as the eternal villain, just as we must avoid exalting any other as the eternal victim. Rather, we must regard the experiences in question as generic to humanity as a whole and consider how to overcome the problems from that point of view.

2. "Our" History Is Everyone's History

While each community's or ethnic group's history is in an obvious sense its own, it is also part of the history of all ethnic and national groups and of the world as a whole. Although it is certainly important to have pride in one's own country and culture, at the same time one must therefore respect the fact that people in other countries, too, have pride in their cultures. If one recognizes the value of one's own country's constructive nationalism, one must acknowledge the same value in other countries. It is dangerous to try to describe one's own country's history as if it were completely self-contained and detached from world history; such a version of history would be far removed from reality.

The history of Northeast Asia, centering on Japan, China, and Korea, is a case in point. It is impossible to describe the history of any individual country in the region separately from that of the others. In order to get as close as possible to the truth, it is necessary to incorporate the point of view of other countries into any single country's historical record.

3. Reconciliation over the Past Is a Process

That historical issues are heating up does not mean that they will directly trigger war. However, as Yang points out in his analysis of the case of Japan and China, under certain circumstances historical animosity makes war more likely, and once a conflict rooted in such historical enmity does erupt it could easily become a quagmire from which neither party can easily escape.

Promoting collaborative efforts toward reconciliation over issues of the past would thus contribute greatly to ensuring peace and stability. Such reconciliation is a long-term process; there will be no quick, comprehensive settlement or all-encompassing instances of forgiving and forgetting. The dynamics of truth-telling, memorialization, compensation, and accountability will vary from case to case. Unless the process is begun, however, no visions of peace or coexistence will take root and germinate and no linkages between civil societies will be able to form.

4. There Is No Universal Formula

While acknowledging the ubiquitous nature of historical issues, we must, at the same time, analyze and take into account the separate and specific circumstances under which each violation of human rights took place. It is essential to advance the process of reconciliation while weighing various conditions surrounding each case, including historical factors, geopolitical conditions, degrees of economic development and economic disparity, levels of democracy, and the state of domestic politics. In this regard, no universal formula exists that can be applied in all parts of the world at all times.

5. Reconciliation Must Be a Joint Effort by Victimizers and Victimized

Unless the process of reconciliation over issues of the past leads to a concrete legal judgment and a clear sense of justice having been done, there will be no real forgiveness of the victimizers by the victimized. At the same time, however, overemphasizing the aspects of law and justice will hinder development of the kind of mutual empathy needed for all parties to work together in fostering reconciliation. Efforts toward reconciliation will not take proper root unless they are made by both the victimizers and the victimized, working in collaboration.

It is important to recognize that the terms *victim* and *victimized* do not represent absolute concepts. Even so, we must not pretend that they are the same. Because the anguish of the victimized differs in nature from that of the victimizer, to pay equal attention to both at the outset of a reconciliation process would be to risk artificially conflating two fundamentally distinct kinds of pain.[4] Although consideration must be given to both sides, it must be given with the utmost care and prudence and with a clearly defined order of priorities. Attention must first be devoted to creating some peace of mind and "peace of heart"[5] on the victimized side. Furthermore, the victimizers' efforts to achieve their own peace of mind must be made in a spirit and in a form that will win the understanding of the victimized side.

6. Use a Forward-Looking, Realistic Approach

The philosopher David Crocker, noting that "moral questions have a habit of not going away," suggests that as long as there remain in people's minds grudges, animosity, and moral doubt over whether or not either victimizers or victimized have been properly dealt with, it will be impossible to establish long-term sustainable peace.[6] It is only on the strength of its moral basis that any attempt at reconciliation will be viable.

At the same time, however, arguments on the moral aspects inherent in historical issues are not necessarily an effective way of transcending the problems of the past. In all countries and contexts, people tend to become overly idealistic and moralistic in discourse about reconciliation over the past. What we need instead is more discussion on how to resolve these problems concretely, beginning with taking whatever steps can be taken, however small, and working together with a common vision.

A weakness of moral idealism is its assumption that people are perfect. As long as efforts are based on this unrealistic expectation, they will not yield a sustainable program of reconciliation. Society simply cannot live up to such ideals. Pertinent here are the following words by Martin Buber, a Jewish German who served the cause of peaceful coexistence of Jews and Arabs: "Can I be so presumptuous to forgive. . . . My heart understands the weakness of man and refuses to condemn my neighbor for his unwillingness to become a martyr."[7] This view of human beings as neither fundamentally evil nor fundamentally good but rather fundamentally weak is a productive one.

In the current age of globalization, historical issues have a strong tendency to be recast in emotional terms as a nation-uniting theme, and to be championed with populist rhetoric. Discussion of the topic often swiftly becomes impassioned and ideologically slanted. Accordingly, there is a need to bring the issue back into the context of diplomacy and to calmly reassess what is to be gained or lost in terms of enlightened national interests. Considerable intelligence and discretion must be exercised to create a climate that will engender opportune moments for positive action. As in politics, so in the field of reconciliation, timing is crucial to success.

In this respect, and as demonstrated by the example of Germany's reconciliation with its West European neighbors, the fostering of cooperation and confidence-building measures in areas such as the economy and security is very important. Reconciliation should be built on the foundation of common interests while being driven by, and responsive to, emotional needs. Reconciliation over the past should be undertaken with a forward-looking, realistic approach. This means developing an approach to reconciliation in which the interests of both parties are interwoven as closely as possible.

7. Cultivate Democracy

In order for reconciliation over the past to take firm root, it is important to expand and strengthen the institutions of democracy in each society involved. The protection of human rights is one of the most important values underpinning democracy. Reconciliation over the past is ultimately aimed at learning the lessons of past violations of human rights and ensuring that such violations do not recur. It is only when democracy is firmly entrenched that both human rights and reconciliation over the past can also take lasting root.

In addition, democracy fosters the kind of political culture in which the perspectives and interests of other parties are taken into account and in which compromise is encouraged. This kind of outlook is essential in fostering reconciliation over the past. Furthermore, the political leaders elected in a democratic system are unlikely to make up for their lack of legitimacy by resorting to xenophobic nationalism. A major factor in the progress toward reconciliation made by Japan and South Korea, for example, has been the fact that South Korea has become a bona fide democracy with a democratically elected president. One of the reasons that earlier attempts at reconciliation between Japan and South Korea proved difficult was that previous ROK governments often used antiforeign (and more specifically anti-Japanese) nationalism to compensate for their lack of political legitimacy.

Also important in this respect is the role played by nongovernmental organizations (NGOs) and other institutions within civil society. In the case of reconciliation between Germany and Poland, dialogue on issues of the past began with appeals by the Catholic Church. In the case of Japan and South Korea, the development in the late 1980s of schemes for joint action through associations of environmental groups and other organizations on both sides brought about a significant change in mutual perspectives. Numerous NGOs have also been involved—in Japan and elsewhere—in highlighting past violations of human rights and in seeking compensation for the individuals who were victimized.

8. The Approach Should Be Based on Multilateralism and Regionalism

Efforts to promote bilateral reconciliation over the past should seek to reinforce the processes and frameworks of multilateralism and regionalism. In the Asia-Pacific region, multilateralism and regionalism have been gradually developing since the early 1990s through such institutions as the Asia-Pacific Economic Cooperation Conference (APEC), the ASEAN

Regional Forum, the ASEAN+3 summit meeting, the summit meetings involving Japan, China, and the ROK, and cooperation among the countries of Southeast Asia in the field of finance.

In the meantime, the cooperation of Japan, the United States, and the Republic of Korea in security matters and the coordination of policy with China are indispensable for the reconciliation of Japan and North and South Korea. The aim should be to work toward a framework for multilateral policy dialogue centering on the Korean peninsula, to promote the process of reconciliation while securing the foundations for an enduring multilateral framework.

A crucial part of multilateral cooperation is the nurturing of a "culture of dialogue" and a "custom of dialogue." In advancing the process of reconciliation between Japan and China, the culture of dialogue should be steadily built up by such efforts as including China in the World Trade Organization (WTO), promoting policy coordination under APEC and ASEAN+3, and gradually expanding the three-way policy talks among Japan, China, and the United States.

As fellow democracies, Japan and South Korea should work together toward a common vision of democratic peace. That is, they should confirm their commitment to developing the kind of Western-style relations of peace and security that help to explain why democratic countries rarely go to war against one another.

In relation to China, which is not a democratic country, the corresponding aim should be to develop a vision of peace through economic interdependence. This means ensuring that the increased economic interdependence of Japan and China contributes to lasting stability between the two countries.

9. Political Leadership Is Key

Whatever vision is pursued, the process of reconciliation over the past will not move forward without appropriate political leadership of a high intellectual and moral caliber. Behind every case of successful advancement of reconciliation in the post–World War II era there have been leaders of preeminent political skill, among them the West German chancellors Konrad Adenauer (in the normalization of relations between Germany and France) and Willy Brandt (in the normalization of relations between Germany and Poland); the Chinese premier Zhou Enlai (in the normalization of relations between China and Japan); the South African president Nelson Mandela (in the abolition of apartheid and the creation of a democratic South Africa); and the South Korean president Kim Dae Jung (in the promotion of peace on the Korean peninsula and reconciliation with Japan).

Even gifted and committed politicians, however, cannot necessarily overcome widespread popular resistance to the idea or to the practicalities of reconciling with longtime adversaries. In Israel, for example, a fatal gap existed between Prime Minister Yitzhak Rabin's vision of reconciliation with Palestine and that of the Israeli people. A similar gap may exist between, on the one side, President Kim Dae Jung's policy of embracing North Korea and his plan for reconciliation with Japan, and, on the other side, public opinion in South Korea.

10. Individual Initiative Is Essential

Progress toward reconciliation over the events of the past depends considerably on the quality of political leadership, but the key to success in the process lies in the commitment of individuals.

The German chancellor Helmut Kohl once referred to the "grace of a late birth," by which he meant the "blessing" that Germany's postwar generations enjoyed in being exempt from direct responsibility for the Holocaust, unlike their parents and grandparents, who must bear that guilt as adult citizens of German society during the Nazi era. Today, people born after World War II make up the majority of the population in all countries. As individuals, these people feel no guilt for the colonialism, aggression, atrocities, large-scale human rights violations, or other crimes their countries may have committed in the past. There is no such thing as *collective guilt* that makes the nation as a whole culpable for past invasions or colonial rule and extends to successive generations. This does not mean, however, that one does not or need not feel any sense of shame or responsibility for past injustices in which one was not directly involved. That is, there is such a thing as *collective liability,* whereby one feels responsible for past wrongs committed by one's country even if one was not even born at the time they occurred. At the very least, each individual citizen is caught up in this issue and cannot escape its implications. Tessa Morris-Suzuki defines this notion as "acknowledging the existence of a conscious connection with the past and the reality of being an accessory after the fact."[8]

What can the individual do to overcome these problems? The first step is to take a fresh look at history and to learn from it. We must study what is to be recognized and remembered as truth and pass those facts down to successive generations. Second, we must examine whether the injustices of the past are the sources of continuing political and economic injustices and disparities, and, if they are, make appropriate efforts to redress them. Third, we must enhance dialogue and exchange with people in neighboring countries and work with them in building frameworks for security, democracy, and economic development—the foundations on which reconciliation can rest.

11. Our Behavior Should Reflect the Kind of Nation We Hope to Build

Facing up to history and transcending the lingering troubles of the past are tasks that should not be approached passively. The way in which we tackle these issues will itself make up a part of our identity. That identity will be either broadened or narrowed depending on whether or not our society can become an open one, both internally and externally. In attempting to confront and overcome the past with an open mind, we should start not with extravagant ideals and unrealistic ambitions but with a commitment to taking concrete, practical steps. For each of us, loving one's country should not mean idealizing it or its past. Ultimately, the task of reconciliation requires the kind of grace that in individuals arises at the intersection of heartfelt remorse and heartfelt forgiveness.

Democracy is the apparatus by which anyone can freely contribute to and partake of such an experience. Whether that apparatus is made broadly accessible and is structured to allow movement to and from the outside world depends on the capacities and broad-mindedness of the people. In order to pursue deeper reconciliation, democracy is a basic requirement. Only a democratic system can ground the reconciliation process at the level of people-to-people contact.

The manner in which a nation faces up to history reflects what kind of country it wants to be and how its people as an ethnic group want to be remembered by future generations.[9]

Appendices

The following three commentaries were given at the International Conference on Reconciliation in the Asia-Pacific, held February 16–17, 2001, at the International House of Japan in Tokyo.

The Process of German-Polish Reconciliation

Frank Elbe

I don't think that European experiences can be translated into Asian terms. Asia has to develop its own approaches. But I would like to invite you to engage in a friendly comparison between the progress toward reconciliation that's been made in Asia with the progress we've achieved in Europe.

At the end of 1999 I participated in an inauguration ceremony for a joint Danish-Polish-German army corps at the headquarters in Szczecin, or Stettin, a former German town. It sent a thrill down the back of even experienced diplomats: Danish, Polish, and German troops had lined up in a former German town, and a Polish officer reported their presence to the president of Poland using the NATO language, English. The French celebrate their national day, the 14th of July, with a great parade on the Champs-Elyssées. For a couple of years now German soldiers and tanks have taken part in this parade. Can you imagine having a trilateral Japanese-Chinese-Korean army corps with its headquarters in Pusan? Can you imagine Japanese tanks parading on Tiananmen Square?

Reconciliation with our Western neighbors in the 1950s was facilitated, if not determined, by outside factors, namely, the European security issue and the prospects of economic cooperation.

The geographic proximity of the military threat of Stalin's expansionism made the countries of Western Europe band together shortly after the end of World War II, with NATO being formed in 1949. Bonn, Amsterdam, and Brussels were only 250 to 400 kilometers away from the massive presence of the Soviet military forces; Soviet tanks could have reached the Rhine River within five to six hours. Another important factor that brought former adversaries even closer together originated in Asia. The war in Korea created the need for an integrated command structure within the North Atlantic Alliance and, above all, for a German military contribution to the defense of Europe. The presence of German forces and their integration into NATO—the process of turning former foes into brothers-in-arms—became an important mechanism for reconciliation. Furthermore, in the early 1950s ideas emerged in Western Europe to optimize the production of steel and coal. The Montan Union, a union of France, the Benelux states, and Germany, was created and became the foundation stone for the integration of Europe.

The history of German-Polish reconciliation was a long and agonizing one, but it was a more structured process compared with the process of reconciling with Germany's neighbors in the West, such as France and the Benelux countries.

People know little about the colossal sufferings of the Poles during World War II. Poland lost six million people, of whom three million were Jews. The Nazis systematically eradicated the political and intellectual leadership of the country, killing one million Polish citizens in the process. Such a toll gave little hope for forgiveness.

Germany, too, experienced unprecedented suffering, which later complicated reconciliation with Poland. As a result of decisions by the wartime Allies, Germany had to cede one-fourth of its territory to Poland and to the Soviet Union. Two million Germans—one-sixth of the population living in the eastern provinces—lost their lives fleeing or while being expelled from their homes; most were women, children, and elderly men. They became victims not only of the bestiality of the Soviet army but also of Polish people taking revenge for the atrocities that had been committed earlier by the Nazis

The Cold War prevented any political dialogue on normalization of relations between Poland and Germany—let alone reconciliation between the two countries—for more than twenty-five years after the end of World War II. The Polish Stalinists used the suffering of the Polish people under Nazi occupation for their own political purposes. They sought to compensate for their lack of democratic legitimacy by depicting the Germans as the archenemy, as the eternal threat to the security of Poland. They succeeded in embedding hostility deep in the hearts and minds of Poles.

However, in 1965 the Catholic bishops of Poland sent a unique, unexpected, and unprecedented message to the German bishops. They wrote: "We hold our hands out to you, we grant forgiveness and we ask for your forgiveness." Forgiveness for the millions of crimes committed during the Nazi occupation of Poland? How could that be possible? Who was granting forgiveness to whom?

The New Testament calls on victims to forgive victimizers, just as Jesus Christ forgave his torturers while he was crucified. The Polish Catholic Church introduced a religious dictum into practical politics. The Polish bishops did not act on biblical grounds alone. They were guided by their responsibility for the security of the Polish people and for the creation of peace in Europe.

It was a bold move and without parallel in the twentieth century. The gesture of the Polish bishops created an uproar in Poland. The communists were infuriated and called Cardinal Wyszinski a traitor. Of course, they felt threatened by the church, which dared to take away the only source of legitimacy for communist rule, namely, fear of the Germans. But it was not only the communists who objected: one-third of Polish Catholic priests disagreed with their bishops.

In 1970 Willy Brandt signed the German-Polish treaty on normalization. He got on his knees when he visited the memorial for the Jewish martyrs. Brandt was an innocent man who had proved his moral integrity by fighting the Nazis. Yet, he knelt and thus accepted responsibility for the crimes committed by Germans. The communist propaganda machine concealed Brandt's important gesture from the Polish public: films of the German chancellor at the memorial showed only the top half of Brandt's body.

From 1972 to 1976 I served as a young diplomat in Warsaw. In those years very little progress was possible in reconciling Germans and Poles. I learned a lot about honest approaches, but also a lot about cynical attitudes and false tones. The communists in Poland had no real interest in engaging in a meaningful process of normalization with Germany. A top diplomat made it quite clear to me that the treaty on normalization with Germany meant no more than establishing a beginning for normalization;

the end was not in sight and might never be in sight. Normalization, he said, had to be deserved by the nation of the perpetrators! And he added that Brandt had actually knelt in front of the wrong monument—by which he meant that Brandt should have got on his knees at a Polish, not a Jewish, place of worship. But one important step was achieved during communist rule: Poland and Germany agreed to set up a Schoolbook Commission to revise the texts on history in their schoolbooks.

When, in 1989, Poland again became a free country, the process of reconciliation gained new momentum. Today, reconciliation between our two nations can be considered a successful process. It became a success because it was based on a structured dialogue and a few important principles. Again, the bishops from both countries took the lead, issuing a joint declaration in 1995 that stated, "We remember all the wrong that has been done during the war. Only the truth can make us free, a truth that does not add and does not omit anything, a truth that does not conceal anything, a truth without reckoning."

At the end of World War II, the dark chapters of our history left the German people with little hope for reconciliation with their victims. In the early 1950s, the German-Jewish philosopher Martin Buber asked, "Can I be so presumptuous to forgive?" But then he continued, "My heart understands the weakness of man and refuses to condemn my neighbor for his unwillingness to become a martyr."

Reconciliation is a process between two parties, but reconciliation begins at home. It stems from the ability and readiness of a society to be at peace with its moral constitution. What kind of country do we want to be, as Gareth Evans asked [in his presentation to the conference] yesterday. The only meaningful offering Germany could make to gain forgiveness or to atone for the crimes committed under National Socialism was to accept responsibility for what happened and not to forget, to strive for the establishment of a democratic society and to assure our neighbors by our acts and deeds that they no longer needed to live in fear of the Germans. This was more important to the process of reconciliation than the massive compensations that Germany paid from the beginning of the fifties and that until today amount to 124 billion German marks.

German history cannot and will not make a detour around Auschwitz. Its history passes right through the Nazi camps of extermination, but neither has it begun there nor does it end there. An understanding that accepts liabilities of the past makes a society free again and restores its dignity. It allows a nation to play a role as a meaningful partner in politics. Our European friends would never have tolerated Germany playing a major role in promoting the integration of Europe if they had not have been confident that indeed we had accepted responsibility for the past. And they would not have consented to German unification if it had been otherwise.

One last observation: The process of reconciliation is a contribution to peace in a region. It pushes the door open for regional cooperation, which is a source of political stability, economic prosperity, and good neighborliness. However strong the forces may be that stem from the revenge cycles or from a false pride or from the notion of losing face, we should not miss the chance of keeping our planet intact and establish cooperation by all means—that includes reconciliation.

The Processes of Reconciliation Are Diverse

Yukio Sato

Ambassador Sato discussed his personal experiences of dealing with the past in the context of Japan-Dutch issues. The following is a summary of his comments.

During World War II, Japan occupied Indonesia, or what was then known as the Dutch East Indies. At the time, there were 120,000 Dutch under Japanese control, including women and children.

The manner in which the Dutch have approached reconciliation after World War II has been very impressive. There are, for instance, sixteen Dutch organizations representing Dutch victims. One example of the Dutch approach is particularly worth recounting. At the Dutch-German border there is a war museum, and inside the museum there is one room where the pictures on display are only of prisoner camps—Dutch, German, and Japanese. At the entrance to the museum there is a photograph of a nineteenth-century Dutch newspaper telling the story of Dutch people harassing Jews. According to the director, as some Dutch will leave the museum hating the Germans it is helpful to let them know that the Dutch also share some guilt.

Another story concerns a Japanese journalist who was writing a special article on "comfort women" at a time when the Japanese government was being sued, and who wished to be introduced to a former comfort woman. When one of the organizations was contacted it refused, but it refused on very interesting grounds. The issue, according to the organization, was extremely complex, and although there were women who had been victimized in that manner, this was only one part of the overall suffering for which the Dutch victims were suing the Japanese government. As such, it did not wish to focus solely on this one aspect of their case. Moreover, the organization also suggested that the case was complex because some women had been forced, while others had been involved voluntarily. Such frankness was surprising.

A further interesting aspect of discussions with Dutch survivors is the frequency of the word "recognition." In Dutch, there seems to be a specific word carrying this meaning, and thus a special significance is attached to acts of recognition. Consequently, having the Japanese ambassador recognize the wrongdoings of the Japanese soldiers—recognize the suffering of the Dutch survivors—would help lessen the suffering of these people. It would help them feel easier toward Japan.

For these Dutch survivors, recognition of their suffering, not only by Japan but also by their fellow Dutch, has been a long and arduous process. When many of these Dutch returned to the Netherlands after the war they were told not to talk about their experiences. Holland at that time had just experienced five years of German occupation, and the attitude was that those Dutch had been well off in a faraway colony. It was not until fifty years later that many of these victims publicly came forward to retell their experiences.

Direct contact is vital for achieving reconciliation between Japan and the Netherlands. The impression many Dutch have of Japan continues to be based on the brutality of Japanese soldiers fifty years ago, rather than on the postwar development of Japan into a modern, democratic nation. It is important, therefore, to increase direct people-to-people contacts between the two nations to dispel these views. A good example of such efforts is the sister-city relationship between a town called Middleburg in Zeeland, Netherlands, and Nagasaki in Japan. Middleburg was bombed flat and Nagasaki, of course, was devastated by an atomic bomb. It seems natural that a shared understanding of suffering through such kinds of contact could be therapeutic for the victims of both countries.

It is necessary, however, to be very careful when we talk about victims and victimization. The sister-city relationship between Middleburg and

Nagasaki is a good example of this issue also. At one point, Nagasaki approached Middleburg and asked if the city would like to ring a bell and pray for the victims of Nagasaki on July 9. But when this proposal was raised at the council meeting in Middleburg, a number of people protested, saying that because Japan has not apologized for what was done to the Dutch in Indonesia, the people of Middleburg should not be praying for the people of Nagasaki. This event highlights the manner in which Japanese people tend to "hide behind" the nuclear bombings of Hiroshima and Nagasaki. Playing the victim without recognizing the wrongs one has done to others is a very harmful attitude. Happily, there is an exhibition now at Hiroshima about history before the bombing.

In order to increase the exchange of experiences, the Japanese government has provided funds for Dutch survivors to write their memoirs of the war with Japan. These memoirs, which also include a number of notes written during the war, will be translated into Japanese and published in Japan. It is to be hoped that these accounts of suffering will become lessons for future generations of Japanese. Although the issue of compensation is often the focus of attention, experiences, exchanges, and documents like this are vital parts of the reconciliation process. As much as compensation, such recognition eases the suffering of people.

Extending the notion of recognition from the Dutch case to the broader field of reconciliation, we might ask whether these methods could be applied to other nations. Perhaps. However, the atrocities committed by the Japanese against other nations, particularly China and Korea, were on a much greater scale than those committed against the Dutch. As such, it seems doubtful whether the same method could be applied to these cases with equal success. This highlights the diverse nature of reconciliation processes: there is no such thing as a "typical" reconciliation—each case is different and requires a different approach.

There Is No "Single Truth"

Marianne Heiberg

Dr. Heiberg discussed her experiences of the Israeli-Palestinian conflict, explaining the nature of the conflict and how this has affected reconciliation. The following is a summary of her comments.

Wars between states obviously differ in nature from wars within states (civil wars). These differences also significantly affect the postwar process of reconciliation. First, wars between states tend to last, on average, about one to three years. Civil wars, however, tend to last between ten and fifteen years, sometimes even longer. Second, when wars between states are concluded, either through treaty or through surrender, they tend to be "over." In contrast, there is a strong tendency for civil wars to re-explode. Last, in theory at least, wars between states are supposed to be conducted according to the Geneva Conventions. It is well known that practice often differs from theory, but certain rules for wars between states do nevertheless exist. In civil wars, the Geneva Conventions are irrelevant: it is community versus community and neighbor versus neighbor. Consequently, civil wars tend to be much more brutal. Bosnia, Rwanda, and Sierra Leone are appalling examples of this phenomenon. In civil wars, because the sources of conflict often remain unresolved for a long time after hostilities have ceased, the sense of fear and the sense of insecurity often remain acute, increasing the likelihood of violence re-erupting and creating extra difficulties and obstacles for later reconciliation.

Of all the conflicts in the Middle East, the Israeli-Palestinian conflict most resembles a civil war. Israel's wars with its Arab neighbors were largely wars between states, and the general populations were not engaged in direct battle. However, the Israeli-Palestinian conflict involves the direct confrontation of people-versus-people; while it consists of two nations, they coexist on a territory to which both have traditionally laid *exclusive* claim.

In this context, consider the official guesthouse in Oslo, Norway, late on the night of August 19, 1993, and then early in the morning of the following day. On the evening of the nineteenth, Shimon Peres was on an official visit to Oslo and was given an official dinner at the guesthouse. What was actually happening that night, however (a fact not known to many, although certainly known by Peres), was that another Israeli delegation and a Palestinian delegation would arrive at the guesthouse after the function and sign a document that had been negotiated in Oslo over the previous nine months—the Declaration of Principles.

The guests that night were quite surprised to discover that the function had not only an arrival time (7:30 PM) but also a departure time (10:30 PM sharp!). Once the guests had departed, the two delegations arrived from their hotels and were brought in through the kitchen. The atmosphere was very somber—no sense of celebration. The two leading negotiators sat down at the desk, which had previously been used to sign the Norwegian Declaration of Independence, and initialed the document. The room was completely silent. Perhaps everyone realized that the consensus was being broken and that history was being broken. Those in attendance were witnessing the demise of a consensus based on conflict and confrontation and the assumption that Arabs and Israelis could not live together in peace. The wasted efforts in search for peace seemed at that moment to have reached a critical point and had come crashing down, landing on that old desk and on that particular night, in the guesthouse of the Norwegian government in Oslo.

In the light of this experience, the process of reconciliation seems to consist of two stages, each requiring important ingredients to be completed successfully. The first stage is the initial agreement and the second is turning this agreement into sustainable peace. The initial agreement stage requires good *timing* and strong *leadership;* the second stage requires a political *reaction* and an understanding of *history*. For the Israeli-Palestinian conflict, the first requirement (timing) has consisted of numerous factors. Obviously, the timing of the end of the Cold War, the explosion of the Gulf War, and perhaps the political isolation and virtual bankruptcy of the Palestine Liberation Organization—not to mention the intifada—all contributed to the breakthrough in the talks. However, it is important to remember that these talks were also the product of the previous "unsuccessful" endeavors.

Leadership was the second factor necessary to achieve an initial agreement. Individual personalities are critical in the formation of history. Only recently are historians beginning to rediscover the importance of individual actors in politics, as opposed to process and structures. To achieve an initial agreement it is vital that the leaders are very intensely concerned with the welfare of their societies and realize that the status quo is unsustainable. Politics has been described as the art of the possible. Here, perhaps, politics might be described as the art of making possible that which is necessary; that is, to achieve an initial agreement, it is necessary that leaders have a strong vision for what is necessary and be prepared to take political risks to achieve that vision.

As briefly suggested above, taking a fragile, initial paper agreement and transforming it into a sustainable peace requires a political reaction and historical understanding. The term *political reaction* refers here to the participants developing a shared understanding that continuing the "military option" was unsustainable, then reacting against this status quo of violence. The issue of history, on the other hand, is deeply problematic. The two chief negotiators, for instance, who had spent their lives only half a kilometer apart, had completely different life experiences. While recognizing the inequities of history, therefore, it has been necessary to ignore the historical dimension in order to achieve progress at the negotiations.

The question is how to achieve these abstract objectives of a sustainable peace in practice. Practical policymaking has consisted of two essential elements—the creation of mutual trust and the management of history at the community level. In order to postpone politically impossible tasks, such as the issues of Jerusalem, refugees, and so forth, the negotiators agreed on an interim period of five years. This time, it was thought, would be used to initiate practices of cooperation leading to an ethos of cooperation and, in turn, to a deepening mutual understanding and trust. A whole series of institutions would be set up to manage such matters as security, water, and architecture. Moreover, a people-to-people program was initiated to bring together the Palestinian civil society and the Israeli civil society. Teachers, lawyers, doctors, youth groups, and sporting clubs, among many, were meant to meet, exchange views, and become acquainted as people.

This whole program to achieve mutual trust failed, however. And to gain an insight into the cause of that failure, it might be helpful to again return to the issue of history. On one level, many people talked about rewriting textbooks, of introducing historical works to each other's communities. But it was seen as much too controversial. It just couldn't be done. On another level, it was suggested that each community needed to understand and to take a certain responsibility for each other's historical discourse—to apologize, it was hoped, for the suffering caused. Again, this proved to be totally impossible. Perhaps the whole process was too intellectually difficult. History in the Middle East is an extremely contested field. In a region where property claims might have a three-thousand-year-old basis, where does relevant history begin? Who defines it? In the Middle East, there is no such thing as "the truth." Instead, there are many "truths": some live together well and some live uncomfortably with one another, while others simply contradict and confront one another.

Briefly, in conclusion, a very popular proverb among French peasants about the choice of a wife seems to be an appropriate tool for understanding the problem of "truth" in the Middle East. The proverb says that you may choose a beautiful wife, who may satisfy you, but she will never be faithful. Or you may choose a faithful wife, who may satisfy you, but she will never be beautiful. The quest for a faithful truth in the Middle East may one day be satisfying, but it will never be beautiful.

Notes

Introduction

1. Council on Foreign Relations, Independent Task Force, *Public Diplomacy: A Strategy for Reform,* www.cfr.org/publication.phd?id=4683.

2. See *Christian Science Monitor,* December 6, 2002, www.csmonitor.com/2002/1206/p02s01-uspo.html.

3. Speech at Tsinghua University, Beijing, February 2002, online at www.whitehouse.gov/news/releases/2002/02/20020222.html.

4. See Elazar Barkan, *The Guilt of Nations* (New York: W. W. Norton, 2000).

5. Interview with Carol Gluck, *Asahi Shimbun,* November 24, 1995.

1. Evaluating the Inter-Korean Peace Process

1. For an example of a perspective that focuses on the domestic origins of the Korean War, see Bruce Cumings, *Korea's Place under the Sun: A Modern History* (New York: W. W. Norton, 1997). For an alternative perspective in the field of Cold War international relations, see William Stueck, *The Korean War: An International History* (Princeton, N.J.: Princeton University Press, 1995).

2. For more information on the armistice and its negotiation, see Rosemary Foot, *The Wrong War: American Policy and the Dimensions of the Korean Conflict, 1950–1953* (Ithaca, N.Y.: Cornell University Press, 1985); and C. Turner Joy, *How Communists Negotiate* (New York: Macmillan, 1955).

3. For the full text of the communiqué, see www.korea-np.co.jp/pk/011the_issue/97100103.htm.

4. See Don Oberdorfer, *The Two Koreas: A Contemporary History* (Reading, Mass.: Addison-Wesley, 1997).

5. See Scott Snyder, "The End of History, the Rise of Ideology, and the Pursuit of Inter-Korean Reconciliation," in *Korea Briefing 2000–2001: First Steps toward Reunification,* ed. Oh Kongdan and Ralph Hassig (Armonk, N.Y.: M. E. Sharpe, 2002).

6. Xinhua News Service, "Full Text of DPRK–South Korean Joint Declaration," Pyongyang, June 15, 2000 (from Nexis news service). The first point of the Joint Declaration states: "The North and the South agreed to solve the question of the country's reunification independently by the concerted efforts of the Korean nation responsible for it."

7. Seok-jae Kang, "Koreas Agree on Military Commission," *Korea Herald,* September 26, 2000.

8. See Don Kirk, "The South Korean Spy Chief Who Paved the Way for Thaw with North; Point Man's Worries—Will Hard-Liners Retaliate?" *International Herald Tribune,* January 31, 2001, 2.

9. Francis Fukuyama, *The End of History and the Last Man* (New York: Aron Books, 1993).

10. Joon-seung Lee, "Rival Parties Battle over Diplomacy, Unification, Security Issues," *Korea Herald,* November 15, 2000.

11. Don Kirk, "South Korea Impatient for Return of Prisoners," *International Herald Tribune,* August 30, 2000, 4; and Joon-seung Lee, "President's North Korea Policy Violates Constitution, Kim Y. S. Charges," *Korea Herald,* August 26, 2000.

12. Kim Dae Jung, notes from group meetings with author and others, April 2000 and February 2001.

13. Author's notes from group meetings with Kim Dae Jung, April 2000 and February 2001.

14. See Oknim Chung, "The Role of South Korea's NGOs: The Political Context," in *Paved with Good Intentions: The NGO Experience in North Korea,* ed. Scott Snyder and L. Gordon Flake (New York: Praeger, 2003).

15. For instance, following President Kim Dae Jung's putative promises of assistance as part of his Berlin Declaration in February 2000, the DPRK sought energy from South Korea. See Kim Yong-sik, "Background for DPRK's Electricity Request—Energy Shortage Seems to Have Reached a Limit," *Tong-a Ilbo,* September 29, 2000 (as translated by Foreign Broadcast Information Service [FBIS] under "ROK Daily on DPRK's Electric Supply, N-S Cooperation," FBIS document no. KPP20000930000008).

16. Yonhap News Agency, "President Predicts 'End to Cold War on Korean Peninsula' via Four Party Talks," October 16, 2000 (as translated by FBIS, document no. KPP20001017000004).

17. Byung Joon Ahn, "Sinking the Sunshine Policy," *Straits Times* (Singapore), July 6, 2002.

2. Hypotheses on History and Hate in Asia

1. Driven in part by the salience of ethnic conflict, studies on emotion in international relations as well as on connections between emotion, identity formation, and national histories have only recently come to the fore. See Jonathan Mercer, "Approaching Emotion in International Politics" (paper presented at the conference of the International Studies Association, San Diego, Calif., April 1996); Neta Crawford, "The Passion of World Politics," *International Security* 24, no. 4 (spring 2000); Nancy Sherman, "Empathy, Respect, and Humanitarian Intervention," *Ethics and International Affairs* 12 (1998); Consuelo Cruz, "Identity and Persuasion," *World Politics* 52, no. 3 (April 2000); James Fearon and David Laitin, "Violence and the Social Construction of Identity," *International Organization* 54, no. 4 (autumn 2000); and Robert Jervis, *Perception and Misperception* (Princeton, N.J.: Princeton University Press, 1976), 356–381.

2. Crawford, "Passion of World Politics," 118.

3. See Aaron Friedberg, "Ripe for Rivalry," *International Security* 18, no. 3 (winter 1993–94); Richard Betts, "Wealth, Power, and Instability," *International Security* 18, no. 3 (winter 1993–94); Kent Calder, *Pacific Defense* (New York: Morrow, 1996); Michael Klare, "The Next Great Arms Race," *Foreign Affairs* 72, no. 3 (1993); Christopher Layne, "Less Is More: Minimal Realism in East Asia," *National Interest* 43 (1996); Paul Bracken, *Fire in the East* (New York: HarperCollins, 1999); Richard Bernstein and Ross Munro, *The Coming Conflict with China* (New York: Knopf, 1997); Barry Buzan and Gerald Segal, "Asia: Skepticism about Optimism," *National Interest* 39 (1995); Denny Roy, "Hegemon on the Horizon?" *International Security* 19, no. 1 (summer 1994); and Susan Shirk, "Asia-Pacific Regional Security: Balance of Power or Concert of Powers," in *Regional Orders: Building Security in a New World,* ed. David Lake and Patrick Morgan (University Park, Pa.: Penn State University Press, 1997).

4. What is interesting about the neoliberal position in the context of this chapter is not the well-known argument about economic interdependence but the fact that, much like the realists, neoliberals readily accept the premise that historical animosity inexorably inclines a region to conflict.

5. Peter Katzenstein, *Cultural Norms and National Security* (Ithaca, N.Y.: Cornell University Press, 1995); Peter Katzenstein and Nobuo Okawara, "Japan's National Security:

Structures, Norms, and Policies," *International Security* 17, no. 4 (spring 1993); Peter Katzenstein and Takashi Shiraishi, eds., *Network Power: Japan and Asia* (Ithaca, N.Y.: Cornell University Press, 1997); Desmond Ball, "Strategic Culture in the Asia-Pacific Region," *Security Studies* 3, no. 1 (1993); Thomas Berger, *Cultures of Antimilitarism: National Security in Germany and Japan* (Baltimore: Johns Hopkins University Press, 1998); Thomas Berger, "From Sword to Chrysanthemum: Japan's Culture of Anti-Militarism," *International Security* 17, no. 4 (spring 1993); Amitav Acharya, "Ideas, Identity, and Institution-Building: From the ASEAN Way to the Asia-Pacific Way," *Pacific Review* 10, no. 3 (1997); and Ken Booth and Russell Trood, eds., *Strategic Cultures in the Asia-Pacific Region* (New York: St. Martin's, 1999).

6. As noted above, there has been surprisingly little work concentrated on this issue despite its importance and the degree to which it has been acknowledged as a salient variable in Asia's security landscape. See Gerrit Gong, ed., *Remembering and Forgetting* (Washington, D.C.: CSIS, 1996); and Thomas Berger, "Tangled Visions: Culture, Historical Memory, and Japan's External Relations" (paper presented to the American Political Science Association, Boston, Mass., September 1998).

7. For example, the two states have been staunch allies of the United States and have hosted the mainstay of the American military presence in East Asia. For most of the postwar era, they faced hostile communist adversaries in China, the Soviet Union, and North Korea. They led East Asia as examples of thriving postwar market economies based on state-led industrialization and export-oriented strategies. Their high volume of trade and investment not only attests to the interdependence of the two economies but also has created numerous domestic groups with strong interests in congenial relations. Geographic proximity and a cultural familiarity facilitate ease of travel, communication, and policy coordination. Given these general commonalities, logic suggests that cooperative relations should ensue. This section is based on my book *Alignment despite Antagonism: The United States–Korea-Japan Security Triangle* (Palo Alto, Calif.: Stanford University Press, 1999), chap. 2.

8. Coercive policies largely characterized the initial and latter stages of the occupation (particularly between 1905 and 1919 and after 1934). Japan's colonial policies in the interim period were relatively less harsh, and at times benevolent. Nevertheless, it is the coercive periods that remain most vivid in Korean collective memories. For studies on this period, see Carter Eckert et al., *Korea: Old and New* (Seoul: Ilchokak, 1990), chaps. 15–17; and Chong-sik Lee, *Japan and Korea: The Political Dimension* (Palo Alto, Calif.: Hoover Institution Press, 1995), chap. 1.

9. Negatively constructed nationalisms and nationalist myths are not unique to Korea; however, the degree to which this identity is so viscerally framed against a past aggressor may marginally distinguish the Korean case. In contrast, July 4 is a patriotic institution in the United States, but its construction is as a pro-American holiday more than as an explicitly anti-British one.

10. Cited in Sung-hwa Cheong, *The Politics of Anti-Japanese Sentiment in Korea* (New York: Greenwood, 1991), 104.

11. See Akira Tanaka, "Japan and Korea," *Japan Quarterly* 28, no. 1 (March 1981): 30; Yasuo Wakasuki, "Sasil kwa hogu waui ch'airul ara" (Knowing the difference between fact and fiction), *Hanguk Nondan* (Seoul), March 1992, 48; and Hiroshi Imazu, "A New Era in Japan–South Korean Relations," *Japan Quarterly* 37, no. 2 (April-June 1990): 359.

12. Richard Finn, conversation on February 3, 1949, cited in Cheong, *Politics of Anti-Japanese Sentiment,* 72.

13. Bae-Ho Hahn, "Japan's International Role," in *Korea-Japan Relations in Transition,* ed. Bae-Ho Hahn and Tadashi Yamamoto (Seoul: ARC, 1982), 10–11.

14. For both peoples, this gap in images stems partly from a mutual indifference and ignorance. Newspaper polls consistently find that few Japanese know anything about the occupation and most cannot associate anything of significance with Korea. By the same token, Korean knowledge of Japan is found to be consistently limited.

15. See Kil Sûnghûm, "Han-Il kukkyo chôngsanghwa 20-nyôn ûi pansông" (Reflections on twenty years of normalization between Korea and Japan), *Sin-Tonga* (Seoul), June 1985, 146.

16. Similarly, at the 1951 talks, the chief delegate, Iguchi Sadao, silently listened to a litany of emotional ROK demands (personally written by Rhee) that Japan bear responsibility for "burying the hatchet" of the past. He then responded by asking blandly what "hatchets" the Koreans were referring to (Cheong, *Politics of Anti-Japanese Sentiment,* 104).

17. For the Showa apology, see Ministry of Foreign Affairs (MOFA), *Ilbon kaehwang* (Summary status: Japan) (Seoul Govt. Pub. 17000-20030-67-9607, 1996), 363. For South Korean dissatisfaction with the wording, see Kil Sûnghûm et al., "Han-il kwan'-gye ûi chiha sumaek chindan" (Examining the hidden pulse of Korea-Japan relations), *Chonggyong Munhwa* (Seoul), September 1984. Emperor Akihito's apology in 1990 attempted to address these semantic criticisms by providing a more direct expression of Japanese regret.

18. For a concise overview of this issue, see Lee, *Japan and Korea,* especially chap. 6.

19. For empirical overviews of the current period and improvements in relations between Japan and the Republic of Korea, see Cha, *Alignment despite Antagonism,* chap. 7; and Victor Cha, "Japan-Korea Relations," *CSIS Comparative Connections,* online at www.csis.org/pacfor/ccejournal.html.

20. For a discussion of the position of Japan and Korea over the history controversy in 2001 and the subsequent attempts to improve relations, see Victor Cha, "The

Emperor Has No (Soccer) Shoes," *CSIS Comparative Connections,* first quarter 2002, www.csis.org/pacfor/cc/0201Qjapan_skorea.html.

21. The hot-line decision, for example, was made specifically in response to the inability on the part of the two navies to communicate adequately when DPRK ships intruded into Japanese waters in the fall of 1998.

22. For details, see "Seoul-Tokyo Cooperation on North Korea: Tried, Tested, and True (Thus Far)," *CSIS Comparative Connections,* third quarter 1999, http://webu6102.ntx.net/pacfor/cc/993Qjapan_skorea.html.

23. Cha, *Alignment despite Antagonism.*

24. Michael Armacost, *Friends or Rivals?* (New York: Columbia, 1996), 247.

25. "Japan and Korea Fear a Vacuum If Clinton Turns the US Inward," *New York Times,* November 9, 1992.

26. Analytic distinctions between democratization and democratic consolidation are discussed below.

27. For agreements relating to the Kobe earthquake, civilian nuclear energy, and sea-related search and rescue operations, see MOFA, *Woegyo yônp'yo: 1993* (Diplomatic documents: 1993) (Seoul: Government Publications, 1994), 205–209; and MOFA, *Taehan min'guk choyakjip: Yangja choyak: 1990* (Bilateral treaties and agreements: 1990) (Seoul: Government Publications, 1991), 361–376.

28. Edward Mansfield and Jack Snyder, "Democratization and the Danger of War," *International Security* 20, no. 1 (summer 1995); and Jack Snyder and Karen Ballentine, "Nationalism and the Marketplace of Ideas," *International Security* 21, no. 2 (fall 1996).

29. See Cha, *Alignment despite Antagonism,* chap. 6.

30. See Kil Soong Hoom et al., "Han-Il kwan'gye chiha sumaek ch'indan," 149–150; and "Japan's Korea Boom," *Korea Herald,* September 8, 1988.

31. Dianne Hoffman, "Changing Faces, Changing Places: The New Koreans in Japan," *Japan Quarterly* 39, no. 4 (1992): 489.

32. Lee Jong-suk, "Measures on the Import of Japanese Pop Culture," *Korea Focus* 5, no. 1 (1997): 89.

33. Allan Song, "Diplomacy and Yakuza Films," *Far Eastern Economic Review,* June 12, 1997.

34. In particular, Akihito stated: "I think of the suffering your people underwent during the unfortunate period, which was brought about by my country, and cannot help but feel the deepest regret" (for this text and the apologies by the former premiers, see MOFA, *Ilbon kaehwang,* 365). ROK officials admitted that this was a more direct statement of contrition than was the apology made in 1984 by Emperor Hirohito (see statements by the presidential adviser Kim Chong-whi in *Korea Newsreview,* May 26, 1990). For very favorable ROK reactions to Hashimoto's apology in 1996, see "Looking Ahead," *Korea Herald,* June 25, 1996.

35. See MOFA, *Ilbon kaehwang,* 353–355. The former example refers to agreements made in 1991 that exempted third-generation Korean residents from the fingerprinting registration, with its connotations of criminality, required of previous generations. South Koreans perceived this exemption as an important first step toward more democratic and equitable treatment of the ethnic Korean minority in Japan (also see "Japan Eases Rule on Korean Aliens," *New York Times,* January 11, 1991). Regarding the latter example, in January 1992, historical records were found implicating the Japanese Imperial Army in conscripting Korean women to serve in "comfort stations" during World War II. Tokyo had previously denied any responsibility, asserting that private companies were involved in these practices (*Han'gyôre Sinmun* [Seoul], January 17, 1992; and *Korea Herald,* January 15, and 17–18, 1992). Although this issue was a potential powder keg for relations, the two governments conducted a rational and businesslike dialogue. There were no emotional invectives from Seoul, and immediately after the revelations, Premier Miyazawa of Japan offered an uncharacteristically prompt apology. Tokyo also undertook to revise history textbooks to include explicit recognition of Japanese wartime aggressions and supported compensation of *chôngsintae* victims through private organizations (Cho Jung-pyo, director, Foreign Ministry Northeast Asia Division I [Japan], interview by author, Seoul, February 14, 1992; and Shim Jae-hoon, Seoul bureau chief, *Far Eastern Economic Review,* interview by author, Seoul, March 19, 1992). See *Han'gyôre Sinmun,* January 17, 1992, for criticism by women's and human rights groups of Seoul's atypically rational attitude during this dispute.

36. "Japan Offers Joint History Study with Korea," *Korea Herald,* June 25, 1996; Brian Bridges, *Japan and Korea in the 1990s* (London: Edward Elgar, 1993), 63; *Choson Ilbo* (Seoul), April 15, 1997; and "Korea, Japan to Hold Research Talks," *Korea Herald,* July 15, 1997.

37. Cho Jung-pyo, interview; and official, Japanese embassy (political section), interview by author, Seoul, March 15, 1992.

38. *Choson Ilbo,* October 11, 1998; *Washington Post,* October 8, 1998; and *New York Times,* October 8, 1998.

39. See transcripts of Kim Dae Jung's address to the National Diet, October 8, 1998, and the Joint Declaration, October 9, 1998 (unofficial translations) at www.kocis.go.kr.

40. Jung-Hyun Shin, *Japanese–North Korean Relations* (Seoul: Kyunghee University Press, 1981); Lee, *Japan and Korea;* Chae-Jin Lee and Hideo Sato, *U.S. Policy toward Japan and Korea* (New York: Praeger, 1982); and Bridges, *Japan and Korea.*

41. In early November 1999, Japan partially lifted sanctions against the DPRK, including the ban on charter flights and restrictions on unofficial contacts with DPRK authorities (imposed after the Taepo-dong 1 missile was launched in August 1998). This was followed in early December by a suprapartisan Japanese delegation led by former prime minister Tomiichi Murayama to Pyongyang. The three-day visit was both an exploratory foray and a goodwill visit largely, as described by Japanese officials, to cultivate an "atmosphere" conducive to the resumption of dialogue. The meetings took place without preconditions on either side, and the former premier carried a letter from Prime Minister Obuchi to the DPRK leader, Kim Jong Il, expressing hope for improved relations. Japan subsequently lifted the remaining sanctions (the most significant of which was on food aid) after the Murayama mission.

42. In early March 2000, Japan lifted a three-year suspension on food aid to the DPRK and undertook to provide a hundred thousand tons of rice through the World Food Program, meeting an important precondition for the North to start normalization talks. Pyongyang's reciprocal commitment to look into the issue of abducted and/or missing Japanese made it marginally easier domestically for the Obuchi government to start the talks.

43. For a fuller discussion of Japan's engagement dilemmas with North Korea, see Victor Cha, "The Ultimate Oxymoron: Japan's Engagement with the DPRK" (paper presented at the Conference on North Korea, National Intelligence Council and Library of Congress, Washington, D.C., February 23, 2001), ii.

3. Reconciliation between Japan and China

1. Hotta Yoshie, "Chûgoku o mitsumeru futatsu no me: Moto gunjin no hôkoku kara 'gendai Chûgoku ron' made" (Two perspectives of discovering China: From "reports by former officers" to "treatise on modern China"), May 25, 1959, *Hotta Yoshie zenshû,* vol. 14 (Tokyo: Chikuma shobô, 1997), 466–469. Some information in this essay has previously appeared in my "Mirror for the Future or History Card? Understanding the History Problem in Japan-China Relations," in *Chinese-Japanese Relations in the Twenty-first Century: Complementarity and Conflict,* ed. Marie Söderberg (London: Routledge, 2002), 10–31.

2. A Japanese youth tore down the PRC flag flown outside an exhibition in Nagasaki, leading the Chinese government to terminate bilateral exchanges in protest.

3. Ministry of Foreign Affairs of the People's Republic of China, "Bilateral Relations with Japan: Some Sensitive Issues," www.fmprc.gov.cn/eng/29726.html.

4. For Japanese- and Chinese-language texts of Ambassador Tanino Sakutarô's speech, see Japan, Ministry of Foreign Affairs website, www.mofa.go.jp/mofaj/press/enzetsu/12/sei_0607.html.

5. See Yamada Tatsuo, "Cong jingdaishi kan Zhong-Ri guangxi" (Relations between China and Japan seen from modern history), in *Ri-Zhong guanxi mianmian guan,* ed. Li Tingjiang (Beijing: Zhongguo guoji guangbo chubanshe, 1991), 79–93; and Hatano Sumio, "Nitchû sensô no isan to fusai" (Legacies and debts of the Sino-Japanese War), in *Ajia no naka no Nihon to Chûgoku: Yûkô to masatsu no gendaishi,* ed. Matsuda Hiroshi and Hatano Sumio (Tokyo: Yamakawa shuppan, 1995), 57–76.

6. See Allen S. Whiting, *China Eyes Japan* (Berkeley, Calif.: University of California Press, 1989), 157–161.

7. *Zhongguo qingnian bao* (Beijing), February 15, 1997. Respondents could choose more than one item from the list. Results from this nationwide survey may not be entirely representative as most of the respondents were drawn from the male, educated, urban population.

8. Ambassador Chen Jian, interview by Tahara Sôichirô, TV Asahi, March 20, 2000.

9. Komori Yoshihisa, "Machigaidarage no Chûgoku enjo" (Aid to China that is full of mistakes), *Chûô kôron* (Tokyo), March 2000, 94–109; Miyamoto Yûji, "Tai-Chû keizai enjo dôsuru ka" (What to do with economic aid to China), *Gaikô Forum,* August 2000, 83.

10. Ijiri Hidenori, in *Kingendaishi naka no Nihon to Chûgoku,* ed. Nakajima Mineo (Tokyo: Tokyo shoseki, 1992), 251.

11. The Defend Diaoyu Islands Movement (*bao-Diao yundong*) is a grassroots movement that started in Hong Kong and Taiwan in the early 1970s.

12. Nicholas D. Kristof, "The Burden of Memory," *Foreign Affairs* 77, no. 6 (November-December 1998): 38, 47.

13. In addition to Whiting, *China Eyes Japan,* see Caroline Rose, *Interpreting History in Sino-Japanese Relations: A Case Study in Political Decision-Making* (London: Routledge, 1998); and Ian Buruma, *Wages of Guilt: Memories of War in Germany and Japan* (New York: Farrar, Straus and Giroux, 1994).

14. For an English text of the communiqué, see Japan, Ministry of Foreign Affairs website, www.mofa.go.jp/region/asia-paci/china/joint72.html.

15. Hotta Yoshie, "Wasureru koto to wasurerarenai koto" (The forgettable and the unforgettable), in *Shanhai ni te* (Tokyo: Chikuma shobô, 1973), 203–204. This was first published in the monthly *Sekai* (Tokyo) in March 1958.

16. Toynbee made this comment in 1968 in an article for *Mainichi Shimbun,* quoted in Albert Axelbank, *Black Star over Japan* (New York: Hill and Wang, 1972), 151.

17. Ian Nish, "China-Japan Relations, 1895–1945," in *China and Japan: History, Trends, and Prospects,* ed. Christopher Howe (Oxford: Clarendon, 1996), 43–44.

18. See Michael Scudson, "Dynamics of Distortion in Collective Memory," in *Memory Distortion: How Minds, Brains, and Societies Reconstruct the Past,* ed. Daniel L. Schacter (Cambridge, Mass.: Harvard University Press, 1995), 246–364.

19. Quoted in Yamaguchi Kikuichirô, *Hoshutô kara mita shin Chûgoku* (The new China seen by the Conservative Party) (Tokyo: Yomiuri shimbunsha, 1955), 130.

20. Chalmers Johnson, "The Patterns of Japanese Relations with China, 1952–1982," *Pacific Affairs* 59, no. 3 (fall 1986): 424. To be fair, Johnson did go on to discuss what he termed "collective Japanese amnesia about Asia" after the war.

21. Nakajima Mineo, "Imakoso 'rekishi no chôbo' no kessan o" (Settle the "history account" now), *Shokun* (Tokyo), August 1987, 95.

22. Mo Bangfu, "Nihon no sensô sekinin Chûgoku de susumu kenkyû no 'shin-chôryû" (New trends in ongoing Chinese research on Japan's war responsibility), *Ronza* (Tokyo), May 2000, 146–151.

23. *Dadongya zhanzhen de zongjie* (A summary of the Greater East Asian War), comp. Rekishi Kenkyû Iinkai (Beijing: Xinhua chubanshe, 1997). This is the Chinese translation of *Daitôa sensô no sôkatsu,* published for internal use by government and party officials in China.

24. *Nihon keizai shimbun* (Tokyo), May 2, 1997. A good discussion of domestic political factors in Japan is Mike Mochizuki, *Japan Re-Orients: The Quest for Wealth and Security in East Asia* (Washington, D.C.: Brookings Institution Press, 2001). See also Kabashima Ikuo, "Zenkokkai giin ideorogi chôsa" (An ideological survey of all Diet members), *Chûô kôron* (Tokyo), May 1999, 46–61.

25. Ozawa Ichirô, *Blueprint for a New Japan: The Rethinking of a Nation,* trans. Louisa Rubenfien (Tokyo: Kodansha International, 1994), 128–129.

26. See Carol Gluck, "The Past in the Present," in *Postwar Japan as History,* ed. Andrew Gordon (Berkeley, Calif.: University of California Press, 1993), 64–95.

27. Buruma, *Wages of Guilt,* 122.

28. *Nihon keizai shimbun,* May 2, 1997.

29. *Gaikô ni kansuru yoron chôsa* (Opinion polls concerning foreign relations) (October 2002), online at www8.cao.go.jp/survey/h14/h14-gaikou/images/zu06.gif.

30. Asano Akira, "Nitchû kankei no shinten o motome, chokusetsu kôryû no kakudai" (Seeking development in Japan-China relations, expanding direct exchanges), in *Nihon no gaikô anzenhôsho option* (Tokyo: Nihon Kokusai Kôryû Senta, 1998). Online at www.jcie.or.jp/japan/gt_ins/gti9709/ah1.htm.

31. Chae-jin Lee, *China and Japan: New Economic Diplomacy* (Palo Alto, Calif.: Hoover Institution Press, 1984), 146. On one such figure on the Chinese side, see Kurt

Radtke, *China's Relations with Japan: The Role of Liao Chengzhi* (Manchester, England: Manchester University Press, 1990).

32. Amago Satoshi, "Nitchû kankei—sengo sedai kara no teigen" (Japan-China relations—suggestions from the postwar generation), *Sekai,* July 1988, 258–270.

33. See Elazar Barkan, *The Guilt of Nations: Restitution and Negotiating Historical Injustices* (New York: Norton, 2000).

34. Quoted in the preface to Vamil D. Volkan, Demetrious A. Julius, and Joseph V. Montville, eds., *The Psychodynamics of International Relationships,* vol. 2, *Unofficial Diplomacy at Work* (Lexington, Mass.: Lexington Books, 1991), x.

35. Ann Phillips, "The Politics of Reconciliation: Germany in Central-East Europe," *German Politics* 7, no. 2 (August 1998): 66.

36. David A. Crocker, "Reckoning with Past Wrongs: A Normative Framework," *Ethics and International Affairs* 13 (1999): 43–64.

37. See Susan Dwyer, "Reconciliation for Realists," *Ethics and International Affairs* 13 (1999): 81–98.

38. Okazaki Hisahiko, "Let Historians Handle Japanese History," *Daily Yomiuri* (Tokyo), April 17, 2000.

39. For example, He Fang, "Women neng tong Riben youhao xiaqu ma" (Can we continue to be friendly with Japan?), *Huanqiu ribao* (Beijing), May 11, 1997; and Feng Zhaokui, "Zengyang zuo lingju: Dui shiji zhijiao Zhong-Ri kuanxi de sikao" (How to be neighbors: Thinking about relations between China and Japan at the turn of the century), *Shijie zhishi* (Beijing), January 2000, 28–30. It may be pointed out that the latter piece, published in a popular international affairs magazine, has invited a largely negative response from Chinese readers.

40. Yang Bojiang, "Yi lixin siwei mouqiu Zhong-Ri guanxi de kuashiji fazhan" (Seeking development of relations between China and Japan in the new century with rational thinking), *Xiandai guoji guanxi* (Beijing), September 1999, 1–6.

41. A transcript of Zhu's "town-hall meeting" with a Japanese television audience was made available by the Tokyo Broadcasting System, Inc., at www.tbs.co.jp/zhu/en.

42. Ozawa, *Blueprint for a New Japan,* 128–129.

43. Kono Yohei, speech at Naigai Josei Chôsakai, a foreign policy think tank, on January 23, 2001, online at www.mofa.go.jp/mofaj/press/enzetsu/13/ekn_0123.html. The comparison of relations between Japan and China with those between France and Germany dates back to the prewar era. One example is a piece with racist tones, Edward Hunter, "The France and Germany of Asia," *Esquire,* April 1938, 16–20. Hunter noted that "there are more differences, although they belong to the same yellow race, than between any two variations of the white race." It is subtitled "Contrasting the imitative Japs [*sic*] with the inventive Chinese, you find they have nothing in common but slant eyes."

44. Mochizuki, *Japan Re-Orients.*

45. Ministry of Foreign Affairs of the People's Republic of China, "Bilateral Relations with Japan: Some Sensitive Issues," www.fmprc.gov.cn/eng/29726.html.

46. Kojima Tomoyuki, "Nitchû kankei 'atarashii hatten dankai" (New stage of development in relations between Japan and China), in *Ajia jidai no Nitchû kankei,* ed. Kojima Tomoyuki (Tokyo: Simul, 1995), 32. He considered the fiftieth anniversary to be "perhaps the last chance."

47. For an account by one of the activist Japanese lawyers supporting the Chinese, see Uchida Masatoshi, "The Hanaoka Incident: Corporate Compensation for Forced Labor," www.iwanami.co.jp/jpworld/text/nanaoka01.html. For a recent Chinese popular assessment, see Hao Zi, *Zunyan: Zhongguo minjian dui-Ri suopei jishi* (Honor: A truthful account of nongovernmental Chinese efforts to seek compensation from Japan) (Beijing: Zhongguo gongren chubanshe, 2002).

48. For a persuasive discussion of the need for Japan to pay compensation to Asian victims, see Ônuma Yasuaki, "Sengo hoshô to kokka no hinkaku" (Postwar reparations and a country's character), in *Tokyô saiban kara sengo sekinin no shisô e,* 4th ed. (Tokyo: Tôshindo, 1997), 331–346.

49. Ministry of Foreign Affairs of the People's Republic of China, "Bilateral Relations with Japan: Some Sensitive Issues," www.fmprc.gov.cn/eng/29726.html.

50. *Zhongguo qingnian bao* (Beijing), February 15, 1997.

51. Zhu Jianrong, "Rekishi o wasurezu, 'toku o motte rin o nasu' kankei e" (Not forgetting history, toward a relationship of ethical neighbors), *Sekai* (Tokyo), February 1999, 76–77.

52. Zhu Jianrong, "Chûgoku ga 'Chûka shisô' o kokufuku suru hi" (The day China overcomes the "Zhonghua thought"), *Chûô kôron* (Tokyo), February 2001, 180–190.

53. Japan, Ministry of Foreign Affairs, "Proposal Summary by the Deliberation Council on Economic Assistance to China in the Twenty-first Century," www.mofa.go.jp/mofaj/gaiko/oda/seisaku/seisaku_1/sei_1_13_2.html.

54. Barry Buzan, "Japan's Future: Old History versus New Roles," *International Affairs* 64, no. 4 (autumn 1988): 570.

55. I have discussed some of the specific related issues in "Historians and the Nanjing Massacre," *SAIS Review* 19 (summer-fall 1999): 133–148.

56. Joseph V. Montville, "The Arrow and the Olive Branch: A Case for Track-Two Diplomacy," in *Unofficial Diplomacy at Work,* vol. 2 of *Psychodynamics of International*

Relationships, ed. Vamik D. Volkan, Demetrios A. Julius, and Joseph V. Montville (Lexington, Mass.: Lexington Books, 1991), 7.

57. Masahide Shibusawa, "Japan's Historical Legacies: Implications for Its Relations with Asia," in *The Process of Japanese Foreign Policy: Focus on Asia,* ed. Richard L. Grant (London: Royal Institute of International Affairs, 1997), 25–36.

58. See Kimijima Kazuhiko, "The Continuing Legacy of Japanese Colonialism: The Japan–South Korea Joint Study Group on History Textbooks," in *Censoring History: Citizenship and Memory in Japan, Germany, and the United States* (Armonk, N.Y.: M. E. Sharpe, 2000), 203–225; and "Seoul, Tokyo Have Long Way to Go to Reach Shared View on Korea-Japan History," *Korea Times,* May 31, 2000.

59. In the wake of the 1982 textbook controversy, a group of Japanese historians hosted one such symposium on comparative history and history education with Chinese and Korean historians. See Hikakushi Hikaku Rekishi Kyôiku Kenkyûkai (Society of Comparative History Education), comp., *Kyôdo tôgi Nihon Chûgoku Kangoku: Higashi Ajia rekishi kyôiku sinpojûm kiroku* (Joint discussion, Japan, China, Korea: Record of an East Asia history education symposium) (Tokyo: Horupô shuppan, 1985). Unfortunately, there does not seem to have been any successful effort to follow up on this initiative.

60. A useful place to start is Laura Hein and Mark Selden, eds., *Censoring History: Citizenship and Memory in Japan, Germany, and the United States* (Armonk, N.Y.: M. E. Sharpe, 2000).

61. *Encyclopedia Britannica,* which has been published in both Japan and China, serves as an example of reference works that can help internationalize history education in both countries.

62. UNESCO aims at eradicating from school textbooks "factual errors, erroneous ideas, controversial interpretations . . . all of which might have given an unfair and pejorative image of a people or a civilization and hence embitter relations between countries." UNESCO, *Guidelines for Curriculum and Textbook Development in International Education,* online at www.unesco.org/education/pdf/34_71.pdf.

63. Japan, Ministry of Foreign Affairs, www.mofa.go.jp/mofaj/press/enzetsu/12/sei_0607.html.

64. "Japan in the Right," *Economist,* December 5, 1998.

65. Phillips, "The Politics of Reconciliation," 64–85.

66. On the importance of a healthy market and democracy to community formation, see Funabashi Yôichi, *Nihon no taigai kôsô* (Tokyo: Iwamani shoten, 1993), 41–42.

67. For example, see Qian Liqun, "'Bôkyaku' o kyohi suru" (Refusing to "forget"), trans. Maruyama Noboru, *Sekai* (Beijing), February 2000, 194–202. Noting that Japan has been rightly criticized for lack of repentance for its aggression in China, Li went on to point out that although the Chinese people have all the more reason to repent for their own wrongs against fellow Chinese, they have not done so. Li Shenzhi, "Fengyu canghuang wushinian" (Fifty years of turmoil), online at www.taiwan-strait.net/forum/phpBB/viewtopic.php?topic=2100&forum=5.

68. Brandt's motivation was a complex one: "Oppressed by memories of Germany's recent history, I simply did what people do when words fail them. My thoughts dwelt not only on the millions who had been murdered but also the fact that, Auschwitz notwithstanding, fanaticism and the suppression of human rights persisted." Willy Brandt, *Willy Brandt: People and Politics: The Years 1960–1975,* trans. J. Maxwell Brownjohn (Boston: Little, Brown, 1978), 398–399.

69. Phillips, "The Politics of Reconciliation," 64–85. For a slightly different view that depicts a somewhat uncertain future, see Andrei Markovits and Simon Reich, *The German Predicament: Memory and Power in the New Europe* (Ithaca, N.Y.: Cornell University Press, 1997), 109–117.

70. Ogawa Akira, "Nitchû kyôdô no bunkateki sôzô no hôkôsei to sono junbi toshite no Nitchû wakai" (Directions of Japan-China joint cultural creation and Japan-China reconciliation as a preparation) (paper presented at the second Japan-China Young Researcher Forum, Beijing, 1998), online at www.glocomnet.or.jp/okazaki-inst/jcbunka.ogawa.html.

71. Nishio Kanji, "Nihon kigyô ni taisuru baishô seikyû wa kokusaihô no jôshiki o mushishita bôkyo de aru" (Demands for compensation against Japanese corporations in an outrage that ignores the common sense of international law), *Nihon no ronten 2000* (Tokyo: Bungei shunjû sha, 2000), 181. Nishio, born in 1935, is a professor of German philosophy and author of *Kokumin no rekishi,* a popular history of Japan aimed at inspiring pride among the Japanese. *Bokumetsu* can also be translated as "destroy" or "exterminate," whereas the term *riteki kôi* has fallen out of use since the war. For a pointed rebuttal of such attacks, see Kuroda Tamiko, "Rekishi o hihanteki ni mirukoto wa 'jikyaku' dewa nai" (Viewing history critically is not "masochistic"), *Ronza* (Tokyo), July 1997, 52–57.

72. Zhu, "Rekishi o wasurezu, 'toku o motte rin o nasu' kankei e," 77.

4. Overcoming the Difficult Past

1. For a detailed account of the 2-28 Incident, see Lai Tse-han (Lai Zehan), Ramon H. Myers, and Wei Wou, *A Tragic Beginning: The Taiwan Uprising of February 28, 1947* (Palo Alto, Calif.: Stanford University Press, 1991); and Xingzhengyuan yanjiu er'erba shijian xiaozu (2-28 Incident Research Subcommittee of the Administrative

Yuan), *Er'erba shijian yanjiu baogao* (The 2-28 Incident Report) (Taipei: Shibao chuban gongsi, 1992).

2. Thomas Gold, *State and Society in the Taiwan Miracle* (New York: M. E. Sharpe, 1986), 51.

3. "Horiokosareru Kurai Kako, Taiwan No. 228 Jiken" (Taiwan's 2-28 Incident: Dark past dug out), *Asahi Shimbun,* March 18, 1992.

4. Li Dongming, "Guangfu hou Taiwan renkou shehui zengjia zhi tantao" (A study of the social increase of Taiwan's population after the Restoration), *Taipei Wenxian* (Taipei Archives), nos. 9–10 (December 1969): 223.

5. Xingzhengyuan yanjiu er'erba shijian xiaozu (2-28 Incident Research Subcommittee), op. cit. (n. 1), 367.

6. He Yilin, "Taiwanjin no seijishakai to ninihachijiken" (Taiwanese political society and the February 28 Incident) (Ph.D. diss., University of Tokyo, 1998), chap. 3. Japan and its people had no direct role in the 2-28 Incident and its aftermath, as Japanese colonial rule had ended in August 1945 and almost all the Japanese had left the island by the end of 1946. However, the Japanese occupation (the "Japan experience") did have some influence, for Japan had left a legacy that affected the national and ethnic identity of the Taiwanese. On this point, He Yilin gives us an excellent description: "The 2-28 Incident was a tragedy in which the Taiwanese lives were sacrificed when policies of 'nation creating' by Japan and that of China clashed and yet Japan and the Japanese could not be involved directly. In this sense, the tragedy of the 2-28 Incident was a legacy left by the Japanese colonial rule" (ibid., p. 383). The "Japan experience" has continued to be one of the issues of identity politics in contemporary Taiwan.

7. Masahiro Wakabayashi, *Taiwan: Bunretsukokka to Minshuka* (Taiwan: Democratization in a divided country) (Tokyo: University of Tokyo Press, 1992), 11–12.

8. Wang Fu-chang, "The Unexpected Resurgence: Ethnic Assimilation and Competition in Taiwan, 1945–1988" (Ph.D. diss., University of Arizona, 1989), chap. 3.

9. The number of Mainlanders in the whole population of Taiwan was 0.9 percent in 1947, 8.0 percent in 1952, 15.7 percent in 1969, and 13.6 percent in 1990. See Li Dongming, op. cit. (n. 4), 223, for 1947; and Gong Yijun, *Wailai zhengquan' yu bentu shehui* (Foreign regime and the native society) (Taipei: Daoxiang Chubanshe, 1998), 222, for the remaining years.

10. See Masahiro Wakabayashi, "Taiwan wo meguru identity politics heno shikaku" (Democratization, ethnopolitics, and the remaking of state and nation in contemporary Taiwan), *ODYSSEUS* (Bulletin of the Department of Area Studies, Graduate School of Arts and Sciences, University of Tokyo), no. 5 (2000).

11. Er'erba hepingri cujinhui (2-28 Memorial Day Promotion Society), ed., "Zouchu er'erba de yinying Er'erba shijian sishi zhounian jinian zhuanji" (Footfalls of the 2-28 Incident: Anthology for the fortieth anniversary of the 2-28 Incident), *Ziyou shidai zazhishe* (Liberty Times Magazine) (Taipei) (1987): 59.

12. The following description of the process of the rectification movement up to the end of 1990 is based on Er'erba hepingri cujinhui (2-28 Memorial Day Promotion Society), ed., *Zouchu er'erba de yinying Er'erba hepingri cujin yundong shilu, 1987–1990* (Footfalls of the 2-28 Incident: Records of the "2-28 Memorial Day" Promotion Movement, 1987–1990) (Taipei: Zili wanbao wenhua chubanbu [Independent Evening Post Cultural Publications Dept.], 1991), 21–94.

13. Taiwan's Presbyterian Church played a significant role from the outset of the movement. See Zhuang Tianci, "Zhanglao jiaohui yu Er'erba pingfan yundong (1987–1990)" (Taiwan's Presbyterian Church and the rectification movement of the 2-28 Incident), *Taiwan Shiliao Yanjiu* (Taiwan Historical Material Studies), no. 12 (November 1998).

14. Lin Zongyi, "Kangzheng yihuo fuhe?" (Confrontation or rapprochement?), in *Er'erba shijian yanjiu lunwenji* (Studies in the 2-28 Incident: An anthology), ed. Zhang Yanxian, Chen Meirong, and Yang Yahui (Taipei: Wu Sanlian Taiwan Shiliao Jijinhui [Wu Sanlian Foundation for Taiwan Historical Materials], 1998), 382, 392.

15. Chen Shouguo, "Li zongtong: Jiejue er'erba shanghen de shiji chengshoule" [President Lee: Time is ripe for solution of 2-28 wounds], *Zhongguo Shibao* (China Times) (Taipei), March 5, 1991.

16. The following description of the events up to enactment of the Act on the Settlement and Compensation for the 2-28 Incident is based on Zheng Mingde, "Woguo zhengfu yu minjian shehui dui er'erba shijian de shanhou chuli: 1987–1997" (Our governmental and nongovernmental aftertreatments for the 2-28 Incident: 1987–1997) (M.A. thesis, National Sun Yat-sen University, Gaoxiong, 1997), 81–113, 128–129. For the discussion in the Legislative Yuan, see Lifayuan mishuchu (Secretariat of the Legislative Yuan), ed., *Er'erba shijian chuli ji buchang tiaoli an* (The minutes of the deliberation on the Act on the Settlement and Compensation for the 2-28 Incident) (Taipei: Lifayuan mishuchu, 1996).

17. Lai Tse-han's remark at the fifth session of the joint committee on internal and judicial affairs (Lifayuan mishuchu, op. cit. [n. 16], 199).

18. A remark by one of the representatives of the bereaved families at the second session of the public hearing on the problem held by the Central Policy Committee of the KMT; see Zhongguo guomindang zhongyang zhengcehui bian, *Er'erba shijian chuli (shanhou) wenti gongtinghui jish* (Minutes of the public hearing on the question of the settlement of the 2-28 Incident, edited by the Central Policy Committee of the KMT) (Taipei: Zhonguo guomindang zhongyang zhengcehui, 1994), 56.

19. Texts of these drafts can be found in Lifayuan mishuchu, op. cit. (n. 16), 1–20.

20. The text of this draft can be found in ibid., 329–349.

21. The text of the 2-28 Act passed that day can be found in ibid., 540–543.

22. "Li zongtong zai er'erba jinianbei jiemu dianli shang de jianghua" (Speech by President Lee at the unveiling ceremony of the 2-28 memorial monument), *Zhongguo Shibao,* March 1, 1995.

23. Gen Tsukamoto, "Ninihachi jiken gojushunen to Taiwan shakai" (Fiftieth anniversary of the 2-28 Incident and Taiwan society), *Sekai* (World Monthly), August 1997, 327.

24. Hong Mingqin, "Er'erba guanban beiwen chongxian" (Official version of the inscription on the 2-28 Incident monument plaque reappears), *Zhongguo Shibao,* May 24, 1999.

25. Cai Zizhen, "Ma yingjiu: Waisheng zuqun bu ying beifu yuanzui" (The Mainlanders shuold not be burdend with "original sin" of 2-28 Incident), *Zhongguo Shibao,* March 1, 1999.

26. Announcement on the website of the 2-28 Incident Memorial Foundation, www.228.org.tw/07.htm.

27. Tsukamoto, op. cit. (n. 23), 325–326.

28. Li Jianrong, "Zhengyuan tongguo er'er ba dashe-an" (Administrative Yuan decided to grant a general amnesty to those who were charged in the 2-28 Incident), *Zhongguo Shibao,* June 13, 1997.

29. Texts of these acts can be found at the website of the Foundation for Compensating Improper Verdicts on Sedition and Communist Espionage Cases during the Martial Law Period, www.cf.org.tw.

30. Opposition demonstrators and police clashed on the World Human Rights Day, December 10, 1979. Opposition leaders at the time were rounded up and arrested. The incident is known as the Formosa Incident.

31. "Introduction," Foundation for Compensating Improper Verdicts, op. cit. (n. 29).

32. FTV news, May 23, 2002, www.ftvn.com.tw/Politics.

33. Robert Edmondson criticized the attitude of Lee and the KMT toward rectification of the 2-28 Incident as "Bitburg history," likening it to the invitation extended by Chancellor Helmut Kohl of West Germany to Ronald Reagan, then the U.S. president, to visit a cemetery for German soldiers, including Nazi SS soldiers, on the fortieth anniversary of V-E day in 1985. See Robert Edmondson, "The February 28 Incident and National

Identity," in *Memories of the Future: National Identity Issues and the Search for a New Taiwan,* ed. Stephane Corcuff (New York: M. E. Sharpe, 2002), 37.

34. Some family members of the victims tried several times to bring a criminal charge against him, but to no avail. See Li Shuhua, "Peng Yingang bei ti gongsu" (Peng Yingang [son of Peng Mengji] indicted for slander), *Zhongguo Shibao,* June 3, 1998.

35. This account is based on the author's on-the-spot observations in Taipei in the days immediately following the election on March 18, 2000, and on news reports in Taipei papers, mainly *Zhongguo Shibao.*

36. See Zhuang Mingren, "Li Denghui bei bo hong-moshui" (Lee Teng-Hui hit by red ink), *Zhongguo Shibao,* May 28, 2000; and Liu Tianzai, "Yangqi duili, chaoye liwei dahejie kafei" (Legislators of ruling and opposition parties drink coffee for reconciliation), *Zhongguo Shibao,* June 1, 2000.

37. News reports in Taipei papers, December 2, 2001.

5. Cambodia

1. On August 16, 2001, President Khieu Samphan of Democratic Kampuchea, in a "Letter appealing to all of my compatriots," claimed that he had had no authority to order any killing, and declared: "To those who lost their loved ones to the regime, I am sorry. It was my fault for being so foolish, and [I] failed to keep up with the real situation. I tried my best for the sake of our nation's survival, so that we might develop and prosper like other nations. I deeply regret that this turned out to be genocide." The letter was written in Pailin, Western Cambodia, and faxed to the Documentation Center of Cambodia, Phnom Penh.

2. I am indebted to Youk Chhang, director of the Documentation Center of Cambodia, for this and many other insights.

3. Christopher Cox, "Cambodian War Crimes Are Going Unpunished," *Boston Herald,* March 17, 2002, 4.

4. As reported by Reuters, September 3, 2002.

5. Chea Vannath, president, Center for Social Development, Phnom Penh, described "[t]he apology [as an intrinsic part of] Cambodian society. For example, in the daily Buddhist prayer, there are invocations to apologize to the Buddha, dharmas, and sangha for our wrongdoing, if any. During the Khmer New Year and other occasions, it is the tradition that people ask for forgiveness for their previous improper actions or activities (intentional or unintentional) [with regard] to the elderly. This also applies when someone is getting very sick and may think that she will die. That person will ask family and friends for forgiveness. In the Khmer Rouge context, people who suffered from the Khmer

Rouge atrocities get angry because they feel that the Khmer Rouge commit crimes and never admit [them], nor ask for forgiveness." Laura McGrew and Hang Path, *Discussion Guide: Truth, Justice, Reconciliation, and Peace in Cambodia, Twenty Years after the Khmer Rouge* (Phnom Penh: Canadian Embassy, November 1999–February 2000), 6.

6. King Norodom Sihanouk, private conversation with author, Phnom Penh, December 27, 2000.

7. "Hun Sen Flays UN for Hypocrisy, Failure in Cambodia," Agence France-Presse, January 23, 2001.

8. Qin Huasun, China's ambassador to the United Nations, said, "China strongly opposes any act by the international community to impose an international tribunal on Cambodia and is not in favor of the proposed establishment of such an international tribunal by the Security Council or the General Assembly." See United Nations Development Programme website, March 19, 1999, www.undp.org/missions/china/khmer.htm.

9. Phelim Kyne, "China Enraged by Alleged Link to S-21," *Phnom Penh Post,* November 24–December 7, 2000; Youk Chhang, director of the Documentation Center of Cambodia, interview by author, January 2, 2001.

10. Rithy Panh, "Cambodia: A Wound That Will Not Heal," *Courier* (UNESCO) (December 1999): 30–32.

11. "UN Receives Letter from Cambodia Asking Help in Trying Khmer Rouge," Associated Press, June 23, 1997.

12. "Cambodia's Tattered Judiciary to Try Khmer Rouge—but Can It?" Associated Press, March 25, 2001.

13. "Opposition Leader Speaks Out against Khmer Rouge Trial Plan," Agence France-Presse, March 7, 2001.

14. "Tom Fawthrop: No Reason for Standoff on KR Law," *Phnom Penh Post,* March 2–15, 2001.

15. Associated Press, June 25, 1999.

16. "China Won't Back Pol Pot Tribunal," *Chicago Tribune,* June 25, 1997.

17. During a visit by An Min, China's deputy minister for foreign trade and economy, Hun Sen accompanied him to Kompong Speu and urged him to carry a message to the world's Chinese community. "I want investment from mainland China but I also want to send a message to ethnic Chinese living around the world . . . especially those living in countries where they are discriminated against, to come to Cambodia and bring capital and technology," Hun Sen said. Reported by Associated Press, April 3, 2001.

18. Statement by UN legal counsel Hans Corell at a press briefing at UN Headquarters in New York, February 8, 2002, www.un.org/News/dh/infocus/cambodia/corell-brief.htm.

19. Ibid.

20. "Cambodia Trial to Shock World—Khmer Rouge Chief," Reuters, December 23, 2002.

21. Njabulo S. Ndebele, "South Africa: Quandaries of Compromise," *Courier* (UNESCO) (December 1999): 22–23.

22. Vannath, quoted in McGrew and Path, *Discussion Guide,* 5.

23. Center for Social Development, "Public Forum on 'Khmer Rouge and National Reconciliation,'" *Bulletin* (Phnom Penh: Center for Social Development, February 2000).

24. Purported to be a history of Vietnam-Cambodia relations, the *Livre Noir* is a fanciful account designed to justify the launching of Khmer Rouge attacks on Vietnam to preempt the historical "swallower" of Khmer lands.

25. Nayan Chanda, *Brother Enemy: The War after the War* (New York: Harcourt Brace Jovanovich, 1986), 251.

26. Ben Kiernan, holding that the two most important themes in the history of the Pol Pot regime are the race question and the struggle for central control, observed that "the KR conceptions of race overshadowed those of class." *The Pol Pot Regime: Race, Power, and Genocide in Cambodia under the Khmer Rouge, 1975–79* (New Haven, Conn.: Yale University Press, 1996), 26. For his account of the nationwide campaign to eliminate the Vietnamese and people tainted by association with the Vietnamese, see ibid., 296–298 and 423–427.

27. David Chandler, *Voices from S-21: Terror and History in Pol Pot's Secret Prison* (Berkeley, Calif.: University of California Press, 2000), 151.

28. Cambodian Institute of Human Rights, *Minorities of Cambodia: A Textbook on Cambodia's Minority Groups, Designed to Teach Tolerance in the Schools,* www.ned.org/grantees/cihr/minority.html#IV.

29. Youk Chhang, "The Right to Life" (address to Women International Group [WIG], Konrad Foundation, Le Royal Hotel, Phnom Penh, Cambodia, September 4, 2002).

6. East Timor

1. Paula Escarameia, "The Meaning of Self-Determination and the Case of East Timor," in CIIR/IPJET (Catholic Institute for International Relations/International Platform of Jurists for East Timor), *International Law and the Question of East Timor* (London: CIIR/IPJET, 1995), 119–150.

2. *Tempo* magazine, February 8, 1999; see also Law no. 7 of 1976.

3. Jose Ramos Horta, conversation with author, c. 1979.

4. See, for example, Peter Carey, *Generation of Resistance: East Timor* (London: Cassell, 1995), 10.

5. George J. Aditjondro, "Prospects for Development in East Timor after the Capture of Xanana Gusmao," in CIIR/IPJET, *International Law,* 57.

6. Various parties, conversations with author, Kupang, East Nusa Tenggara (West Timor).

7. Author, personal observation during visits to Irian Jaya, 1982–92.

8. Carey, *Generation of Resistance,* 9, 42–43.

9. Ibid., 45–55.

10. The author was to be one of the speakers at the seminar. The cancellation of the conference was regarded as a slap in the face for the Indonesian government.

11. Carey, *Generation of Resistance,* 51.

12. The performance of the National Commission on Human Rights was, according to the Human Rights Watch, "better than expected."

13. For Habibie's views on East Timor, see Dewi Fortuna Anwar, "Habibie and East Timor," *Tempo* magazine, February 8, 1999.

14. Some said that Foreign Minister Ali Alatas and General Wiranto, the military chief, were not consulted by Habibie before he announced the two options. The author's requests for confirmation from Alatas and Wiranto received no response.

15. As reported in *Tempo* magazine, February 8, 1999.

16. KPP HAM Timtim, *Executive Summary Report on the Investigation of Human Rights Violations in East Timor* (Jakarta: KPP HAM Timtim, January 31, 2000).

17. See ibid.

18. National Commission on Human Rights, *Statement,* September 8, 1999. See the report at www.hrw.org/press/2000/09/timor0908.htm.

19. Decree no. 770/TUA/IX/99, passed on September 22, 1999. This decree was amended with Decree (Kep) no. 797/TUA/IX/99, dated October 22, 1999.

20. The members of KPP HAM were Albert Hasibuan (chairman), H. S. Dillon, Koesparmono Irsan, and Asmara Nababan representing Komnas HAM. The other members were Todung Mulya Lubis (vice chairman), Nursyahbani Katjansungkana, Zoemrotin, and Munir. The investigation of human rights abuses began, and one by one the allegations of "collusion" that were made in the UN Human Rights Commission's resolution were proved.

21. KPP HAM Timtim, *Executive Summary Report.* Under universal jurisdiction in international law, all states have the right to prosecute perpetrators, no matter where the crime took place.

22. Todung Mulya Lubis, "Civil Military Relations Revisited: A Human Rights Perspective" (draft paper, 2000).

23. KPP HAM, *Executive Summary Report.*

24. Barry Wain, "Will Justice Be Served in East Timor?" *Asian Wall Street Journal,* April 14–15, 2000.

25. James Dunn, *Timor: A People Betrayed* (Gladesville, Australia: Jacaranda Press, 1983), 1–2, quoting Alfred Russel Wallace, *The Malay Archipelago* (London: Macmillan, 1869), 18–19.

26. Dunn, *Timor,* 60, 63.

27. The investigation conducted by KPP HAM of the military and the militias suggests that, on the pretext of avoiding prolonged bloodshed, there was indeed a thorough plan to evict as many East Timorese as possible, should the referendum be won by the pro-independence group.

28. KPP HAM, *Executive Summary Report.*

29. *Far Eastern Economic Review,* October 12, 2000.

30. "Reconciliation as Refugees Return to East Timor," *Irish Times,* August 1, 2002.

31. See www.easttimor-reconciliation.org/mandate.htm.

32. "East Timor—Justice Denied?" *Sunday,* July 7, 2002.

33. United Nations, Office of the High Commissioner for Human Rights, *Report of the International Commission of Inquiry on East Timor to the Secretary General,* January 2000, available online at http://www.unhchr.ch/huridocda/huridoca.nsf/(Symbol)/A.54.726,+S.2000.59.En?OpenDocument.

34. "Call to Support or Scrap Crimes Unit," *Sydney Morning Herald,* May 25, 2001.

35. East Timor NGO Forum, "Expression of Concern at Xanana's Statement Regarding an International Tribunal," press release, April 23, 2001.

36. "Hopes Dim for International Tribunal in Thoenes Case," *Christian Science Monitor,* June 25, 2002.

37. International Crisis Group, Indonesia Project, "Situation Report," May 6–17, 2002.

38. "Prosecutors Request 10-Year Sentence for Former East Timor Police Chief," Associated Press, July 25, 2002.

39. See, for example, ibid.; and "Indonesia Puts Top East Timor Suspect on Trial," Reuters, July 10, 2002.

40. See Richard Lloyd Parry, "Australians Covered Up East Timor Terror Plot," *Independent* (London), March 15, 2002.

41. Ibid.

42. East Timor NGO Forum, "Expression of Concern at Xanana's Statement Regarding an International Tribunal," press release, April 23, 2002.

43. See www.unhchr.ch/huridocda/huridoca.nsf/TestFrame/d4018877e47d4134c1256bb2004ab94a?OpenDocument.

44. East Timor Action Network, "UN Human Rights Commission Abandons Justice for East Timor," press release, April 22, 2002.

45. Sidney Jones, *Indonesia: Implications of the Timor Trials* (Brussels: International Crisis Group, May 2002) 1; online at www.crisisweb.org/projects/asia/indonesia/reports/A400643_08052002.pdf.

46. Ibid., 12.

47. Ibid., 13.

8. Conclusion

1. Lee made these observations during the International Workshop on Reconciliation in the Asia-Pacific, held February 16–17, 2001, at the International House of Japan in Tokyo.

2. Heiberg, speaking at the International Workshop. A summary of her remarks is one of the appendices to this book.

3. Solomon, opening remarks to the International Workshop.

4. These comments are based on observations made by Daqing Yang at the International Workshop.

5. The phrase "peace of heart" was used by Ambassador Elbe at the International Workshop.

6. David Crocker, "Reckoning with Past Wrongs: A Normative Framework," *Ethics and International Affairs* 13 (1999).

7. As quoted by Elbe in the first appendix to this volume.

8. Tessa Morris-Suzuki, "Hihan sozoryoku no kiki" (Crisis of critical imagination), *Sekai* (Tokyo), January 2001.

9. As was noted by Gareth Evans during his keynote speech to the International Workshop.

Index

United States Institute of Peace

The United States Institute of Peace is an independent, nonpartisan federal institution created by Congress to promote the prevention, management, and peaceful resolution of international conflicts. Established in 1984, the Institute meets its congressional mandate through an array of programs, including research grants, fellowships, professional training, education programs from high school through graduate school, conferences and workshops, library services, and publications. The Institute's Board of Directors is appointed by the President of the United States and confirmed by the Senate.

Reconciliation in the Asia-Pacific

This book is set in American Garamond; the display type is Eurostile. Hasten Design Studio designed the book's cover; Mike Chase designed the interior. Helene Y. Redmond made up the pages. Frances Bowles copyedited the text, which was proofread by Karen Stough. The index was prepared by Sonsie Conroy. The book's editor was Nigel Quinney.